A Volume in
Research in Social Education

Editor: Merry Merryfield, The Ohio State University

Critical Issues in Social Studies Research
for the 21st Century

Printed in the United States of America

Library of Congress Control Number: 2001090933

CRITICAL ISSUES IN SOCIAL STUDIES RESEARCH FOR THE 21ST CENTURY

Edited by

William B. Stanley
University of Colorado at Boulder

INFORMATION AGE
PUBLISHING

411 West Putnam Avenue
Greenwich, Connecticut 06830

Lynn—to love, companionship, and better days.

CONTENTS

LIST OF CONTRIBUTORS

Keith C. Barton	University of Cincinnati
Michael J. Berson	University of South Florida
Catherine Cornbleth	School of Education; University of Buffalo
John K. Lee	Georgia State University
Linda S. Levstik	University of Kentucky
Merry Merryfield	The Ohio State University
Jack L. Nelson	Carlsbad, CA (Emeritus) Rutgers University
Walter C. Parker	University of Washington
E. Wayne Ross	State University of New York at Binghamton
Ellen M. Santora	Warner Graduate School; University of Rochester
James P. Shaver	Utah State University
William B. Stanley	University of Colorado at Boulder
Daniel W. Stuckart	King High School and University of South Florida
Kevin D. Vinson	University of Arizona

ACKNOWLEDGEMENTS

This book would not have been possible without the inspiration, encouragement, support, and patience of the Series Editor, Merry Merryfield. I also wish to thank the chapter authors for their many thoughtful contributions and critical dialog with the editor throughout this project. The following deserve special thanks for their various contributions to this project: Patricia Avery, Cynthia Carter, Maureen Connors, Pamela Ford, Maria Franquiz, Steven Fuller, Dan Liston, Hope Longwell-Grice, Patty McDonald, Rebecca Martusewicz, William F. Pinar, Cinthia Salinas, Kristian Stanley, John Stanley, Jon Stanley, Marc Swadener, and James A. (Tony) Whitson. Finally, I wish to thank George Johnson for his many helpful suggestions, support, and patience while this project was in process.

CHAPTER 1

SOCIAL STUDIES: PROBLEMS AND POSSIBILITIES

William B. Stanley

Social Studies remains a field in search of an identity. Or to put things more accurately, social studies is a field struggling to reconcile multiple and, at times, conflicting rationales. As we enter a new century, it is an appropriate time to reflect on the condition of social studies. Where have we been? Where are we now? What should we do in the future? The essays in this book explore possible answers to these questions as they apply to critical areas of concern for social studies educators.

Social studies is, by definition, an eclectic field that draws on a wide range of disciplines and other fields. It is this enormous range of knowledge that makes social studies such a rich and dynamic curriculum area. The field includes the social science disciplines (e.g., anthropology, economics, geography, political science, psychology, sociology) and the humanities (e.g., history, law, literature, philosophy). But social studies also include the interdisciplinary study of other disciplines' or fields (e.g., the history and philosophy of science; literary criticism; critical race theory; ethnic studies; bisexual, gay, lesbian, transgendered, and queer studies; multicultural education; and women's studies), as well as other fields of study such as communications, semiotics, or systems theory. Keep in mind that each of the disciplines or interdisciplinary fields that contribute to the social studies curriculum has itself been the locus of considerable debate regarding its methods, purposes, and boundaries.

Given this wide and varied knowledge base, it is not surprising that there has been so much debate over the definition and purposes of social studies. While the level of debate might be understandable (and some would argue beneficial), the lack of consensus has made the social studies vulnerable to political attack and manipulation. Is such political manipulation

1

unique to the social studies? I think not; the evidence points in another direction. We have witnessed over three decades of "reading wars," and more recently what some have called the "science wars." Within English education, the debates over literary criticism and the literary canon are now well known. Even mathematics, a curriculum area usually seen as well defined, has been plagued with debates over "new math," and more recently "fuzzy math." Nevertheless, one might argue that the social studies has been unusually prone to such debate and fragmentation.

Fragmentation and lack of consensus has had its consequences. For example, the very existence of "social studies" as a legitimate curriculum area has been called into question. The rhetoric of the standards movement over the past two decades has focused on national or state discipline standards (e.g., history, geography, political science, and economics), not social studies standards. About eight years ago, I served as co-chair of one of four state curriculum committees to design K–12 content standards. There was an English/Language Arts committee, a Mathematics committee, a Science committee, and a History, Geography, Political Science, and Economics committee. We were given an explicit charge not to use the term social studies as a curriculum committee descriptor.

Service on the History, Geography, Political Science, and Economics curriculum standards committee was an interesting experience. Over time, I came to realize that most of the historians, geographers, political scientists, and economists on the committee were interested in promoting interdisciplinary, inquiry-based, approaches to instruction that I would have called social studies. In other words, we tended to argue more about terminology than instructional approach. In contrast, some of the members of the committee who supported teaching social studies recommended rather low-level, fact-based, (even anti-intellectual) approaches to instruction. These distinctions were never clear-cut for either group. Nevertheless, in an effort to promote what I thought were more progressive approaches to curriculum (irrespective of the terminology used), I often found myself siding with representatives of the various disciplines and opposing some who considered themselves social studies advocates.

It is also interesting to note how only history and certain social science disciplines appear to have had a significant stake in social studies curriculum debates. The national associations of anthropologists, philosophers, psychologists, and sociologists have not lobbied very hard for inclusion in the social studies curriculum. Scholars from these disciplines seem content to leave the domination of the K–12 curriculum to historians, geographers, political scientists, and economists. While it is evident that history, geography, political science, and economics dominate the social studies curriculum, it is not clear why the four favored disciplines deserve priority consideration. In fact, one might question how well educated students would be if they only studied the national standards of the four of the disciplines available to constitute the social studies curriculum.

Of course, the problem has never been that simple. For example, proponents of history as the core discipline of social education (the single most influential group throughout the past 150 years) often argue that history is the best discipline for introducing students to ideas from anthropology, philosophy, psychology, sociology, and other studies of human behavior. Since history is, broadly speaking, the history of everything, it should be able to accommodate this ambitious goal. Geography educators have made similar arguments. Of course, this sort of thinking is in tension with those who advocate that students need to understand the unique structures of the individual disciplines (e.g., Bruner, 1960; Wesley & Wronski, 1958). Conversely, the dominance of history, geography, political science, and economics has been challenged by other educators, for example, the social reconstructionist Theodore Brameld (1965) who argued that anthropology should serve as the core discipline of social studies.

In contrast, the K–12 science education curriculum is dominated by a unitary view of "science," (Matthews, 1994; Siegel, 1997; Stanley & Brickhouse, 2001) while simultaneously accepting that there are many sciences (e.g., Astronomy, Biology, Chemistry, Geology, and Physics). There is nothing analogous to this way of thinking with regard to history and the social sciences. This is not to say that attempts to imitate the natural sciences and unify the social sciences have not been made. Indeed, for much of the past century, history the social sciences have suffered from "physics envy" and sought to emulate the natural sciences (Fuller, 2000). However, the desire to aspire to the unity and legitimacy of the natural sciences has not been realized. Nor is it clear that this aspiration makes sense. Part of the so-called "science wars" has been an attempt to problematize the idea that the sciences themselves really have a unified approach to understanding the natural world. In fact, the science war debates have called into question many of the strong realist assumptions that underlie the unity of science position (e.g., Fuller, 2000; Harding, 1998; Margolis, 1993; Stanley & Brickhouse, 2001).

Fragmentation and lack of consensus notwithstanding, the National Council for the Social Studies (NCSS) has developed its own standards that are interdisciplinary, and thematic. More important, the National Association for the Accreditation of Colleges of Teacher Education (NAACTE) has adopted the NCSS standards as the basis for accrediting the social studies programs at Schools and Colleges of Education. It is conceivable that this decision by NCSS might reflect a logistical (as opposed to philosophical) consideration. After all, it would be extremely complicated to have the four dominant professional organizations in this curriculum area (American Historical Association, National association of Geographers, American Political Science Association, and American Economics Association) collaborate on program reviews for NCATE. In addition, many states want their social studies teachers to be able to teach a wide variety of social sciences as well as history. Without a broad-based conception of social studies, it would be difficult to staff public schools, especially in rural areas. Consequently, State requirements often amount to tacit (if not philosophical) endorsements of "social studies" as a major curriculum area. Whatever the actual motivation, NCATE has opted for a more integrated definition of "social studies" standards.

However, when one moves beyond the definitional debates, it is clear that social studies (or whatever terminology we use) does not receive a high priority in most of the K–12 curricula throughout the United States. One way to confirm this assertion is by looking at the high-stakes standardized tests most K–12 students are required to take. In the main, we test student's knowledge of reading, writing, and math. This rather narrow conception of "what knowledge is of most worth" sends a clear signal to students and parents. The exclusion of social studies from most high-stakes testing confirms that literacy and mathematical knowledge have far greater legitimacy and public support as core curriculum areas.

The problem is even worse when one considers how social studies would be tested if it were a higher curriculum priority. The vast bulk of high-stakes standardized testing is aimed at measurable, low-level, forms of knowledge (e.g., Kohn, 2000). This low-level approach to social studies is antagonistic to developing the competencies one needs to function in a democratic culture and society (Stanley, 1992). Thus, one could argue that we might be better off not testing student's social studies knowledge this way. Yet the failure to test social studies continues to signal that this curriculum area is not as important as literacy and mathematics, a peculiar idea in an allegedly democratic society.

The authors of the nine other chapters in this book have struggled with the issues discussed above in several different ways. The chapter authors represent a wide range of views and expertise within the field of social studies. Some have been leading social studies scholars for three or four decades. Other authors represent new voices that have begun to shape the direction social studies will take in the future. The topics examined here include the debate over how to define social studies, social studies and the impact of the standards/accountability movement, the contextual constraints/restraints on teaching social studies, education for democracy, rationales for teaching history, multicultural education, global education, social studies and educational technology, and the nature and effectiveness of social studies research.

Given the wide and varied social studies knowledge base, the authors have drawn upon recent developments in interdisciplinary knowledge and research that transcends particular disciplines and fields. Certainly, the attempt to incorporate such a wide range of knowledge poses significant problems for social studies scholars. We live in a culture of academic specialization in which narrowly focused scholarship tends to receive the greatest rewards. However, social studies, by its very nature, cannot afford too much specialization or narrowness. The best social studies research needs to risk the challenges posed by multi and interdisciplinary analysis.

In Chapter 2, Jack L. Nelson focuses on defining the social studies, and how definitional distinctions have influenced the course of research in the field. Nelson argues that social studies is not only a subject taught in many schools, it is also the subject of intense intellectual debate stemming from its roots in social welfare activism of the middle nineteenth century and the progressive education movement of the twentieth century. Censorship has had a major impact on social studies. The arts and humanities suffer from forms of censorship motivated by political forces on the right and left. The sciences suffer from religious and political censorship. The applied fields suffer from a lack of academic respect.

But in Nelson's view, the raging attacks on the very existence and definition of social studies surpass the debates over what should be included in or how we should teach other school subjects. The very core idea of social studies has been under scrutiny from its earliest days. Nelson examines various approaches to defining the field over the past century. He is particularly critical of the negative influence of historians on the nature of social studies curriculum and practice. Nelson recognizes the importance and value of history, but he rejects the attempts to use history in a narrow disciplinary sense or as a form of nationalist education. Defining any field of study is crucial to its content, methods, scholarly work, legitimacy, and development. According to Nelson, examining the definition of social studies and issues that surround it is fundamental to understanding the field and its scholarship. And in spite of the many problems caused by debates over the nature of social studies, Nelson also sees such debates as a sign of the field's importance and intellectual vitality.

In Chapter 3, Kevin Vinson and Wayne Ross also examine the nature of social studies, but extend this analysis to the context and impact of the recent national and state standards and accountability movements. Like Nelson, they argue that the social studies curriculum is the most inclusive of all school subjects. Determining the boundaries of what is taught in social studies requires decisions about what social knowledge is most important, which skills and behaviors are most valuable, and what values are most significant. As a result, the curricular terrain of social studies education is continually contested in the political arena. Yet, the large-scale studies of the field conducted in the last quarter of the twentieth century have suggested the appearance of uniformity in basic topics, sequences, course titles, and textbook content and instructional practices of social studies teachers. Despite these findings, Vinson and Ross argue that there is enormous diversity within the enacted social studies curriculum as a result of the curricular decisions made by individual teachers.

In recent years, standards-based curriculum initiatives have become ubiquitous. For example, they are manifested in a number of recent policy statements produced by the National Council of the Social Studies and by various frameworks established among the states. These standards-based curriculum reforms are often linked with high-stakes tests as part of an accountability system intended to assure their inclusion in the enacted curriculum of social studies classrooms. Vinson and Ross present a review of what we know about the nature of social studies curriculum; how the roles of people both in and outside classroom shapes the curriculum; and the issues social studies curriculum workers/researchers will face in coming years. Their critical overview of past large-scale studies of the social studies curriculum is augmented by analysis of the impact of standards-based curriculum reforms on student's experience in social studies classrooms.

In Chapter 4, Catherine Cornbleth presents an analysis of the how social studies is affected by the cultures of constraint and restraint. Cornbleth examines the social and political constraints and restraints on social studies education. Her analysis is oriented by anthropologist Jules Henry's claim in *Culture Against Man (1952)* that the purpose of public elementary and secondary schooling has been to transmit the national culture, not to transform it. Henry believed that social studies, in particular, teaches students to be stupid, that is, to accept the culture as given, not to question it. A half-century later, it could be argued that little has changed in this regard, even to the extent that the culture being transmitted by social studies is a decade or two behind the lived cultures of students and teachers outside of school. In some contrast to the argument presented by Vinson and Ross in Chapter 3, Cornbleth argues that, despite various reform efforts, the status of social studies education conveyed by Shaver, Davis, and Helburn (1979) more than twenty years ago is out-of-date in relatively few schools and social studies classrooms across the nation. To understand the holding power of the kind of social studies education portrayed by Henry and Shaver et al., Cornbleth critically examines the research evidence regarding external influences, constraints, or controls on teachers and teaching, especially social studies teachers and teaching, and the internal restraints (e.g., self-censorship) felt by social studies teachers with respect to curriculum practice (i.e., what they teach and how they teach it). In particular, she examines the impact of the bureaucratic emphasis on law and order, the conservative pressure to maintain the status quo, the external threats to shape the curriculum, the focus on students as pathological, and our cultural preoccupation with schooling as competition. Cornbleth's critical analysis reveals specific social and political obstacles to progressive curriculum and instruction reform in social studies education and how some of these obstacles might be undermined by social studies educators in the future. She reminds us all of the powerful influence of our wider cultural on social studies research and practice.

In Chapter 5, Walter C. Parker explores education for democratic citizenship in light of the diverse and changing social contexts in which citizenship education takes place. He argues that there has been a relatively stable consensus regarding the centrality of citizenship to social studies education. However, our understanding of citizenship education has changed significantly since World War II from the "three traditions" described by Barr, Barth, and Shermis (1977) to the critical/noncritical framework stressed by Giroux (1988), and, now, to one dominated by the cultural politics of identity and the contest between participatory civics and transmission civics. Meanwhile, the social contexts of citizenship have also shifted. The rhetoric of "decline" (as in "the decline of community") has been popular with scholars, political candidates, and average citizens alike, yet community life is not declining so much as *changing*. The resurgence of nationalism, separatism, and gated suburban communities makes one set of examples, globalization another, and disinvestment in public institutions, such as schools, still another.

Citizenship education also takes place across a shifting array of social settings. Parker focuses on a comparison of citizenship learning outside of school (e.g., religious organizations, clubs, neighborhood hangouts, social class) with citizenship learning inside school, both formally (e.g., civics curriculum) and informally (classroom climate and school governance). He compares these school and non-school sites to a third, powerful predictor of citizenship outcomes: school attendance. Neither inside nor outside school, attendance (called "educational attainment" by researchers) refers simply to the number of years a citizen has gone to school. Parker examines the possible effects of a broader, multifaceted, school and community linked approach to citizenship education.

Parker also describes three pervasive problems that distort citizenship education: First, we have a tendency to treat democracy as an accomplishment rather than an aspiration. Second, we often conflate the cultural with the political as opposed to seeing the two as parallel. Third, we often operate on the assumption that our democratic system is neutral, thereby masking its ethnocentric and androcentric origins and effects.

Finally, Parker calls our attention to the unresolved (and often unexamined) tensions between multicultural education and education for democracy. He argues that both elements of democratic education are essential for a robust democratic culture and illustrates how more dialogue between proponents of both positions would strengthen social studies education.

In Chapter 6, Linda S. Levstik and Keith Barton analyze four different ways we might use the past and the implications for social studies education. As noted earlier, history has long been considered a central (if not the central) discipline of the social studies. But even if one were to accept this position, it would not explain how history should shape the curriculum. Levstik and Barton, use a sociocultural theory to examine how the teaching and learning of history is influenced by a variety of socially defined purposes. They compare international studies of research on children's historical thinking and examine how the social purposes of history vary across contexts and how the multiple goal underlying historical learning reflect complex and often contradictory "stances" toward the topic. The chapter describes four overlapping positions toward the past; each defined by a particular "act" related to historical thinking, that is, *exhibition, identification, analysis,* and *understanding.* Each position is described in terms of its prevalence in schools and other educational settings, the multiple purposes which can accompany the position, the extent to which it influences students' ideas about the past, and the potential drawbacks to overemphasizing that position in educational settings. Levstik and Barton compare the four positions and evaluate each with regard to their ability to expand student's use of history a guide to action in the present. They also offer suggestions for how educators might make more reasoned decisions regarding meaningful historical approaches in their own contexts of practice (e.g., teaching, curriculum development, research). They argue for an approach to curriculum that is focused on humanistic education for the social good.

Education in a multicultural society has presented special challenges to social studies educators. In Chapter 7, Ellen Santora, examines the problems and possibilities of multicultural education. She maintains that today's social studies has the mission of providing students with the dispositions, knowledge, skills, and practices necessary for citizenship in a non-hierarchical, culturally pluralistic democracy. As such, social studies should model inclusive habits of mind and civility while providing equitable opportunities for all students to learn about realities of global interdependence, the development of the human condition, and the struggles for American democracy in culturally and gender inclusive ways. In practice, however, social studies has focused on the assimilation of students from different cultures to the mainstream culture.

Following a brief overview of the history of multicultural education research, Santora, focuses on research related to four principal ideas connecting multicultural education and social studies education. Santora examines research concerning the complex web of sociocultural conditions influencing the development of students' identities. She also explores research linking social studies curriculum content and materials, teachers' beliefs, and instructional approaches to hierarchies of race, class, and gender in school and society. Santora outlines theory and research relating students' and teachers' epistemological orientations to each other and to social studies content and processes as these orientations may shape students' attention to and perspectives of social studies content as well as their civic habits of inclusion/exclusion. Because unity and diversity are fundamental to the existence of a cultural democracy, she pays particular attention to theory and research that explores the nature of culturally diverse, democratic communities. She highlights the lack of research on cross-cultural dialog and how often recommended multicultural instructional strategies fail in practice. One reason for such failures is the tendency for white teachers to lack consciousness of their own racism. Another problem is the tendency of dominant student groups to marginalize students who are not part of the mainstream culture. This landscape of research relating multicultural education to social studies education provides a backdrop for examining critical issues in the field as well as proposing an agenda for future research. It is instructive to compare Santora's analysis of multicultural education with the one presented by Parker in Chapter 5.

In Chapter 8, Merry M. Merryfield calls our attention to the changing nature of global education and the implications of such changes for social studies. Over the last thirty years, scholars from international studies, area studies, intercultural and cross-cultural education, postcolonial theory, peace education, environmental education, and people working for local/ global equity, diversity, and justice have developed a rich knowledge base from which teachers can learn and teach about the world and its peoples from a global perspective. But, according to Merryfield, global education within the social studies has remained a rather parochial and stagnant field uninformed by research and conceptual literature beyond that generated by social studies educators. She points out the dysfunctional nature of a conception of global education rooted in the negative language of imperialism and the cold war, and makes a persuasive argument for the reconceptualization of global education in ways more consistent with a postcolonial era. Her chapter also examines recent research from several fields that can inform and strengthen the development of global K–12 social studies teachers and teacher educators, and presents the implications for future research on social studies teaching and learning.

Computer technology has had a powerful, albeit unclear, impact on society and education. In Chapter 9, Michael J. Berson, John K. Lee, and Daniel W. Stuckart present a critical analysis of the integration of computers in social studies instruction and learning. A critical evaluation of research on computer use in the social studies includes the current pedagogic application of technology through Internet and web-based approaches, tele-collaborative teaching, simulations, drill and practice activities, games, tutorials, databases and archives, word processing, and graphing. Although an increasing body of research suggests that technology can improve academic achievement, Berson, Lee, and Stuckart argue correctly that changes in social studies instruction based on these findings must be balanced with a consideration of issues concerning the practice and purpose of social studies as it relates to the application of computer technology. In this regard, the issues raised by the other chapter authors are directly relevant to the application of technology in social studies instruction.

The authors examine questions regarding the efficiency and effectiveness of computer technology applications in social studies classroom, the role of teacher education institutions and school settings, the unrealized potential of technology and the overlooked consequences of technological development on children and youth with regard to their social development, interpersonal interactions, and global understanding. In addition to evaluating technology as a tool of instruction in the social studies, the authors focus on the significant effects that these resources have had on the political, social, and economic dimensions of our society. Berson, Lee, and Stuckart also consider the precursors of the digital divide, which separates those who are information rich through their access to telecommunications, computers, and the Internet from the information and technologically poor. They examine the differential impact of privileged access to these resources in the early stages of development and the continuing consequences of this separation of "haves" and "have-nots" on economic success, civic influence, and personal advancement. Ultimately, as Berson, Lee, and Stuckart argue, technology must be harnessed as a tool to reinforce our democratic culture.

In chapter 10, James P. Shaver presents a provocative argument as to why research on social studies has not been particularly productive, either in terms of theory development or for practical assistance to social studies educators. The reasons for the limited impact of social studies research identified by Shaver are numerous, and include confounding of the roles of professional educator and scholar/researcher; lack of clarity in regard to educational research as science, with resultant epistemological confusion; inappropriate methodology, such as statistical significance testing; difficult-to-control study environments; lack of sustained, long-term research efforts built on theory and prior research findings; inconstant, non-validated outcome assessments; failure to recognize ontological reality; and the pursuit of inappropriate research goals.

As part of his analysis, Shaver reviewed articles that appeared in *Theory and Research in Social Education* (TRSE) from 1995 through 1999. He found only one explicit report of effect sizes, but without consideration of the relationship of effect-size magnitude to educational significance. And while the number of qualitative research articles in TRSE have increased significantly in recent years, Shaver argues there appears to be little evidence that the impact of this form of research on educational practice is any greater than for quantitative research.

Shaver's suggestions for a more productive social studies research future include abandonment of the concept of social studies research as science; research efforts focused on the practical goal of verifying what is good about social studies and how it can be generalized and improved; adoption of an appropriate epistemological frame, with methods appropriate to educational settings and relinquishment of the qualitative-quantitative distinction and disputation; efforts directed at the social validation of outcome assessments; and adoption of a strategy for the production of coordinated, long-term research findings. Shaver looks to engineering and technology as opposed to natural or social science as a better model or approach to research in social studies.

This revised focus for social studies research would emphasize how to obtain specific social goals. Social studies educators, irrespective of their epistemological orientations, tend to agree that their research should help social studies teachers. If social studies researchers could reach consensus on this more practical, problem-focused approach to research, they are likely to reduce fragmentation and make more progress. Certainly, Shaver's views will provoke significant debate. We might question his dismissal of the impact of qualitative social studies research, as he seems to employ the same critical criteria he uses to analyze quantitative research when analyzing the latter (e.g., see the chapters by Santora and Merryfield). His epistemological claims with regard to relativism will also raise the ire of some readers. Nevertheless, his case for the historical failure of social studies research, as presently conceived, poses a challenge to the other chapter authors and the field in general by one of its most important scholars.

Twenty years ago, Howard Mehlinger (1981) described what he saw as "gulfs and priorities" for the social studies. In Mehlinger's estimation, the social studies were close to being dead, or at least on a life support system. He emphasized the gulf between social studies professionals and the wider public, between the leaders and followers (teachers) of social studies, and between social studies educators and the rest of the academic community. In particular, Mehlinger believed that the lack of consensus regarding what social studies should be and the confusion regarding how we should deal with values posed a direct threat to the field. Reading the authors in this book, one might conclude that not much has changed over the past two decades. On the other hand, social studies continues to exist as a significant element of the K–12 curriculum. It has not died. Certainly, social studies continues to fall short of our best visions of what it could be. But it persists nonetheless; and there is a trace of hope embedded in this persistence.

The domination of history and the social science disciplines notwithstanding, an integrated conception of social studies remains alive, if not especially well. Much of what has characterized the attack on social studies by critics like Bennett, Bestor, Cheney, Hirsch, Nevins, Ravitch, and others can be understood within a wider attempt to preserve traditional foundations for Western culture and the nature of knowledge. A constant theme embedded in this ongoing debate, is a fear of relativism, or what Bernstein (1983) called the "Cartesian anxiety," that is, the fear that either we have objective foundations for truth or we must fall into the abyss of relativism, skepticism, and nihilism. This dysfunctional mode of "either or" thinking is rejected by Bernstein as it was long ago by Dewey (1929).

It is important to note that either or thinking has infected scholars on both the political right and left (Stanley, 1992). In social studies, the debate has often bogged down around arguments for neutrality (e.g., values clarification, attempts not to teach values) or socialization (cultural transmission) to maintain the status quo, or "counter socialization," which emphasizes teaching "progressive democratic" values and ways of life in opposition to dominant conservative values that reinforce an oppressive system. Each of these arguments has led to an intellectual cul-de-sac. This is not to assert that values are irrelevant to social studies education and research.

There is no way to construct a neutral curriculum. At best, we can work to inform ourselves and our students of the ideology that shapes our thought and practice. The objectivism/relativism dichotomy is false, because human knowledge, while never foundational, can be more than arbitrary. Dewey's conception of warranted assertability is one way to view this issue. Human knowledge in a democratic culture is always partial and provisional. But this knowledge should reflect our best estimations of the practices we should follow to realize the social good. Values are always present in any culture and they always influence how we think and act. But we need not take such values as given a priori. Rather, each generation in a democratic culture must construct (or reconstruct) its own values. The appeal to taken-for-granted core values like social justice is not intrinsically more defensible than the taken-for–granted values of a market economy. While traditional values will always be passed on via schooling and other institutions, democratic citizens must develop the critical competence to determine if they should continue to follow those values or alternatives, and how the values we choose will be applied in our lives. If we fail to exercise this critical competence as citizens, we fall prey to an unreflective acceptance of tradition.

The collective work of the chapter authors in this book represents an attempt to grapple with such issues as we begin the next century of social studies education. It is hoped that a critical examination of issues central to social studies education will promote continued dialog aimed at improving research and practice in the field.

REFERENCES

Barr, R.P., Barth, J.L., & Shermis, S.S. 1977. *Defining the social studies.* Bulletin 51. Arlington, VA: National Council for the Social Studies.

Bruner, J.S. 1960. *The process of education.* Cambridge, MA: Harvard University Press.

Dewey, J. (1929). *The quest for certainty: A study of the relation of knowledge to action.* New York: Putnam Press.

Fuller, S. (2000). *Thomas Kuhn: A philosophical history for our times.* Chicago: The University of Chicago Press.

Giroux, H.A. 1988. *Schooling and the struggle for public life. Critical pedagogy in the modern age.* Minneapolis: University of Minnesota.

Harding, S. (1998). *Is science multicultural? Postcolonialisms, feminisms, and epistemologies.* Bloomington: Indiana University Press.

Henry, J. (1963). *Culture against man.* New York: Random House.

Kohn, A. 2000. *The case against standardized testing: Raising the scores, ruining the schools.* Portsmouth, NH: Heinemann.

Margolis, J. (1993). *The flux of history and the flux of science.* Berkley: University of California Press.

Matthews, M. (1994). *Science teaching: The role of history and philosophy of science.* New York: Routledge Press.

Ravitch, D., & Finn, C.E. 1987. *What do our 17-year-olds know?* Albany: State University of New York Press.

Shaver, J.P., Davis, O.L., & Helburn, S.W. 1979. *An interpretive report on the status of pre-collegiate social studies education based on three NSF-funded studies.* Washington, DC: National Science Foundation.

Siegel, H. (1997). Science education: Multicultural and universal. *Interchange, 28,* 97–108.

Stanley, W.B. (1992). *Curriculum for utopia: Social reconstructionism and critical pedagogy in the postmodern era.* Albany: State University of New York Press.

Stanley, W.B., & Brickhouse, N.W. (In press). Teaching sciences: The multicultural question revisited. *Science Education.*

Wesley, E., & Wronski, S. 1958. *Teaching social studies in high schools.* Boston: D.C. Heath.

CHAPTER 2

DEFINING SOCIAL STUDIES

Jack L. Nelson

PURPOSES, DEFINITION, AND DEBATE

Definitions are significant. Our individual lives and our multiple cultures are intertwined with definitions. Language use requires them; interpretation involves them; judgment depends upon them. Our perspectives, political and educational, are colored by our definitions. Further, our concepts of quality and significance, whether in theory, scholarship, or practice, are based on definitional considerations; some things are valued more than others, depending on definition. Our basic principles—justice, democracy, equality, integrity, loyalty, and honesty—are all dependent upon definition and evolving definition.

Definitional questions are more than esoteric disputes among theoreticians. Knowledge is essentially a set of definitional statements, always under scrutiny and subject to change. Certainly, the body of social studies content consists of definitions from the most trivial to the most significant for individuals and for society. Social studies, itself, is the subject of definition and debate about definition, as are all vital subject fields. The definition of social studies has significant implications for the school curriculum, teacher/classroom practice, the teacher education curriculum, and the forms of research valued in the field. These are solid grounds for examining again the definitions of social studies, and presuming that this examination will not be the last. Redefining, of course, honors previous efforts at definition; it suggests an evolution, with debate as an avenue for improvement.

Defining social studies is not an easy task; it is encumbered by a confounding history, conflicting conceptual ideas, and strong ideological divergence in both political and educational philosophy. Even the question

of whether social studies is a singular or plural term has political overtones—singular suggesting the field is an integrated study of social knowledge and plural suggesting that it is a collection of several separately-
defined subjects. More important, the several definitions of social studies
cover a political-educational gamut from right-wing conservative traditional to left-wing liberal progressive. They range from definitions that
would eliminate social studies entirely (e.g., Bestor, 1953; Keller, 1991), to
one that identifies social studies as virtually all social knowledge—the most
inclusive, overarching field that envelopes content from all other subjects
(Stanley & Nelson, 1994). That is a broad spectrum of definitions, from
zero to all-inclusive and all infused with political overtones. This is not neutral territory; it is fraught with ideological baggage. This chapter, along
with most of the writing about defining any fields of study, is itself informed
by a perspective.

In addition to ideological overtones, differing definitions of the field
incorporate disparate criteria that make it difficult to make consistent comparisons; the definitions sometimes involve school or social purposes,
methods of study, expected personal or social outcomes, and imbedded
values. For example, some definitions:

- use basic purposes of the field as paramount defining criteria (e.g.,
  citizenship, social criticism, social responsibility, civic competence,
  cultural stability or change, personal character, self-respect).
- use knowledge structure dimensions to define social studies (e.g.,
  social sciences, history, law-related education, behavioral studies, global education, humanities, integrative social knowledge).
- use instructional or curricular criteria for definitional differences
  (e.g., critical thinking, issues-centered, multicultural studies).

The following terms have been used as defining characteristics for social
studies (listed alphabetically; citations refer to source information, not necessarily to author's position):

- Character/Moral/Values education (Kohlberg, 1976; Leming, 1985;
  Raths, Harmin, & Simon, 1978).
- Citizen Transmission, Social Sciences, Critical Thinking (Barr, Barth,
  & Shermis, 1977).
- Citizenship, Civics (*Education for Responsible Citizenship*, 1977; Shaver,
  1996).
- Critical Theory (Cherryholmes, 1988; Gibson, 1999; Giroux, 1988;
  Giroux & Penna, 1979).
- History (Bestor, 1953; Keller, 1991; Levstik, 1996; Ravitch, 1985;
  Whelan, 1992).
- Integrated Study of Subject Fields for Civic Competence (NCSS,
  1993).

- Issues-Centered Study (Evans, 1992; Evans & Saxe, 1996; Oliver & Shaver, 1966).
- Policy Study (Parker & Zumeta, 1999).
- Practical Reasoning/Phronesis (Stanley, 1992; Whitson & Stanley, 1988).
- Reflective/Critical Thinking; Decision Making; Citizen Action (Engle, 1971; Engle & Ochoa, 1988; Hunt & Metcalf, 1955; Massialas & Cox, 1966; Newmann, 1975; Vinson, 1999).
- Reconstructionism (Counts, 1932; Stanley, 1981a,b, 1992).
- Social Criticism (Engle, 1977; Nelson, 1985; Nelson & Ochoa, 1987).
- Social Sciences, including history (Keller, 1961; Lowe, 1969).
- Social Welfare, Social Problems (Saxe, 1991a,b, 1992a,b).

ESTABLISHING SOCIAL STUDIES

Social studies has been disputed academic terrain for over a century. A committee of The Progressive Education Association published a report in 1938 that included this historical note:

> The social studies began to appear sporadically as separate subjects in the secondary school about 1830 ... toward the end of the century a number of national committees attempted to bring order out of the existing confusion and to design a solid base for the social studies curriculum. Of these committees, the two most important were the Committee of Ten of the National Education Association, which reported in 1893, and the Committee of Seven of the American Historical Association, which reported in 1899. (*The Social Studies in General Education*, 1939, pp. 2, 3)

The confusion identified in the quote above rests on definitional elements; is social studies the same as history and geography—two subjects dating back into eighteenth-century American school curriculums—or is social studies an integrating field of knowledge devoted to study of human society and its problems and found in philosophic or social welfare literature also dating back to the eighteenth or nineteenth century in America? Or is social studies something else entirely?

An example of the confounding politics of historical attempts to define social studies occurs in a dispute over how social studies emerged as a field of study and how it came to be known as a school subject. Some popular literature in the field often portrays the term as emerging from a document published in 1916. This traditional view is that social studies became a widely accepted curricular field through the relatively progressive 1916 Report of the Committee on Social Studies of the National Education Association Commission on the Reorganization of the Secondary School (Hertzberg, 1981; Lybarger, 1991). The recommended curriculum of that report had history and geography as the subjects most frequently taught, with a course in American social problems as the 12th grade capstone. That report called the purpose of social studies to be good citizenship within the school's mission of social efficiency. The 1916 curriculum proposed remains substantially in use today, with history continuing as the dominant subject studied, and citizenship is often claimed as the primary purpose for teaching it. One definition of social studies that arose out of this report is "the social sciences simplified for pedagogical purposes," but history was the main subject taught (Wesley & Wronski, 1958).

More recent scholarship raises questions about that founding perspective, noting that social studies and social science organizations evolved more than three decades before the 1916 Report. More important, they have a core based on social problems rather than social transmission of historical/cultural information (Saxe, 1991a,b, 1992a,b). Saxe (1991b) notes that social studies was a term in use in schools in England by 1884, the same year that the American Historical Association (AHA) was founded at an annual meeting of the American Social Science Association, a group itself founded in 1865 to address social problems. The establishment of social studies from this perspective identifies the field as a part of a social science/social problems movement intended to be useful in dealing with social problems. It is a much more activist approach and doesn't depend on historical teachings to convey social values. Shaver (1967) noted a definition different from the earlier 'social studies as simplified social sciences': social studies as general education to prepare citizens for participation in democratic society—a definition that makes it an integrating field, selecting from all fields material that could help develop active citizens and more consistent with the social problems founding perspective.

In 1921, The National Council for the Social Studies (NCSS), presumably the organization with the most interest in advocating social studies as a curricular term, was founded with help of the American Historical Association (AHA). The NCSS and the AHA met jointly in the early years, and historians have continued to be particularly influential in the leadership of NCSS. History has been the dominant subject studied in the social studies curriculum, and state social studies teacher licensing requirements reflect that domination in history course credit mandates for social studies teachers. The conventional wisdom, along with the popular 1916 Report curricular structure that featured history, places the history establishment as parent-guardian of social studies, and results in support for the primary location of history in social studies, and in the corollary interest in transmitting socially and historically acceptable traditions to young people. From this perspective, social studies owes its beginnings and academic substance to history and history properly continues its dominant influence on social studies. In the main, this definition of social studies is based on the essentially uncritical transmission of historical information, wherein traditional historians determine appropriate knowledge and social studies teachers simply transmit it to youth.

The influence of the history establishment on the practical definition of social studies is shown in more than the AHA involvement in establishing NCSS. The first NCSS yearbook was apparently intended to deal with "some aspects of the social sciences," but it has four chapters on history teaching and only one chapter on social studies, focused on the junior high school. One of the featured chapters is "History and Patriotism," which argues against the excessive use of ethnocentric history but admits that much history education is of that form (*First Yearbook*, 1931). The second NCSS yearbook, presumably devoted to problems in teaching "the social sciences" actually contains seven chapters on history education, two on geography, one on testing, and only one on citizenship (*Second Yearbook*, 1932).

NCSS was a department of the National Education Association (NEA) at that time, but was strongly influenced by the professional historian movement; for example, the first official NCSS journal for social studies teachers was titled *The Historical Outlook* and the later NCSS journal, *Social Education*, carried a formal tribute to the AHA in each issue until the 1960s, even though the AHA had no involvement with or support for the journal. It was not until the 6th NCSS yearbook that the term social studies becomes important enough to specify: "This year the Yearbook is directly devoted to the Social Studies [caps in original]" (*Elements of the Social Studies Program*, 1936, Foreword). This was the first yearbook to seem to worry about confusion in defining the term: "...barely two decades ago that the phrase 'social study' made its appearance" (p. 8), and "That committee [Committee on Social Studies of the NEA] used a 'cryptic' description: the term 'social studies' is used to include history, civics, and economics" (p. 9). However, by 1913, the U.S. Bureau of Education had already defined social studies much more broadly as "subject matter which relates directly to the organization and development of human society, and to man as a member of social groups" (*Bulletin No. 41*, 1913, p. 16).

Clearly, this bifurcated history lends itself to conflicts in conceptual rationales for social studies, as well as to ideological debate couched in political and educational philosophy. Some might argue that it is not important which account of the founding of social studies is more accurate; as a mere matter of archival information, it has limited importance. But a basic undercurrent in the continuing dispute over a definition and the resulting practice of social studies in the schools reflects the essential difference between these founding perspectives: (1) the view that social studies is the product of historians and is a form of junior history, consisting mainly of historical information defined and described by university historians for transmission as cultural heritage by precollegiate teachers, and (2) the view that social studies is the product of interests in social progress involving broader social and intellectual concerns, and including the active or critical study of social issues by precollegiate teachers and students.

This disparity in founding orientations and in current practice incorporates ideological positions that use political and educational theory as frameworks. One view holds that social studies should be abolished in schools because it is a product of progressive-liberal school ideas that corrupt academic study and threaten traditional values (Bestor, 1953). Another view holds that social studies offers a rare opportunity to improve society by critical study and social action (Engle, 1977; Nelson, 1991). There are many other views. Unfortunately, the positions have hardened so that a clear determination of which founding tradition is more accurate would not be likely to change positions on the debate over purposes and practices of social studies. It would, however, help scholarship in the field to continue research on this topic. Defining knowledge, as in social studies, is a worthy effort beyond mere historical accuracy.

FINDING DEFINITIONS AND TRADITIONS

Barr, Barth, and Shermis (1977) identified three historical traditions of social studies practice: citizen transmission, social science, and reflective thinking. Their analysis concluded that transmission of citizenship was the most widely held tradition, with social science next, then critical thinking. Engle (1977) and others argued in addenda chapters published in the Barr, Barth, and Shermis book that the provided definitions were inadequate in conceptualization, completeness, and logical consistency. Among the disputed points were that the identified traditions ignored other social studies traditions, for example, social criticism, that lay outside of very mainstream concepts and that separating social sciences from critical thinking is illogical.

Other efforts to organize the various definitions of social studies occur in Brubaker, Simon, & William, 1977), Nelson and Michaelis (1980), Goodman and Adler (1985), and Martorella (1996). Martorella, for example, identified the definitions as: citizenship transmission, social sciences, reflective inquiry, informed social criticism, and personal development. Vinson (1998) used Martorella's categories of definition to test empirically teacher perceptions of the nature and purposes of social studies. Vinson found, in opposition to the conclusions of Barr, Barth, and Shermis, that "informed social criticism" was identified more often (25%) than either citizen transmission (10%) or social science (4%).

Not only is there dispute about commonly perceived purposes of social studies, the three traditions identified by Barr, Barth, and Shermis mirror a perplexing and internally inconsistent mix of definitional criteria used in much of the social studies literature. Definitions rest on differing claims of purposes, instructional method, historical derivation, curricular design, knowledge base, and perspective. Disparities in criteria and organizing elements among defining principles make a comparative analysis of definitions of social studies difficult; there are few common groundings. That, in itself, does not diminish the value of revisiting definitions of social studies in order to rethink scholarly and applied work in the field. Indeed, every vital field of knowledge periodically revisits its own definitions. A static definition defines a moribund field. The current confusing mix of definitional criteria suggests that a new effort at definition should provide a set of grounds on which definitions are set and compared. This is a task worth doing in the field. The need for a "logical organization of subject matter" rests on a concern for reflective thinking in the "growth of the mind" (Dewey, 1933, p. 46). Definition is basic to that logical organization.

Barth (1996), attempted to describe the "nature" of social studies as part of the 75th anniversary of the National Council for Social Studies. He did not try to reconcile various sides in the debate, but defined the "essential elements" in social studies as: improving social welfare, meeting student needs for problem solving, and developing democratic citizens. These purposes are helpful as criteria for examining any definition of the field, but do not resolve the key disputes over definition.

KNOWLEDGE AS A SOCIAL CONSTRUCT

Knowledge is not a set of obvious bits of evidence—unsullied by ideology or values. Our definition of what constitutes knowledge is a social construct, relying on fundamental belief of some type—belief in the supernatural or religious, belief in a charismatic leader, belief in sensory perception, belief in reason, belief in scientific principles or practitioners, belief in physical evidence, belief in intuition, or belief in some combination of these. Definitions of knowledge are the product of history and ideology, and this is nowhere more true than in the social sciences and social studies. Subject boundaries usually represent traditional views and ideological commitments.

The social subjects are not clear, unambiguous, pristine, logically tight, and mutually exclusive categories of knowledge; they are sloppy, overlapping, unclear and indistinct in many facets, self-perpetuating, and often intellectually limiting definitions of subjects of study. Many advocates of these subjects engage in actions to gain power in the academic market, a form of academic imperialism wherein one subject controls another. Definitions, and denials of definition, of social studies have suffered this form of dispute wherein partisans from inside and outside the field exclude, ignore, or vilify social studies in an effort to gain academic power in the curriculum (Barth, 1991; Brady, 1993; Dynneson, 1993; Nelson, 1991).

Knowledge is what we agree to make of it; it is not an entity separate from human invention and intervention. What we define as knowledge, then, is of special importance as knowledge itself increases in importance. For subjects of study in all levels of schooling, definitions of knowledge become particularly important. Not only are the definitions used to structure the ways of thinking for younger generations and to continue those definitional characteristics onward into the future, these definitions become the acceptable scholarly terrain for research, for organizing by department or program in academe, and as a basis for holding relative status in the academic hierarchy. To be ignored or rejected as a result of definition is to have no apparent substance as a subject of study, to have no body of scholarly examination, no guild of scholars and teachers attesting to value of the field and continuing the turf battles over academic terrain. The politics of the academy require subject fields to have a recognizable outline and a number of advocates to maintain viability. The status of academic "discipline" conveys numerous advantages in the scholarly world. Disciplines, of course, depend on definitions.

DISCIPLINE AND DISCIPLINES

The mainstream concept of disciplines in academe implies a clarity of definition with distinct separation from other disciplines, clearly established boundaries of study and content, a well-documented and organized body of literature, and a scholarly orientation that is parallel to other disciplines in its power and focus. However, those experienced in academic politics and those with intellectual interests beyond any individual topic of study recognize that the academic disciplines are not obviously distinct areas of knowledge with clear boundaries and unique bodies of literature or modes of scholarly inquiry. As Michel Foucault (1972) noted: "Disciplines constitute a system of control in the production of discourse, fixing its limits through the action of an identity taking the form of a permanent reactivation of the rules" (p. 224).

One of the arguments made about the defining of social studies is that it is not a discipline, and that argument is used as a means for defining the field out of existence or marginalizing it in academic discussion. If social studies is not a discipline, and disciplines are the basic work taught in schools, social studies is automatically defined as a frill or extracurricular topic easily eliminated. This makes the question of discipline important for defining social studies, or any subject of study.

What is a discipline? The idea of an academic discipline as a uniquely separate field of study is widely held, though inherently faulty. The logical and rigorous tests proposed by Jerome Bruner (1960) or Paul Hirst (1974) for separate identification as disciplines require a discipline to (1) have derived a unique set of principles or laws, and (2) use a distinct mode of inquiry. One could make an argument that there is a small shred of evidence of basic laws and separable modes of inquiry in certain of the natural sciences, but, even there, the separations between them are not so discrete as to render each an entirely closed system, as proposed by this definition of discipline. The social and historical sciences, despite efforts to claim otherwise, have even less separation among themselves on basic principles of structure or methodology. The only law that seems to come from study in history and social science is that things change, a modification of scientific information from long ago and a concept scarcely limited to the work of any one social science or to traditional history.

Bruner (1960) contributed most to the discipline-oriented curricular developments in "New Social Studies" of the 1960s by using this rigorous notion of discipline as a means for developing instructional and curricular ideas from each separate discipline. Many disciples became active advocates (e.g., Lowe, 1969), of Bruner's ideas and tried to define social studies by separating the several so-called disciplines, self-defined by scholars in those separate fields who would organize teaching around the "structure and methods" of each field. That effort, strongly supported by U.S. government grants, failed for a variety of reasons, including the lack of intellectual rigor in trying to sustain the separation of social study disciplines on the grounds laid down by Bruner. Bruner himself finally recognized the serious limitations of his own structure in maintaining distinctions among fields of social study and their methods (Weltman, 1999). Almost ironically, one of Bruner's most important contributions to social education is the intellectually challenging and nondisciplinary MACOS project for elementary school students;

It is clear that the fields of history, the individual social sciences, and social studies do not meet the high standard for definition as a discipline posed in early Bruner, Hirst, and some of the philosophic literature (Kincaid, 1996; Nelson, 1991; Wisdom, 1987). Scholars in history, the social sciences, and social studies cannot demonstrate unique sets of principles and mode of inquiry; rather, they offer few, if any, fundamental principles, none of which is unique to that field, and they use many common methods of research and sets of theories in organizing and conducting their work. Scholars in history, the social sciences, and social studies have developed general ideas or theories that have some use in explanation, for example, manifest destiny, scarcity as basic to supply/demand, the social contract, critical thinking dependent upon problems and evidence. But these concepts do not rise to the level of basic principles as found in several of the sciences and mathematics, and each concept is challengeable on solid scholarly grounds as inadequate for fundamental explanation of social phenomena. In addition, such concepts as manifest destiny, social contract and critical thinking are not unique to any specific field of social knowledge. These are working hypotheses or concepts to help organize and manage knowledge. Such concepts as time, place, self, and society are not restricted to the boundaries of history, geography, psychology or sociology; they are important ideas that transcend disciplines into the nondisciplinary.

In methods of study, history is not the only field to study trends and periods or to use archival data over time; sociology is not the only one to examine social conditions or use survey instruments; economics is not the only subject to study relative value or use statistics. While it is true that some fields are known for the use of some methods of study to construct or test theories much more than others, it is not the discipline structure that requires it, it is the choice of certain of the scholars in the field and the force of tradition. Thus, historians commonly use documentary study with dates as key indicators while sociologists and psychologists commonly use observational techniques and statistical analysis—but some historians use field observations and statistics and some sociologists and psychologists use historical data and analysis. There is a political geography of history, a history of politics, a history of economics, an anthropology of language and culture, a philosophy of history and a history of philosophy, a sociology of history and knowledge, a psychology of politics, and on into any number of combinations. According to the most stringent criteria for determining disciplines, separations among history, the social sciences and social studies are intellectually false and academically misleading; they separate information by narrow categories that are not mutually exclusive (American history, sociology, political science, economics, etc.), while impeding the synthesis of that information into broader and more intellectually challenging knowledge categories. Departmental and professional structures of separation limit scholars and students.

Instead of meeting the more rigorous criteria for definition as a discipline, the fields of history, the many social sciences (e.g., economics, anthropology, political science, sociology, women's studies, psychology, global studies, law, education, geography), and the humanities (e.g., philosophy, literature, arts) meet a much less rigorous standard—traditional practice or common public understanding. The term discipline is defined in dictionaries as: "a branch of knowledge involving research" (*Webster's New Collegiate Dictionary*). Under this definition, social studies fits the criteria for a discipline at least as well as most of our companion fields of study. Kline (1995), studying 20 years of experience in the well-reputed multidisciplinary program in Science, Technology, and Society at Stanford University, argues that "discipline" not be given a tight definition because that constrains thinking. He calls a discipline a "subject of study of a university department (or major sector of a department) in a late twentieth-century university. This implies that a discipline possesses a specific area of study, a literature, and a working community of paid scholars and/or practitioners" (p. 3). Under this definition we can place the social sciences, social studies, and history as disciplines, but none more than others except by size or traditional institutional power. Kline concludes his book with an important point about one of the defects of disciplines in the construct of knowledge: "The results of this book dispute over-claims that have long been seen as true by many disciplinary experts about what their particular discipline can do. Discipline experts have tended to dismiss, out of hand, comments from anyone who is not a "member of the club" (Kline, p. 310). What we usually call "disciplines" is the result of historical accident in higher education and the politics of special interest groups and advocates rather than the result of intellectual examination or knowledge-based determinations and definitions that are empirically verifiable.

Fields of study are interdependent in one form or another; the social and humanities fields of study are obviously interdependent. It is often useful and appropriate to differentiate among fields of study in order to provide clarification, simplify, conduct narrow scholarly inquiry, develop explanatory ideas for certain phenomena, or provide for clear educational explanation for students. Thus, having some separation among the social sciences, history (ies), and social studies can be useful for students, teachers, and scholars. But that does not make a hierarchy of disciplines or argue that one of those fields is not a discipline. Further, the separation among fields can be detrimental to long term student understanding and scholarly work when the interdependence and interrelationships among fields of social knowledge are not recognized and when the needed synthesis of information from the available subject field fragments is restricted by "disciplinary" blinders.

The argument that history, but not social studies, is a discipline is actually an ideological and political construct. The claim that history is superior on some grounds of disciplinary knowledge is simply academic imperialism, not the result of intellectual examination. Knowlton (1936) described a similar academic phenomenon in the 6th NCSS Yearbook: "A subject occupies territory not by decree or proclamation, but by active exploitation. In a sense a subject is what it is; it is what its creative scholars really make it, not what the writers of texts define it to be or what they aspire to have it become" (p.17).

Educationally, it may not be a great concern whether social studies or history or economics is a discipline until a threat arises because of the claim that only disciplines should be taught in schools and, by definition, one of these is not a discipline. What should be at issue for determining what deserves to be taught in the schools are such factors as the social and educational purposes of a field of study, its organizing and synthesizing frameworks, its understandability, its comprehensiveness, and its usefulness in life or in advanced academics.

SEMANTICS, TRIVIALITY, AND SOCIAL KNOWLEDGE: SOCIAL STUDIES AND HISTORY

We sometimes dismiss disagreements on definitions by simply classifying them as "semantic arguments," as though semantics were an insignificant concern, making the disagreement appear trivial. There are, of course, many trivial disputes that deserve simple dismissal, but semantics is not the proper category into which they should be put. Semantics is of particular importance in understanding human discourse and social scholarship. Semantics is the study of meanings for terms, the way words are used to shape our thoughts, ideas, and perspectives—a word for definition. Using the phrase, "it is only a semantic argument," to trivialize an otherwise important distinction in the meanings of words is a good illustration of the importance of semantics—it changes the meaning of the word semantic to connote triviality and to demean an opposing position. Such is the case with the dispute over defining social studies as an approach to curriculum and pedagogy in schools. It is not merely a trivial matter of finding a socially respectable or traditionally popular title for this part of the school curriculum.

Even more, the debate is not a simplistic rhetorical issue that some have posed between (1) a small group dedicated to a mythology of social studies and a significant community of historians (Keller, 1991), (2) those who would merely or malevolently politicize the school curriculum against real historical knowledge (Mehlinger, 1992), or (3) those who ignore practical schooling matters in order to further their theoretical interests (Davis, 1993). In each of these published efforts to trivialize or mediate the argument between social studies and history, the author has demonstrated a personal strong support for history rather than social studies as the organizing framework for social studies. Keller (1991), for example, merely dismisses social studies as a myth and unworthy of academic argument, proposing that we should just give it up and accept history as the savior field. Rather than address the serious limitations and restrictive traditions of a history framework for teaching in schools and rather than arguing over the potentials of a good social studies framework, these authors imply that the debate is trivial or unworthy. However, these semantic issues deserve further examination, especially in the context of efforts to impose a set of national standards on schools and the recent ideological furor over the American history standards.

Definitions have great influence on how social studies is approached, organized, taught, and evaluated in schools. The study and teaching of history differ in some significant ways from the study and teaching of social studies. These differences deserve exploration in terms of their impact on the purposes, practices, and potential consequences of education. History can be defined as a systemic method of study rather than a discipline; it is a very important aspect of all fields. Thus we have a history of science, history of art, history of philosophy, and history of social studies.

History of all topics should be better taught in schools and can incorporate critical and problem-based approaches (Whelan, 1992). But traditional history as taught in schools has significant defects, limiting purposes, stultifying practices, and anti-intellectual consequences (Nelson, 1991; Thornton, 1990). That does not argue for elimination of history, only for more critical examination of the kinds and uses of historical study involved in meeting broader definitions of social studies. Social studies, under most definitions, includes authentic historical study. Differing social studies defining characteristics like social criticism, issues, values education, reflective thinking, critical theory, and citizenship all require examination and use of historical evidence for reasoned study. In comparison with traditional history education with its transmission purposes, social studies purposes are more consistent with democratic principles, social studies methods of instruction are more progressive and integrative of knowledge, and its potential consequences more liberating for students and teachers. These are significant definitional positions that orient how scholars, practitioners, and students see the field.

The differences between history and social studies deserve exploration in terms of the interrelationships among social, ideological, and educational contexts for schooling. Questions on the purposes, practices, and potential consequences of schooling decisions arise within this social and ideological context. While one can argue that good education is good education regardless of historic period or particular location, it would be foolish to ignore the extensive influence that time and location have on educational questions. A society that expects its schools to train youth in militaristic manners and morals, as in Sparta, would disdain an argument that good education requires free-form individualistic creativity. Aristotle, the first Western political theorist, clearly argued that "The citizens of a state should always be educated to suit the constitution of the state ... the oligarchical type creates and sustains oligarchy" (1962, p. 332). By "constitution" Aristotle meant more than political structures; he included the general way of life in a state—its social, political, economic and ideological context.

PURPOSES FOR SOCIAL EDUCATION

This concept, that social and ideological contexts orient the general purposes and practices of educational systems, echoes throughout political and educational literature (e.g., Apple, 1993; Aquinas, 1960; Dewey, 1916; Montesquieu, 1949; Nelson, Palonsky, & Carlson, 2000; Rousseau, 1947; Ulich, 1954). Montesquieu (1949) in logic similar to Aristotle's, noted, "The laws of education will therefore be different in each species of government: in monarchies they will have honor for their object; in republics, virtue; in despotic government, fear" (p. 29). For the United States, de Tocqueville's (1969) analysis is apt: "The first duty imposed on those who now direct society is to educate democracy" (p. 12).

DeTocqueville's point offered a great opportunity for the United States to provide mass education suited to critical examination of social issues and active, enlightened self-governance: democratic education. Critical examination of social issues and active civic participation, is of course, an example of a good social studies framework for schooling. Traditional history has been less consistent with this opportunity. Unfortunately for public education, schooling traditions in place in early America were designed for social control by elites, instilling social and religious values, and developing nationalistic pride (Giroux, 1988; Katz, 1968, 1971; Nelson, 1978; Tyack, 1967). As a result, the early social curriculum of schools in the United States depended heavily on nationalistic history and geography, taught as truth and moralism and designed to produce docile and hard-working "good citizens." Critical thinking, controversy, and social issues were kept outside the school, designed only for social elites destined for leadership positions. The history-based social curriculum was deemed use-ful in Americanizing youth through patriotic sloganeering, limiting dis-sent, producing passive but morally righteous citizens, and convincing the masses of the virtues of work and proper status of the upper classes (Nay-lor, 1974; Nelson, 1976, 1978). This illustrates the complex relationship between social ideology and social curriculum and the intellectually cor-rupting influence of special interests such as the state itself. Bertrand Rus-sell (1928) noted the bleak side of this relationship:

> This institution [universal education] once firmly established, was found by the state to be capable of many uses. It makes young people more docile, both for good and evil. It improves manners and diminishes crime; it makes the community responsive to direction from a centre ... State education has acquired a certain bias. It teaches the young (so far as it can) to respect exist-ing institutions, to avoid all fundamental criticism of the powers that be, and to regard foreign nations with suspicion and contempt ... The damage to individual development comes through the undue stress upon authority ... disagreement with prevailing beliefs is severely repressed. Uniformity is desired because it is convenient to the administrator, regardless of the fact that is can only be secured by mental atrophy. (p. 128)

The Russell admonition is a legitimate warning of the high potential for intellectual corruption in social education, the area of schooling which is most directly involved in either state-supportive or state-critical education. One of the key concerns in determining a proper framework for school instruction in social subjects is to judge which academic title(s) would be most likely to succumb to the anti-intellectual and state-biased education Russell warns against.

The school subject of history, unfortunately, has its own long and sordid history of being corrupted for political ends. Historical education, as Nietzsche (1949) suggested, may be simply a major mechanism of political manipulation. There is a vast literature and a long historical record of nationalistic and propagandistic history teaching in the schools (Beale, 1936; Billington, 1962; Dance, 1960; Gellerman, 1938; Hayes, 1930; Mer-riam, 1931; Nelson, 1976, 1978, 1982; Pierce, 1926). Certainly, any social curriculum is subject to corruptibility for ideology, but school-taught history has demonstrated little capability for rising above political manipulation.

British Historian E.H. Dance (1960) notes this problem:

...if there is a record, it has a recorder, whose views and prejudices enter into his record and colour it ... Historians (honest or dishonest) are no more objective than witnesses (honest or dishonest) in a law-court; no two of them give the same account of the same thing ... In our days the whole world has become familiar with deliberate manipulation of history for the purposes of political propaganda. It is less frequently realized that every history book, from *The Decline and Fall* to *Little Arthur's England* puts forth a point of view which is consciously or unconsciously biased. (pp. 9, 16)

And Will and Ariel Durant (1968), suggest that we "respect one another's delusions" about knowledge, counseling modesty in the use of history because of its defects, stating:

To begin with, do we really know what the past was, what actually happened, or is history a fable not quite agreed upon? Our knowledge of a past event is always incomplete, probably inaccurate, beclouded by ambivalent evidence and biased historians, and perhaps distorted by our own patriotic or religious partisanship. Most history is guessing, and the rest is prejudice ... The historian always oversimplifies, and hastily selects a manageable minority of facts and faces out of a crowd of souls and events whose multitudinous complexity he can never quite embrace or comprehend. (Durant & Durant, 1968, p. 12)

Following his examination of civic education in various nations, the widely respected political scientist Charles Merriam (1931) noted that the least useful civic education practices were "pseudo-scientific historical propaganda and rigid indoctrination of ideologies" (p. 362).

Merriam was also among the authors of 16 fine scholarly products, mostly by noted historians, produced from the first and far more significant National Commission on the Social Studies in the Schools during the 1930s (Beard, 1934; Curti, 1935; Merriam, 1934). That Commission concluded wisely that it would not be wise to attempt to impose a restricted, history-bound curriculum on the social studies.

The recent public debate over national standards in United States history could have been based on differing intellectual or scholarly views of historical knowledge; however, the debate was, and is, plainly a political argument over which ideology gets transmitted to and implanted on youth. In the long run of that debate, the professional historians who initially developed the national standards to include more minority views and a more realistic portrayal of events in U.S. history, capitulated to a loud political furor from the right wing and modified the standards to reflect more "acceptable" and traditional views (Crabtree & Nash, 1994; Ravitch, 1994; Winkler, 1995). A public dispute among social education scholars on the quality or validity of the standards proposed in history, civics, geography, social studies, or any other social field would have been very suitable; instead, social studies advocates were excluded from participation in establishing or developing the standards and were ignored in the political debate over them. Historians dominated the political scene in the establishment and development of social education standards and historians prepared the content of the standards, but political pressure from right wing groups forced the historians to change and present much more conservative material.

There is an ironic quality to the notorious public debate over national history standards, an ideological battle between two narrowly constituted groups of special interest history advocates. The irony lies in the fact that this argument is not an intellectual debate about the quality of historical scholarship or an educational dispute over the best pedagogical ideas for examining historical issues. Instead, the battle illustrates one of the most serious traditional defects in history as a framework for social education— its use as propaganda in political and nationalistic education. Each of the sides primarily expresses an ideological position.

Any determination of superiority of history or social science or social studies for schooling should rest on reasoning about educational, political, and social purposes. The larger social purposes, critical stance, and democratic focus of social studies suit it better as the school framework to be used in social education. Despite its many potential defects, social studies offers more potential for fulfilling the democratic ideal of civic competence without the intellectual restrictions and historically negative baggage of school history (Stanley, 1992; Whitson & Stanley, 1988; Wraga, 1993). Defining and redefining social studies offers opportunity to clarify and enhance these ideals.

In the United States, where the ideal of democracy is strong and the structure of government is that of a republic, the form and purpose of education should be consistent. Following the points made by Aristotle and Montesquieu, embellished and enhanced by Dewey (1916), Bastian (1985) and Gutmann (1987), education in the United States should focus on democratic values, including rights to criticize and dissent, and virtues, including active membership in the society and in its improvement. The determining requirement for democratic society is citizen freedom and knowledge; an ignorant or restricted populace cannot sustain democracy. Dewey (1936) stated it succinctly: "Since freedom of mind and freedom of expression are the root of all freedom, to deny freedom in education is a crime against democracy" (p. 36). Education in a democracy demands access to and examination of knowledge, freedom to explore ideas, and development of skills of critical study. All school subjects should incorporate elements of democratic education, but the social subjects have a primary responsibility for liberating students from ignorance on social topics and developing critical thinking for making social decisions.

DEFINING KNOWLEDGE

Through defining, we stake claims on relative values, perspectives, and quality. We define people, events, time, and space in terms that can include, exclude, ignore, idealize, or vilify. Immigrant is a term that defines those who moved in after a nation-state was organized. Citizen includes those who met certain criteria at a particular time in a particular place; slaves and women were not defined as citizens of Greece, Rome, or the United States though they may have been born and lived entire lives within the existing boundaries. Boundaries themselves are definitional statements. Space defined by national and cultural political boundaries, though they are not physically obvious from a space vehicle, still serves as a passionate basis for warfare, ethnic cleansing, massacre, and economic exploitation. Racism and other forms of discrimination are based on definitional elements. Events can also define people as heroes or fools, depending on perspective. Rebels in the American Revolution were heroic to some, fools and traitors to others, by definition. Defining time by decades, for example, the 20s or 60s, may not be historically logical but provides intellectual comfort to many people.

Definitions in the realm of knowledge are also of great significance. Knowledge is basic to human preservation and development; survival requires knowledge, as does social improvement. As societies move from an agrarian to an informational age, defined in the social scientific literature as a shift from focus on food and shelter to technological competence, knowledge becomes even more important. Cultural epochs are identified and structured through scholars in archaeology, anthropology, history, economics, geography, sociology, political economy, philosophy, and others; these subjects, themselves, are also the result of definitions, a set of categories of knowledge intended to assist in the organizing of what we think we know. Definitions and delineations of knowledge structure our thinking and our work (Durant & Durant, 1968; Heilbroner, 1995; Keynes, 1890; Kline, 1995; Martin, 1957; Randall, 1940; Toffler, 1970; Wells, 1920).

Over the period of dramatic social change from clans and agrarian life to a global village and high technology, the nature and form of knowledge also changed. Trial-and-error practical knowledge required for survival became classified, defined, organized, tested, and catalogued. More esoteric knowledge emerged to provide structure and explanation for physical, mental, and spiritual phenomena beyond basic survival. In periods when survival was the paramount activity, it was not consequential to use particular definitions for the categories of knowledge. Determining which plants were edible, which animals were predatory, and which groups peaceable did not require thinking botanically, biologically, or politically; it just required thinking. Names and categories came later to help sort out knowledge and provide a cultural tradition.

The evolution of natural sciences, counterposing evidentially determined and tested information against religious or common sense claims, is the dominant trend since the Renaissance in the Western concept of knowledge. The sciences emerged with a new sense of truth and proof, positive knowledge that offered principles and laws along with methods of study that offered critique of accepted ideas. There is general agreement now on the organization of scientific knowledge, but disputes still arise over ideological views of the nature, role, and consequences of scientific work. The debate over value-laden and value-free scholarship, illustrated in the diverse views of Edward Teller and J. Robert Oppenheimer on the role of moral responsibility in scientific knowledge, tells us that some scientific scholars may claim neutrality in their research, but that there is no such thing. In a similar vein, Feynman (1998) describes the "uncertainty of science" and the dilemma posed by the relation of scientific knowledge to humanities knowledge as a contentious point in contemporary society. These are social studies concerns as well, since social studies can be defined as the study of human issues and conflicting interests. Definitions of social phenomena and constructs, and arguments about the definitions, are in the proper realm of social studies.

The social sciences attempted to emulate the natural sciences in identifying, classifying, predicting, and controlling social phenomena. The sciences of social phenomena were derived, as were the natural sciences, from philosophy but at a much later time and after the natural sciences had survived attack from religion and had gained distinction in the search for verifiable knowledge. The social sciences emerged in the mid 19th century through professionalization of the fields, disciplinization by specialties (e.g., economics, sociology), and the organization and departmentalization of universities in a period of great expansion (Open the Social Sciences, 1996). But social scientific knowledge has not enjoyed the same level of prestige, clarity, consistency, or vision—and it has not demonstrated the same level of scholarly agreement on laws, methodology, or orientation. Unmet claims of science, neutrality, and truth have haunted social sciences. Fundamental disputes over knowledge values, methodology, and social implications of results have threatened the tenuous nature of the social science professions and their definitions of knowledge; this is exemplified in the continuing debate over functionalism and critical theory in the social sciences and social studies (Apple, 1993; Aronowitz & Giroux, 1983; Giroux, 1988; Gouldner, 1970; Young, 1971) Disagreements in social scientific literature have led some to question whether such information should be called knowledge, for example, "Thus there is an ambiguity inherent in the name of the field itself. Whether 'knowledge' should include the products of the social sciences, whether this 'knowledge' is distinct from knowledge in the natural sciences, and, later, whether the common-sense knowledge of social actors is also 'knowledge' has been at issue since the nineteenth century" (Hekman, 1986, p. 14).

CONCLUSION

More scholarly attention to definitions of social studies as perceived, understood, and acted upon would be a contribution to literature in the field. Definitions change as terms are used, understood, acted upon. In addition, many political-ideological dimensions of knowledge definitions become clearer as they are popularized, for example, the use of the term ideology itself changed from a relatively neutral term referring to the study of ideas to become a highly value-charged term often used popularly to deprecate strong or oppositional ideas.

It is important to note again that substantial disagreement in scholarly work is positive. It demonstrates the vitality of the field, and recognizes the worthiness of examination and criticism. The nature of scholarly work is critique and continuous challenge. Petty disputes over terrain, personalities, or items of little consequence may not add to the quality of discourse in a field, but reasoned disputation is at the center of scientific and social scientific study. Disputes over social studies definitions, excepting unreasoned or excessively simplistic ones, are worthy and important parts of development of the field. There is a pertinent and valuable dialectic that works in legitimate and open disagreement over what social studies is or should be. It improves our thinking about the field.

REFERENCES

Apple, M. (1993). *Official knowledge: Democratic education in a conservative age.* New York: Routledge.

Aquinas, T. (1960). *Philosophical texts* (Trans. T. Gilby). New York: Oxford University Press.

Aristotle. (1962). *The politics* (Trans. E. Barker). New York: Oxford University Press.

Aronowitz, S., & Giroux, H. (1983). *Education under siege: The conservative, liberal and radical debate over schooling.* Granby, MA: Bergin and Garvey.

Barker, E. (Ed.). (1947). *Social contract.* New York: Oxford University Press.

Barth, J. (1991). Beliefs that discipline the social studies. *International Journal of Social Education, 6,* 19–24.

Barth, J. (1996). NCSS and the nature of social studies. In O.L. Davis (Ed.), *NCSS in retrospect.* Washington DC: National Council for the Social Studies.

Barth, J., & Shermis, S. (1970). Defining the social studies: An exploration of three traditions. *Social Education, 34,* 743–51.

Barr, R., Barth, J., & Shermis, S. (1977). *Defining the social studies.* Bulletin 51. Washington DC: National Council for the Social Studies.

Bastian, A. et al. (1985). *Choosing equality: The case for democratic schooling.* San Francisco: New World foundation.

Beale, H. (1936). *A history of freedom of teaching in American schools.* New York: Scribners.

Beard, C. (1934). *A charter for the social sciences in the schools. New York:* Charles Scribners.

Bestor, A. (1953). *Educational wasteland: The retreat from learning in our schools.* Urbana: University of Illinois Press.

Billington, R.A. (1962). *The historian's contribution to Anglo-American misunderstanding.* New York: Hobbes, Dorman Co.

Brady, H.R. (1993). The nature of social studies and the problem of definition. *International Journal of Social Education, 8,* 7–22.

Brubaker, D., Simon, L.H., & William, J.W. (1977). A conceptual framework for social studies curriculum and instruction. *Social Education, 41,* 201–205.

Bruner, J. (1960). *The process of education.* Cambridge, MA: Harvard University Press.

Bulletin No. 41. (1913). Washington, DC: U.S. Bureau of Education.

Cherryholmes, C. (1988). *Power and criticism: Post-structural investigations in education.* New York: Teachers College Press.

Counts, G. (1932). *Dare the schools build a new social order?* New York: John Day.

Crabtree, C., & Nash, P. (1994). *National standards for United States history.* Los Angeles: National Center for History in the Schools.

Curti, M. (1935). *The social ideas of American educators.* New York: Charles Scribners.

Dance, E.H. (1960). *History the betrayer: A study in bias.* London: Hutchnison.

Davis, O.L. (1993). Theoretic storm over practical reality: The nonproductive dispute between school history and social studies. *The International Journal of Social Education, 8,* 23–30.

Dewey, J. (1916). *Democracy and education.* New York: Macmillan.

Dewey, J. (1933). *How we think.* Lexington, MA: D.C. Heath.

Dewey, J. (1936). The social significance of academic freedom. *The Social Frontier, 2,* 136.

Durant, W., & Durant, A. (1968). *The lessons of history.* New York: Simon and Schuster.

Dynneson, T. (1993). Reform and social studies: What's at stake? *International Journal of Social Education, 8,* 42–49.

Education for responsible citizenship: The report of the national task force on citizenship education. (1977). New York: McGraw-Hill.

Elements of the social studies program. (1936). 6th Yearbook of the NCSS. Philadelphia: National Council for the Social Studies/McKinley Publications

Engle, S. (1971). Exploring the meaning of the social studies. *Social Education, 35,* 280–288, 344.

Engle, S. (1977). Comments of Shirley Engle. In R. Barr, J. Barth, & S.S. Shermis (Ed.), *Defining the social studies.* Washington, DC: National Council for the Social Studies.

Engle, S., & Ochoa, A. (1988). *Education for democratic citizenship.* New York: Teachers College Press.

Evans, R. (Ed.). (1992). Defining issues-centered social studies education. *The Social Studies, 83*(special issue), 93–124.

Evans, R., & Saxe, D. (1996). *Handbook on teaching social issues.* Washington, DC: NCSS.

Feynman, R.P. (1998). *The meaning of it all.* Reading, MA: Perseus Books.

First yearbook: Some aspects of the social sciences in the schools. (1931). Philadelphia: National Council for the Social Studies/McKinley Publications.

Foucault, M. (1972). *The archaeology of knowledge and the discourse on language.* New York: Pantheon.

Gellerman, W. (1938). *The American legion as educator.* New York: Teachers College Press.

Gibson, R. (1999). Paulo Freire and pedagogy for social justice. *Theory and Research in Social Education, 27,* 447–471.

Giroux, H. (1988). *Schooling and the struggle for public life.* Granby, MA: Bergin and Garvey.

Giroux, H., & Penna, A.N. (1979). Social education in the classroom. *Theory and Research in Social Education, 7,* 21–42.

Goodman, J., & Adler, S. (1985). Becoming an elementary social studies teacher. *Theory and Research in Social Education, 13,* 1–20.

Gouldner, A. (1970). *The coming crisis of western sociology.* New York: Basic Books.

Gutmann, A. (1987). *Democratic education.* Princeton, NJ: Princeton University Press.

Hayes, C.J.H. (1930). *France: A nation of patriots.* New York: Columbia University Press.

Heilbroner. R. (1995). *Visions of the future.* New York: Oxford University Press.

Hekman, S.J. (1986). *Hermeneutics and the sociology of knowledge.* Oxford: Polity Press.

Hertzberg, H. (1981). *Social studies reform: 1880–1890.* Boulder, CO: Social Science Education Consortium.

Hirst, P. (1974). *Knowledge and the curriculum.* London: Routledge.

Hunt, M., & Metcalf, L. (1955). *Teaching high school social studies.* New York: Harper and Row.

Katz, M.B. (1968). *The irony of early school reform.* Cambridge, MA: Harvard University Press.

Katz, M.B. (1971). *Class, bureaucracy, and schools.* New York: Praeger.

Keller, C. (1991). It is time to abolish the mythology that the social studies constitute a discipline. *The International Journal of Social Education, 6,* 69–77.

Keller, C.R. (1961). Needed revolution in the social studies. *Saturday Review, 16,* 61

Keynes, J.N. (1890). *The scope and method of political economy.* London: Macmillan.

Kincaid, H. (1996). *Philosophical foundations of the social sciences.* Cambridge: Cambridge University Press.

Kline, S.J. (1995). *Conceptual foundations for multidisciplinary thinking.* Stanford, CA: Stanford University Press.

Knowlton, D.C. (1936). The social studies and their scope. In *Elements of the Social Studies Program.* Philadelphia: National Council for the Social Studies/McKinley Publications.

Kohlberg, L. (1976). Moral reasoning. In D. Purpel & K. Ryan (Eds.), *Moral education.* Berkeley, CA: McCutchan.

Leming, J. (1985). Research on social studies curriculum and instruction: Interventions and outcomes in the socio-moral domain. In W. Stanley (Ed.), *Review of research in social studies education, 1976–1983* (Bulletin 75). Washington, DC: National Council for the Social Studies.

Levstik, L.S. (1996). NCSS and the teaching of history. In O.L. Davis (Ed.), *NCSS in retrospect.* Washington, DC: National Council for the Social Studies.

Lowe, W. (1969). *Structure and the social studies.* Ithaca, NY: Cornell University Press.

Lybarger, M.B. (1991). The historiography of social studies. In J. Shaver (Ed.), *The handbook of research on social studies teaching and learning.* New York: Macmillan.

Martin, W.O. (1957). *The order and integration of knowledge.* Ann Arbor: University of Michigan Press.

Martorella, P. (1996). *Teaching social studies in middle and secondary schools.* New York: Merrill.

Massialas, B., & Cox, C.B. (1966). *Inquiry in social studies.* New York: McGraw-Hill.

Mehlinger, H. (1992). The National Commission on Social Studies in the Schools: An example of the politics of curriculum reform in the United States. *Social Education, 56,*149–53.

Merriam, C. (1931). *The making of citizens.* Chicago: University of Chicago Press.

Merriam, C. (1934). *Civic education in the United States* New York: Charles Scribners.

Montesquieu, d. (1949). *The spirit of the laws* (Trans. T. Nugent). New York: Hafner Publishing.

National Council for the Social Studies 37th House of Delegates Assembly. (1993). *Social Education, 58,* 199–205

Naylor, D. (1974). *An in-depth study of the perceptions of public school educators and other significant school-related groups concerning aspects of nationalistic education.* Unpublished doctoral dissertation. Rutgers University, New Brunswick, NJ.

Nietzsche, F. (1949). *The use and abuse of history* (Trans. A. Collins). Indianapolis, IN: Liberal Arts Press.

Nelson, J. (1976). Nationalistic versus global education. *Theory and Research in Social Education, 4,* 33–50.

Nelson, J. (1978). Nationalistic political education: An examination of traditions and potentials. *Cambridge Journal of Education, 8,*142–151.

Nelson, J. (1982). Research paradigms in nationalistic education. *Review Journal of Philosophy and Social Science, 6,* 58–71.

Nelson, J. (1985). New criticism and social education. *Social Education, 49,* 368–371.

Nelson, J. (1991). Discipline, knowledge, and social education. *The International Journal of Social Education, 6,* 41–50.

Nelson, J., & Michaelis, J. (1980). *Secondary social studies.* Englewood Cliffs, NJ: Prentice-Hall.

Nelson, J., & Ochoa, A. (1987). Academic freedom, censorship, and the social studies. *Social Education, 49,* 424–427.

Nelson, J., Palonsky, S., & Carlson, K. (2000). *Critical issues in education* (4th ed.). New York: McGraw-Hill.

Newmann, F. (1975). *Education for citizen action.* Berkeley, CA: McCurchan.

Oliver, D., & Shaver, J. (1966). *Teaching public issues in the high school.* Boston: Houghton Mifflin.

Open the social sciences. Report of the Gulbenkian Commission on the Restructuring of the Social Sciences. (1996). Stanford, CA: Stanford University Press.

Parker, W., & Zumeta, W. (1999). Toward an aristocracy of everyone. *Theory and Research in Social Education, 27,* 9–44.

Pierce, B. (1926). *Public opinion and the teaching of history in the United States.* New York: Knopf.

Randall, J.H (1940). *The making of the modern mind* (rev ed.). Cambridge, MA: Riverside Press.

Raths, L. E., Harmin, M., & Simon, S. (1978). *Values and teaching* (2d ed.). Columbus OH: Chas. E. Merrill.

Ravitch, D. (1985, November 17). Decline and fall of history. *New York Times Magazine.*

Ravitch, D. (1994). Standards in U.S. history: An assessment. *Education Week, 14,* 40, 48.

Russell, B. (1928). *Sceptical essays.* New York: Barnes and Noble/Unwin.

Saxe, D. (1992a). Framing a theory for social studies foundations. *Review of Educational Research, 62,* 259–277.

Saxe, D. (1992b). An introduction to the seminal social welfare and efficiency prototype: The founders of 1916 social studies. *Theory and Research in Social Studies, 20,* 156–178.

Saxe, D. (1991a). *Social studies in schools: A history of the early years.* Albany: State University of New York Press.

Saxe, D. (1991b). Salient dates and events of social studies. *The International Journal of Social Education, 6*(2), 11–18.

Second yearbook: Classroom and administrative problems in the teaching of the social sciences. (1932). Philadelphia: National Council for the Social Studies/McKinley Publications.

Shaver, J. (1967). Social studies: The need for redefinition. *Social Education, 43,* 588–593.

Shaver, J. (1996). NCSS and citizenship education. In O.L. Davis (Ed.), *NCSS in retrospect.* Washington, DC: National Council for the Social Studies.

Social studies in general education, The. (1939). Report of the Commission on the Secondary School Curriculum Committee on the Function of Social Studies in General Education (rev. ed.). New York: Progressive Education Association.

Stanley, W. (1992). *Curriculum for Utopia.* Albany: State University of New York Press.

Stanley, W. (1981a). The radical reconstruction of social education. *Theory and Research in Social Education, 8,* 55–79.

Stanley, W. (1981b). Toward a reconstruction of social education. *Theory and Research in Social Education, 9,* 67–89.

Stanley W., & Nelson, J. (1994). The foundations of social education in historical context. In R.A. Martusewicz & W. Reynolds (Eds.), *Inside out: Contemporary critical perspectives in education.* New York: St. Martin's Press.

Thornton, S. (1990). Should we be teaching more history? *Theory and Research in Social Education, 18,* 53–62.

Tocqueville, d. A. (1969). *Democracy in America* (Trans. G. Lawrence; Ed. J.P. Mayer). Garden City, NY: Anchor.

Toffler, A. (1970). *Future shock.* New York: Random House.

Tyack, D. (1967). *Turning points in American educational history.* Waltham, MA: Blaisdell.

Ulich, R. (1954). *Three thousand years of educational wisdom* (2d ed.). Cambridge, MA: Harvard University Press.

Vinson, K.D. (1999). National curriculum standards and social studies education. *Theory and Research in Social Education, 27,* 296–328.

Vinson, K.D. (1998). The traditions revisited. *Theory and Research in Social Education, 26,* 50–82.

Wells, H.G. (1920). *The outline of history: Being a plain history of life and mankind* (Vol. 1). Garden City, NY: Garden City Books.

Weltman, B. (1999). The message and the medium: The roots/routes of Jerome Bruner's postmodernism. *Theory and Research in Social Education, 27,* 160–178.

Wesley, E., & Wronski, S. (1958). *Teaching social studies in high schools* (4th ed.). Boston: Heath.

Whelan, M. (1992). History and the social studies: A response to the critics. *Theory and Research in Social Studies, 20,* 2–16.

Whitson, J.A., & Stanley, W. (1988). *Practical competence.* Unpublished paper, National Council for the Social Studies Annual Meeting.

Winkler, K. (1995). Who owns history? *The Chronicle of Higher Education, 41,* A10–11, 18.

Wisdom, J.O. (1987). *Philosophy of the social sciences II: Schemata.* Aldersnot: Avebury.

Wraga, W. (1993). The interdisciplinary imperative for citizenship education. *Theory and Research in Social Education, 21,* 201–231.

Young, M.F.D. (1971). *Knowledge and control.* London: Collier-Macmillan.

CHAPTER 3

IN SEARCH OF THE SOCIAL STUDIES CURRICULUM: STANDARDIZATION, DIVERSITY, AND A CONFLICT OF APPEARANCES

Kevin D. Vinson and E. Wayne Ross

The relation between what we see and what we know is never settled.
—John Berger (cited in Goodheart, 2000, p. A27)

Without a doubt our epoch prefers the image to the real thing, the copy to the original, the representation to the reality, appearance to being. What is sacred for it is only illusion. More than that, the sacred grows in its eyes to the extent that truth diminishes and illusion increases, to such an extent that the peak of illusion is for it the peak of the sacred.
—Fuerbach (cited in *Spectacular Times*, n.d.)

INTRODUCTION

The social studies curriculum is the most inclusive of all school subjects (Ross, 2001a). Determining the boundaries of what is taught in social studies requires decisions about what social knowledge is most important, which skills and behaviors are most valuable, and what values are most significant. As a result, the curricular terrain of social studies education is continually contested in the political arena. Yet, the large-scale studies of the field conducted in the last quarter of the past century (e.g., Morrissett, 1977; National Assessment of Educational Progress, 1980; Schneider & Van Sickle, 1979; Stake & Easley, 1978; Weiss, 1978; Wiley, 1977) suggested the

39

appearance of uniformity in basic topics, sequences, course titles, textbook content, and instructional practices. Despite these findings, we know also that there is enormous diversity within the enacted curriculum as a result of the curricular decisions teachers make (e.g., Thornton, 1992).

In recent years, standards-based curriculum initiatives (i.e., as part of a broader movement toward "standards-based educational reform" or "SBER") have become ubiquitous, manifested, for example, in a number of recent policy statements produced by the National Council for the Social Studies (NCSS; e.g., NCSS, 2000; NCSS Curriculum Standards Task Force, 1994) and by various frameworks established among the states (Finn & Petrilli, 2000). These standards-based curriculum reforms often are linked with high-stakes tests as part of an accountability system intended to assure their inclusion in the enacted curriculum of social studies classrooms.

The intent of this chapter is to review what we know about the nature of the social studies curriculum, the roles of people both in and outside classrooms in shaping the curriculum, and the issues social studies curriculum workers/researchers/teachers will face in coming years. An overview of past large-scale studies of the social studies curriculum will be augmented by an analysis of the increasing number of interpretive portraits of social studies classrooms and by an exploration of the impact of standards-based curriculum reforms on the curricula students experience in social studies classrooms and on how they go about experiencing them.

More specifically, this chapter takes on four key questions: (1) What do we "know" about the nature(s) of the social studies curriculum? (2) What roles do people play with respect to shaping the social studies curriculum? (3) What is/are the contemporary state(s) of social studies curriculum work? and (4) What issues, trends, and possibilities exist as social educators continue to struggle with the everyday problematics of curriculum research, theory, and practice?

We begin with a review of the major perspectives, viewpoints, and frameworks that have been used to characterize social studies, especially vis-à-vis citizenship education. Next we examine existing large-scale studies of the social studies curriculum that provide an empirical base for much of our understanding of the formal and enacted curriculum of social studies. These large-scale studies provide a backdrop for our analysis of the contemporary scene, one that focuses on the debates about curricular uniformity and diversity and that places specific emphasis on the influence of SBER. We close by examining the challenges of social studies curriculum work in the early twenty-first century.

CONTEXTUALIZING THE SOCIAL STUDIES CURRICULUM

The Origins and Purposes of Social Studies

Perhaps the most inclusive definition of the social studies is posed by Stanley and Nelson (1994), who define social education as "the study of all human enterprise over time and space" (p. 266). As such, social studies requires facing key questions about social knowledge, skills, and values, including how best to organize them with respect to specific subject matter and to the unique subjectivities of teachers and their students (Stanley & Nelson, 1994). Given the possibility of such an open-ended definition, it is not surprising then that social studies has been racked by intellectual battles over its purpose, content, and pedagogy since its very inception as a school subject in the early part of the twentieth century.

One of the earliest uses of the term "social studies" to refer to school subjects is attributed to Thomas Jesse Jones in an article that appeared in the *Southern Workman* in 1905 (Tabachnick, 1991). Jones expanded the article into a book, *Social Studies in the Hampton Curriculum*, in which he expressed his concern that young African Americans and Native Americans "would never be able to become integral members of the broader society unless they learned to understand that society, the social forces that operated within it, and ways to recognize and respond to social power" (Tabachnick, 1991, p. 725).

The roots of the contemporary social studies curriculum are found in the 1916 report of the Committee on Social Studies of the National Education Association's (N.E.A.'s) Commission on the Reorganization of Secondary Schools, which Jones chaired. The final report of the committee, *The Social Studies in Secondary Education*, illustrates the influence of previous N.E.A. and American Historical Association committees regarding history in schools, but it also, perhaps more importantly, emphasized the development of "good" citizenship values in students and established the pattern of course offerings in social studies that remained consistent throughout most of the twentieth century.

Few social studies educators disagree that the purpose of social studies is "to prepare youth so that they possess the knowledge, values, and skills needed for active participation in society" (Marker & Mehlinger, 1992, p. 832). Arguments have been made that students can develop "good citizenship" not only through the long-privileged study of history (Whelan, 1997), but also through the examination of contemporary social problems (Evans & Saxe, 1996), public policy (Oliver & Shaver, 1966), social roles (Superka & Hawke, 1982), social taboos (Hunt & Metcalf, 1968), or by becoming astute critics of one's society (Engle & Ochoa, 1988).

Marker and Mehlinger's (1992) review of the social studies curriculum concluded that the apparent consensus that citizenship education is the primary purpose of social studies is "almost meaningless" because of its wide-ranging diversity of goals and methods. Although it is generally agreed that social studies is about citizenship education, clearly both its content and methodologies have been much affected by social and political agendas (Gehrke, Knapp, & Sirotnik, 1992). The question, of course, is whether social studies should promote a brand of citizenship that is adaptive to the status quo and interests of the socially powerful or whether it should promote citizenship aimed at transforming and reconstructing society—a question that has fueled debates since Jones first employed the term "social studies" (see Barr, Barth, & Shermis, 1977; Hertzberg, 1981; Hursh & Ross, 2000; Nelson, 1985, 1990; Ross, 2001a; Saxe, 1997; Shaver, 1977; Stanley & Nelson, 1994). In the section that follows, we examine the various traditions located within social studies education in an effort to make meaning out of the curricular diversity that is a hallmark of the field.

The "Traditions" of Social Studies Education: Diverse Views on What Should be Taught

Because of the diversity of viewpoints on the meaning of citizenship education—and thus diversity in the purposes, content, and pedagogy of social studies education—social studies educators have devoted considerable attention to identifying categories and descriptions of the major "traditions" within the field. Various schemes have been used by researchers to make sense of the wide ranging and often conflicting purposes (e.g., Barr, Barth, & Shermis, 1977; Morrissett & Haas, 1982; Stanley & Nelson, 1994). The most influential of these was worked out by Barr, Barth, and Shermis (1977), who grouped the various positions on the social studies curriculum into three themes: citizenship (or cultural) transmission, social science/ structure of the disciplines, and reflective inquiry.

Martorella (1996) provides a comprehensive framework for understanding the various traditions within social studies education by establishing a five-part framework that extends the work of Barr, Barth, and Shermis and that emphasizes the central, organizing role of citizenship. His framework includes social studies/citizenship education as: (1) citizenship transmission; (2) social science; (3) reflective inquiry; (4) informed social criticism; and (5) personal development. Each perspective is briefly summarized below.[1]

Citizenship Transmission

In this tradition, the purpose of social studies education is to promote student acquisition of certain "American" or "democratic" values via the teaching and learning of discrete, factual pieces of information drawn primarily from the canon of Western thought and culture. Content is based on the beliefs that: (1) certain factual information is important to the practice of good citizenship; (2) the nature of this information remains relatively constant over time; and (3) this information is best determined by a consensus of authorities and experts.

Teachers operating from this perspective utilize two principal instructional methods: description and persuasion. Description is used for content that teachers believe is of intrinsic importance, information that should be transmitted directly and without interpretation. Persuasion is used with knowledge that teachers perceive to be open to multiple understandings when they wish to convince students that only one is "correct" or "true" (e.g., capitalism is the best economic system). Today this approach is perhaps most strongly advocated by social and political conservatives (Adler 1982; Bennett, 1989, 1992; Bloom, 1987; Hirsch, 1987; Ravitch, 2000; Ravitch & Finn, 1987), although pedagogically there are significant differences among its adherents (e.g., Adler, Bennett, & Bloom's focus on "ideas" vs. Hirsch & Ravitch's focus on "facts").

This tradition draws upon scholarship that views American society as a relatively homogeneous culture rooted in the history, literature, and philosophy of Western civilization. From this perspective, diversity of experience and multiculturalism are downplayed, ignored, or actively challenged. Cultural and social unity are proclaimed and praised. In the curriculum, history and literature dominate over such considerations as learner interests, the social sciences, social criticism, and personal-subjective development.

Social Science

This tradition evolved most directly out of the post-Sputnik effort of social scientists "proper" (as opposed, that is, to "educationists") to have a say in the design, development, and (even) implementation of the K-12 social studies curriculum. Simply, from this viewpoint, each individual social discipline (e.g., political science, history, economics, geography, and so forth) can be considered in terms of its own distinct ontological "structure" of concepts, theories, and modes of empirical inquiry. In educational scholarship this idea was most widely and successfully advanced by psychologist Jerome Bruner (1969, 1977) and educator J.J. Schwab (1969); it formed, in part, the basis for what became known as the "new social studies" (see Fenton, 1966; Massialas, 1992).[2]

In this tradition, citizenship education includes "mastering social science concepts, generalizations, and processes to build a knowledge base for later learning" (Martorella, 1996, p. 20). Here, citizenship is best promoted by decision making based on "mastery" of social science concepts, processes, and problems. From the social science viewpoint, social studies education is that which provides students with the social scientific content and procedures for successful citizenship, and for understanding and acting upon the human condition in its historical, contemporary, political, social, economic, and cultural contexts (e.g., Bruner 1969; Feldman & Seifman, 1969; Massialas, 1992; Michaelis & Johnston, 1965; Wesley & Wronski, 1964; Wronski & Bragaw, 1986). In general, instructional methods include those that develop within learners the characteristics of "real" social scientists, characteristics indicative of conceptual understandings as well as modes of strategic inquiry (e.g., an anthropology course might focus conceptually on "culture" and methodologically on "ethnography").

Recently some social studies scholars have moved away from the more traditional social studies as social science approach to disciplinary structure and toward increasingly complex interrogations of the importance of particular and individual constructions of the specific social and historical disciplines. From this newer perspective, academics, teachers, and students all have *some* understanding of the structure of the various social sciences that relates to how they produce, use, and disseminate disciplinary knowledge. These ideas of disciplinary conceptualizations influence all individual modes of teaching and learning. Thus, it is impossible to teach social studies according to any other approach without simultaneously maintaining some structural comprehension of the knowledge and modes of inquiry of the various academic disciplines. There are, however, competing and dynamic possibilities such that teachers and students may each possess a unique orientation. Within the social studies, much of this contemporary work has focused upon history education, and has emphasized multiple, complex instructional approaches, constructivist understandings of meaning, the production and interpretation of text, historical sense-making, and interdisciplinary conceptions of content (e.g., Barton, 1997; Foster, Hoge, & Rosch, 1999; Sexias, 1993, 1998; VanSledright & Afflerbach, 2000).

Reflective Inquiry

This approach to social studies developed originally out of the work of John Dewey (1916/1966, 1933, 1938/1963, 1956), particularly his sociocognitive psychology and his "pragmatic" philosophy of thinking and learning. From this position, citizenship remains the core of the social studies. But unlike citizenship transmission, in which citizenship rests on the acquisition of preestablished values and content, or social science, where citizenship involves the range of academic social disciplines, citizenship here stresses "relevant" problem-solving, or meaningful decision making within a specific sociopolitical context (Barr, Barth, & Shermis, 1977).

From this perspective, then, the purpose of social studies education is nurturing within students those abilities necessary for decision making in some specified sociopolitical context (e.g., liberal democratic capitalism), especially with respect to social and personal problems that directly affect individual students. In the US this presupposes a necessary connection between democracy and problem solving, one in which the key assumption behind this link is that within the American social-political system significant problems rarely imply a single, overt, and/or "correct" solution. Such problems frequently require decisions between several perceived "good" solutions and/or several perceived "bad" solutions. Democracy thus necessitates a citizenry capable of and competent in the identification of problems, the collection, evaluation, and analysis of data, and the making of reasoned decisions.

Dewey's work on democratic reflective thinking led to the evolution of a powerful pragmatic theory of education, prominent during the early to middle post-World War II era, spearheaded by theorists such as Bode (1940), Bayles (1950), and Hullfish and Smith (1961), and in social education by Engle (1987) and Hunt and Metcalf (1968). The continuing influence of this tradition in social studies is found in works by authors such as Evans and Saxe (1996) and Ross (1994). By carrying forward Dewey's legacy, these scholars offer an alternative to the social sciences per se and to contemporary "back to basics" movements, one grounded in reflective decision making centered on so-called "closed areas" representing a precise time and place—or, more precisely, problem solving within a specific sociopolitical context.

Informed Social Criticism

Martorella extends the work of Barr, Barth, and Shermis by adding a fourth category, one which draws on Engle's (1977) analysis of the original Barr, Barth, and Shermis framework and that is rooted ultimately in the work of social reconstructionists (Brameld, 1956; Counts, 1932) and related to the more recent work of "socialization-countersocialization" theorists (Engle & Ochoa, 1988) and critical pedagogues (e.g., Kanpol, 1994; McLaren, 1998.) (Also important here are earlier works by authors such as Anyon [1980]; Bowles & Gintis [1976], Freire [1970], and Willis [1977/1981]). The contemporary literature addresses primarily such themes as the "hidden curriculum," sociocultural transformation, and the nature and meaning of knowledge and truth. The work of Nelson (e.g., 1985, 1990; Nelson & Ochoa, 1987; Nelson & Pang, 2001; Stanley & Nelson, 1986), Stanley (1985),[4] and more recently Hursh and Ross (2000) perhaps best represents the current status of this tradition (see also Cherryholmes, 1980, 1982; Newmann, 1985; Wexler, 1985).

From this standpoint the purpose of social studies is citizenship education aimed at "providing [students] opportunities for an examination, critique, and revision of past traditions, existing social practices, and modes of problem solving" (Martorella, 1996, p. 20). It is a citizenship education directed toward:

> Social transformation [as] defined as the continuing improvement of ... society by applying social criticism and ethical decision making to social issues, and using the values of justice and equality as grounds for assessing the direction of social change that should be pursued. (Stanley & Nelson, 1986, p. 530)

Social studies content in this tradition challenges the injustices of the status quo. It counters knowledge that is: (1) generated by and supportive of society's elites (Ross, 2000); (2) rooted in rationalistic and oppressive forms of logical positivism (Apple, 1993; McLaren, 1998); and (3) consistent with "social reproduction" and the replication of a society that is classist, sexist, and racist. While it is specific to individual classroom settings and students, it can include, for example, "[r]edressing the needs of the disadvantaged, increasing human rights conditions and stimulating environmental improvements [as] ... possible foci" (Stanley & Nelson, 1986, p. 528). Moreover, teachers and students here may claim their own knowledges—their content, their individual and cultural experiences—as legitimate. Instruction methods in this tradition are situational, but are oriented away from lecture and information transmission and toward such processes as "reflective thinking" (Gore, 1993) and the dialogical method (Shor & Freire, 1987), sociocultural criticism, textual analysis/deconstruction (Cherryholmes, 1980, 1982, 1999), problem-solving, critical thinking, and social action (e.g., Stanley & Nelson, 1986).

Personal Development

The final tradition in Martorella's scheme grew out of the work of Nelson and Michaelis (1980), presented in their textbook *Secondary Social Studies*. Focusing again on the role of citizenship education, this position reflects the belief that "citizenship education should consist of developing a positive self-concept and a strong sense of personal efficacy" among students (Martorella, 1996, p. 20). It is grounded in the idea that effective democratic citizenship involves understanding one's freedom to make choices as well as one's obligation and responsibility to live with their ultimate outcomes (i.e., "authenticity"). In a sense, it is related to what Fenstermacher and Soltis (1992) labeled the "therapist" approach to teaching, what Brubaker et al. (1977) defined as social studies in the "student-centered tradition," and what Joyce and Weil (1992) identified as the "personal family" of instruction.

In this tradition content is selected and pursued by the students themselves so that it is embedded in the "nature, needs, and interests" of the learners (Brubaker, Simon, & William, 1977, p. 203). Instructional methods are "shared" between teachers and students, but include techniques such as Kilpatrick's "project method," various forms of individualized instruction, and the Socratic method of dialogue. For in essence, this approach evolved out of the child-centered progressive education movement of the early twentieth century (e.g., Kilpatrick) and within the settings of humanistic psychology (e.g., Maslow and Rogers) and existential philosophy (e.g., Sartre). Its best-known contemporary advocates include Maxine Greene, John Holt, William Glasser, and Nel Noddings (Fenstermacher & Soltis, 1992) and in the social studies scholars such as Pearl Oliner (1983).

Summary

While the traditions described above encapsulate unique visions of citizenship education as well as particular insights into the questions of purpose, content selection, and teaching methods, they do not of course exhaust all the possibilities for classifying approaches to social studies education. One might, for example, identify other orientations such as: "socialization/countersocialization" (Engle & Ochoa, 1988); "citizenship competencies" (Remy, 1980); teaching social issues (Evans & Saxe, 1996); multicultural education (Banks, 1995); global education (Kniep, 1989; Merryfield & Remy, 1995; Tye & Tye, 1992); and/or "democracy and social justice" (Hursh & Ross, 2000). Still, Martorella's conceptions do seem to provide space for the inclusion of these, and other, viewpoints. Further, the categories outlined above are by no means devoid of overlap. It is important here to remember that there is no singular "real world" of the classroom, of teaching and learning, especially with respect to what these might mean for contemporary social studies education (see Note 2).

As is obvious from the overview of the various traditions within social studies education, while nearly all in the field agree that the main purpose of social studies is citizenship education this should not, indeed *cannot*, be considered a sign of curricular uniformity. There has been "continuous and rancorous" debate about the purposes of social studies (Marker & Mehlinger, 1992, p. 832), and the field has appeared to be tolerant of alternative definitions of how one prepares for citizenship and what the content of the field should be. For example, in the late 1980s the NCSS chose to endorse not one, but three different scope and sequence plans for the field. Gehrke, Knapp, and Sirotnik (1992) speculated that the field's tolerance might have multiple sources:

> Perhaps the reason for this tolerance is that social studies draws from and is taught by individuals from a wide array of disciplines. Perhaps it is because the focus on education for democratic participation that pervades the field requires the modeling of consideration of alternative points of view; or perhaps it is because the field is simply as confused about citizenship and education for it as is the greater culture in which it finds itself. In any case there is little consensus among professionals on what should be taught to make one a good citizen … Perhaps labeling [the traditions] gives a sense of control over the field. (p. 58)

In this era of SBER one might suspect the diversity of traditions in the social studies curriculum would be threatened. Most subject matter areas have been marked by a univocal call for and representation of curriculum standards; however, in social studies there are no fewer than seven sponsors of curriculum standards documents competing to influence the content and pedagogy of social education (see Mathison, Ross, & Vinson, 2001).

Is this a sign that the field is resisting the moves toward standardization, which is indicative of the SBER model dominating current curriculum efforts? We think not. The proliferation of curriculum standards per se is more likely to foment lively debate about social education than it is to provide clear directives about the social studies curriculum. The use of high-stakes testing and other reductive accountability systems (e.g., national accreditation of teacher education programs based upon a single set of standards), however, linked as they are to curriculum standards, seriously threatens the diversity that has existed within the formal (or planned) curriculum, and, more important, it threatens the enacted social studies curriculum. For example, in 1994, the NCSS abandoned its tolerance of multiple curriculum frameworks and endorsed a single set of standards for the field. NCSS has also embarked on a campaign promoting the implementation of these standards in K–12 classrooms (e.g., Haas & Laughlin, 1997) and the use of NCSS standards in accreditation of university teacher education programs (NCSS, 2000).

While SBER has threatened the tolerance and diversity that has marked proposals for what should be taught in or as social studies, the enacted social studies curriculum has proven to be remarkably stable over the years, resisting the various calls for diverse approaches to social studies teaching and learning. This fact, which we examine in the next section, contradicts the *appearance* of curriculum diversity as represented by the various social studies traditions.

THE EMPIRICAL BASE: CURRICULAR UNIFORMITY AND DIVERSITY IN SOCIAL STUDIES

Gehrke, Knapp, and Sirotnik (1992) note that, when social studies educators describe the enacted curriculum, they do so primarily on the basis of large-scale studies, which were mostly conducted in the 1970s and based upon surveys of social studies educators (Applebee, Langer, & Mullins, 1987; Morrissett, 1977; National Assessment of Education Progress, 1980; Weiss, 1978) or the analysis of textbooks, curriculum guides, and documents from states and local districts (Weiss, 1978). Three of these studies (Stake & Easley, 1978; Weiss, 1978; Wiley, 1977) were part of a project funded by the National Science Foundation (NSF) and present the most comprehensive portrait of the field ever attempted.

The three NSF studies were reported in nine major documents and have had a significant effect on the social studies literature and research. "A vast portion of the inquiry in social studies done since the appearance of the reports references one or more of the three studies, the NSF report, the Project SPAN reports (Project SPAN, 1982; Lengel & Superka, 1982) that depended heavily upon them, or a summary and interpretation of them by Shaver, Davis, and Helburn (1980)" (Gehrke, Knapp, & Sirotnik, 1992, p. 57). In the two sections that follow these large-scale studies (along with other more focused studies) will be used as the basis for an examination of the curricular patterns in the formal and enacted curriculum of social studies.

Social Studies Curriculum Patterns

While there has been lively debate about what should be taught among advocates of the various traditions within social studies education, *in practice* social studies has been marked more by constancy than change (Cuban, 1991). A paradox of the social studies curriculum is that while the field has seemingly been tolerant of multiple curricular orientations—in theory—the core pattern of teaching practices and curriculum has endured from social studies' inception as a school subject to the present.

Elementary Grades

The NSF and Project SPAN studies documented widespread use of the "expanding environments" curriculum framework for elementary social studies. This pattern begins from the immediate surroundings of the child and moves outward toward ever-widening contexts. Typical grade level themes include:

- Kindergarten   Self, home, school, community;
- Grade 1   Families;
- Grade 2   Neighborhoods;
- Grade 3   Communities;
- Grade 4   Geographic regions & state history;
- Grade 5   U.S. history;
- Grade 6   World cultures/hemispheres.

This framework can be traced backed to the 1916 Report of the Committee on Social Studies (Committee on Social Studies of the National Education Association, 1916), and Hanna (1987) is credited with elaborating and explaining the rationale for this curriculum pattern. Gehrke, Knapp, and Sirotnik (1992) report that while the "K–3 pattern [for social studies curriculum] has been extraordinarily stable across time, the 4–6 level had shown more changes in both curriculum documents and textbooks" (p. 61). For example, state history rather than geography became the main focus of Grade 4 by 1975 and Grade 6 content had changed from a predominantly Western hemisphere focus to an emphasis on world cultures. The latter pattern, they argue, is connected to the concurrent increase in middle schools with a grade 6–7–8 configuration replacing traditional junior highs (grades 7–8). There are also patterns of curricula particular to local interests in various states.

Overall, while the expanding environments framework has received its share of criticism (e.g., Egan, 1982; Mitsakos, 1978), the pattern has endured because, it has been argued, the topics are generalized and nonspecific and allow teachers to incorporate new content and adapt the topics to local needs and interests (e.g., Brophy, 1990; Lengel & Superka, 1982).

Secondary Grades

The curriculum pattern for the upper grades can also be traced back to the 1916 Report. Based upon a logic that is now archaic, the pattern for social studies in grades 7–12 is a twin cycle of "contracting environments."

- Grade 7   World history, cultures, geography;
- Grade 8   U.S. history;
- Grade 9   World history, cultures or Civics/government;
- Grade 10   World history, cultures;
- Grade 11   U.S. history;
- Grade 12   American government or sociology/psychology/economics.

These cycles were planned for the early twentieth century on the basis of school-leaving patterns, and allowed students exposure to world and U.S. history even if they did not go on to high school.

Social Studies Instructional Approaches

Nearly all of the categorizers of the curriculum and instructional traditions in social studies education agree that although various approaches are represented in the enacted and formal curriculum, the most common approach is "citizenship transmission," or "conservative cultural continuity." Conservative cultural continuity means teaching social studies as transmission of citizenship-related information with an emphasis on inculcation of traditional values (Morrissett & Hass, 1982) and facts (Hirsch, 1987; Ravitch & Finn, 1987; see also Leming, 1994, on "traditional social studies instruction").

This conclusion is supported by empirical studies of social studies classroom practices. As Gehrke, Knapp, and Sirotnik (1992) note:

> the three NSF studies, working from different data sources and using different inquiry methods, all concluded that most social studies curricula, in their planned and enacted forms, were aimed primarily at transmitting information and at socialization aimed to prepare students to enter adult life "without a ripple of discontent or change" (Stake & Easley, 1978, preface). (p. 58)

Cuban's (1991) review of research on how social studies teachers taught between the 1940s and the 1980s buttresses the finding that the most durable and common pattern of social studies teaching is the transmission of information.

> [T]he vast majority of teachers [employ] teacher-centered instruction. The pattern includes activities using the textbook and teacher as sources of information for assignments, recitation … tests, and individual seatwork. Talking by the teacher … exceeds talking by students, whose responses are generally

confined to answering the teacher's questions. Occasional use of films, videos, and other devices supplements these activities. This core pattern is most frequently enacted when the entire class is taught as a group. Infrequently at the high school level, but with slightly more frequency at the elementary level, small-group work is a vehicle for classroom activities. (p. 204)

Cuban's review indicates that secondary social studies teachers have consistently relied on textbooks as a primary source of information. These patterns of instruction in conjunction with recent content analyses of social studies textbooks—which illustrate that many texts are marred by an embarrassing combination of blind patriotism, mindless optimism, sheer misinformation, and outright lies (Loewen, 1996), and/or continue to reflect the growing conservatism and influence of the religious right in the United States (Wasburn, 1997)—add to the evidence supporting conservative cultural continuity as the dominant pattern of social studies education.

THE PARADOX OF SOCIAL STUDIES CURRICULUM PRACTICE

The paradox of social studies curriculum and practice is that it is marked by both the *appearance of diversity* (e.g., the various "traditions" or categories proposed for social studies curriculum and instruction) and the *appearance of uniformity* (e.g., stable curricular scope and sequence and entrenched patterns of instruction).

Evidence from large-scale studies (conducted prior to the onset of the SBER movement) indicates that there has long been at least superficial uniformity in the social studies curriculum (e.g., basic topics, sequences, course titles, and textbook contents). In addition, there has been considerable uniformity in the pedagogical practices of social studies teachers. Cuban (1993) argues that the uniformity of social studies teachers' practices over the years could, at least in part, be attributed to certain

[c]ultural beliefs about the nature of knowledge, how teaching should occur, and how children should learn, [that] are so widespread and deeply rooted that they steer the thinking of policymakers, practitioners, parents, and citizens toward certain forms of instruction. (p.14)

Ironically, studies of teacher decision making indicate that the cultural beliefs of teachers are also the basis of teachers' mediation of curricular topics, sequence, textbooks contents, and other learning assignments, which make the enacted curriculum quite diverse (e.g., Anyon, 1980; Cornett, 1990; Cornett et al., 1992; Fickle, 2000; Jenne, 1997; Ross, Cornett, & McCutcheon, 1992; Slekar, 1998; Thornton, 1988, 1992; Vinson, 1998).

As Thornton (1988, 1992) argues, teacher beliefs about social studies subject matter as well as student learning, planning, and instructional strategies, together function to create the enacted curriculum of the class-room—day-to-day interactions among students, teachers, and subject matter. The differences between the publicly declared formal curriculum and the curriculum experienced by students in social studies classrooms are considerable. The key to the curriculum experienced in the classroom is the teacher:

> Teachers' [sic] beliefs about schooling, his or her knowledge of the subject area and of available materials and techniques, how he or she decides to put these together for the classroom—out of that process of reflection and personal inclination comes the day-to-day classroom experience of students. This is not to say that social studies classes are not affected by factors such as the characteristics of the students enrolled, but only to emphasize that the teacher plays the primary structuring role. (Shaver, Davis, & Helburn, 1980)

Sanders and Stone (1987), in a study of 26 high schools in California, presented evidence to confirm that students in different tracks experience very different curricula, with different goals, textbooks, homework demands, and classroom activities. Studies by McNeil (1986), McKee (1988), and Stodolsky (1988; Stodolsky, Salk, & Glaessner, 1991) support these findings as do a growing number of small-scale studies of social studies classrooms (e.g., Wilson & Wineburg, 1988; Thornton, 1988). Teachers' backgrounds, knowledge, beliefs, and perspectives on teaching contexts have proven to be a tremendous influence on the curriculum experienced by social studies students. For example, teachers' disciplinary perspectives (VanSledright & Afflerbach, 2000; Wilson & Wineburg, 1988); life experiences (Jenne, 1997); the organizational and policy contexts of teaching (Fickle, 2000); prior experiences in school (Slekar, 1998); beliefs about the purposes, contents, and methods of teaching (Anderson et al., 1997; Leming, 1989, 1992; Vinson, 1998); and personal theories of teaching (Cornett, 1990; Cornett et al., 1992; Ross, Cornett, & McCutcheon, 1992) have all been demonstrated as important factors in determining the enacted curriculum. Despite wide variations in the social studies curriculum as a function of teacher-related factors there is a convergence on transmission of similar values, an irony we explore in the following section.

UNDERSTANDING THE CONTEMPORARY SCENE: STANDARDIZATION, DIVERSITY, AND IMAGE

The contemporary state of the social studies curriculum—its appearance-of-uniformity-appearance-of-diversity paradox—reflects in part two recent and evolving socio-pedagogical trends: (1) the contradictory commitment to both "standardization" and "diversity" and (2) the increasingly important convergence (or at least coexistence) of "spectacle" and "surveillance." On some level both work to create the conditions by and within which not only social studies but schooling more broadly reflects and is reflected by the characteristics (i.e., political, economic, social, cultural) of the larger (global) society.

That those who run public schooling continue their call for "higher standards," "high-stakes testing," "accountability," and "competition" while simultaneously praising the merits of "individual" and "cultural" differences should surprise no one, and in fact mirrors and is mirrored by not only the current empirical pedagogical debates surrounding uniformity and diversity but also prevailing U.S. societal conditions—especially those reflected *economically* vis-à-vis global, state-sponsored, corporate, "infotech" capitalism and *politically* in terms of an apparent merging of political independence toward a bland and stultifying "centrism" (see, e.g., the "New Democrat," the "Compassionate Conservative," the Blair-Clinton project of "The Third Way," etc.). Taken together, these contexts produce an uneasy and ultimately false coalition of *sameness*, with the politically powerful claiming to promote the common ("mainstream") good while at the same time their corporate/financial allies and supporters pursue profit-seeking policies at the expense of authentic economic opportunity, social justice, meaningful democracy, the environment, and human rights. No wonder cynicism, "voter apathy," and electoral mistrust. With little real difference between the dominant Democratic and Republican Parties (see, for instance, the "lesser of two evils" mentality among many members of the citizenry and the tag-team effort to marginalize third parties), and with their joint endorsement by and of the elite corporate hierarchy, there seems indeed sometimes little or no room for the less wealthy, the less powerful, and the less well-connected.

Clearly, *educational* leaders, including those responsible for establishing, maintaining, and reforming(?) curriculum and instruction are to some extent beholden to the demands of multiple political interests (including those of *government* leaders who, in turn, depend on and benefit from the interests of the economically and culturally powerful, for example in terms of campaign contributions). Yet, these same educational leaders are influenced by (and thus beholden to) a range of additional constituencies. These include, among others, parents and students, teachers, scholars, community leaders, activists, and residents of local neighborhoods, many of whom hold little concern for the politically and economically mighty. That these various groups and individuals present and experience a vastly more diverse reality than that of those who represent the U.S./global corporate-state indeed is an understatement. Yet it explains, in part, the odd and conflicting dual commitments of today's public school managers, existing as they do between the two worlds of elitist-socioeconomic-competitive-standardization and the everyday experiences of grassroots community activism and pluralistic cultural diversity. Perhaps more importantly, though, it hints at the necessary extent to which this paradoxical state of affairs can only be understood contextually.

Contextualizing Standardization

The move toward social studies curriculum standardization can be seen, of course, in the myriad "official" policy statements and content documents created and put forth by an array of professional academic organizations, each of which seeks control over the meaning or "nature" of social education (e.g., Center for Civic Education, 1991, 1994; Geography Education Standards Project, 1994; National Center for History in the Schools, 1994a, 1994b; NCSS, 1981; NCSS Curriculum Standards Task Force, 1994; National Council on Economic Education, 1997). Though it signifies an attempt to mask any real paradigmatic conflict or struggle within the field, ironically SBER (here, especially, curriculum standards and high-stakes standardized testing) may instead reflect a multiplicity of tensions and confusions over the relative place and meaning of not only the range of constituent social studies disciplines but also fundamental questions relative to purpose, content in general, instructional methodologies, and assessment (i.e., What is it that social studies students—citizens—"need" to know? How do/can they come to know it? How can we be sure they have learned it?).[5] As such, this issue—standardization vs. diversity—may in fact be related to and encompass an assortment of other continuous yet equally contentious and relevant issues in terms of social studies curriculum design and development, including the degree to which curricula should be constructed at the "grassroots" level or "hierarchically," the extent to which *purpose* or *testing* should "drive" curriculum and instruction, the relative merits of "progressive" and "traditional" social studies orientations, and the overall pedagogical balance between "discipline-centeredness" (or "disciplinarity") and "a/anti/interdisciplinarity."

At present, this move toward curriculum standardization represents the dominant, status quo viewpoint and its underlying and foundational aims (e.g., Levin, 1998; Tucker & Codding, 1998; for a general overview of national standards as an issue, see, e.g., Wolf, 1998). Its fundamental features include formal and official curriculum standards frameworks, of course, but also a hypercommitment in favor of high-stakes standardized testing and a one-size-fits-all classroom/school conformity. As indicated above, this perspective on social studies education is manifested vis-à-vis a host of policy statements developed at multiple levels, including the national (e.g., Department of Education, 1991; National Commission on Excellence in Education, 1983), the state (Finn & Petrilli, 2000),[6] and the professional academic organization (e.g., NCSS Curriculum Standards Task Force, 1994). It grows out of the current "liberal-conservative consensus" among politicians, corporate leaders, the news media, and educational policy makers (e.g., apparent *liberals* such as Nash, Crabtree, & Dunn, 1997; conservatives such as Ravitch, 2000) that both "higher standards" (read SBER—curriculum standardization and high-stakes standardized testing) and greater "accountability" are *essential* to the well-being and strengthening of US public schools (note that both major party candidates supported "stronger accountability" and more standardized testing during the 2000 presidential campaign). It is grounded in formal reports such as *A Nation at Risk* and reflected, endorsed, and expanded in works of typically conservative (culturally and economically) scholarship (e.g., Hirsch, 1987, 1996; Ravitch, 1995, 2000; Ravitch & Finn, 1987), especially that linked specifically to the social studies.[7]

Though dominant and indicative of a powerfully elitist consensus, the recent move toward SBER—particularly within social education—must and can only be understood contextually and against certain overlapping and contiguous sociocultural, economic, and political currents, including changes in technology, the advent of state-sponsored global-corporate capitalism, and the "triumph" of the U.S. "one party system." More precisely (and significantly), we must understand that SBER reflects and is reflected by such contexts as they produce/construct/create and are produced/constructed/created by a characteristic feature of twenty-first century life in the United States: namely, the imperatives (in terms both of *desire* and *opportunity*) of seeing and of being seen (i.e., both *how* we are seeing and being seen and *that* we are seeing and being seen; one might consider related notions of the "cult of celebrity," Warhol's "fifteen minutes of fame," Orwell's "Big Brother"). These imperatives induce a clear disciplinarity, a conformity, and a perceived necessity to standardize/become standardized.

So, specifically, what are these various contexts and changes? In terms of technology (*here* a sociocultural change) one might consider several fairly recent developments, including the advent of 24 hour per day/7 day per week television "broadcast" via hundreds of cable/satellite channels, the Internet, and the proliferation of such innovations as Webcams—making it possible, of course, both to see and be seen simultaneously and continuously. Economically (again, within the environment of state-sponsored, global, corporate capitalism), for instance, see how daily, round-the-clock updates reveal the scope to which stock prices and market capitalization figures increase for financial "powerhouses" even in the absence of profit or short-term profit potential—here, apparently, corporate *image*, how such institutions are *seen* (their "get rich quick" possibilities and manipulations)—matter more than fundamental soundness or past and present performance (let alone social, political, environmental, and/or cultural *awareness* and *sensitivity*). Similarly, the current race to the "middle" waged between the major political parties (i.e., year 2000 presidential candidates Bush and Gore) depends less on any authentic issue advocacy and more on how they are seen (and how they themselves see things). In effect, this leads to the establishment of a one-party system in which powerful Republicans seek to appease their Right wing (e.g., Patrick J. Buchanan, the Christian Coalition) while simultaneously staking a claim in the "center" (aka "compassionate conservatism"), and powerful Democrats do the same with respect to their Left wing (e.g., Ralph Nader, environmentalists; see the "New Democrat"). As a result real difference is marginalized and traditional allies (e.g., Nader via the Democrats and Buchanan via the Republicans) are forced out and compelled to accept an existence *viewed* as extremist and nonmainstream. This would be, perhaps, not so problematic were it based less on *mere* image (i.e., polling data, focus group results, advertising) and more on a heartfelt dedication to significant issues and differences. For both sides, however, the goal seems to be less one of defending and promoting the collective social good, and instead one of ensuring first that they are in fact seen, and second that how they are seen (Democrats *and* Republicans) is as "conservative" but not "too" conservative and "liberal" but not "too" liberal.

At heart, these contexts—socio-cultural, economic, political—(re)establish the priority of sight—the "gaze"—as a mechanism of discipline and social control. More specifically, they create and are created by the conditions within which the convergence of "surveillance" and "spectacle" occurs, and establish in part the setting for what might be called the "new disciplinarity," a mode of often subtle coercion grounded in the extreme potentials of continual seeing and being seen, of both surveillance *and* spectacle.

According to Foucault (1975/1979):

> Antiquity had been a civilization of spectacle. *'To render accessible to a multitude of men [sic] the inspection of a small number of objects'* [italics added]: this was the problem to which the architecture of temples, theatres and circuses responded. With spectacle, there was a predominance of public life, the intensity of festivals, sensual proximity. In these rituals in which blood flowed, society found new vigour and formed for a moment a single great body. The modern age poses the opposite problem: *'To procure for a small number, or even for a single individual, the instantaneous view of a great multitude'* [italics added]. In a society in which the principal elements are no longer the community and public life, but, on the one hand, private individuals and, on the other, the state, relations can be regulated only in a form that is the exact reverse of the spectacle: 'It was to the modern age, to the ever-growing influence of the state, that was reserved the task of increasing and perfecting its guarantees, by using and directing, towards that great aim the building and distribution of buildings intended to observe a great multitude of men at the same time.' (pp. 216–217)

For Foucault, surveillance represented a disciplinary power built out of the (eventually automatic and invisible) possibilities of the many being visible to the few (a la the architecture of the modern prison created according to the design of Bentham's Panopticon). At present, elements of surveillance exist in such societal features as "Nannycams," "Carnivore" (the FBI's e-mail-tapping framework), and "Echelon" (the government's program for monitoring virtually all worldwide telecommunications).

Spectacle, conversely, presupposed a mode of disciplinarity based on the processes of the few being visible to the many (a la the ancient architectures of theaters, circuses, and temples). Yet according to philosopher Guy Debord (1967/1994) in *The Society of the Spectacle*, it describes contemporary society as well, especially in that:

> The whole of life of those societies in which modern conditions of production prevail presents itself as an immense accumulation of *spectacles*. All that once was directly lived has become mere representation. (p. 12)

Further:

> The spectacle is not [merely] a collection of images; rather, it is a social relationship between people that is mediated by images.... In form as in content the spectacle serves as total justification for the conditions and aims of the existing system. It further ensures the *permanent presence* of that justification, for it governs almost all time spent outside the production process itself. [And, moreover, the] language of the spectacle is composed of signs of the dominant organization of production—signs which are at the same time the ultimate end-products of that organization. (pp. 12–13; see also Bracken, 1997; Debord, 1988/1990; Jappe, 1993/1999)

In today's U.S. society, such conditions exist, for example, via popular television shows (*Survivor, Jerry Springer*) and such technological innovations as "Webcams" (see also Vinson, 1999c).

What makes today unique, however, is the merging or at least coexistence of the two, making it *possible* and among some people (even) *desirable* to see and be seen continuously and simultaneously (i.e., because of the Internet and cable/satellite/wireless technologies). In the extreme, the potential becomes more real that society will (or at least *can*) be understood as nothing but a medium through which everybody *can* watch everybody all the time and across and throughout all space—nothing more than a totality of images and spectacular relationships.[8] Standardization/SBER in fact represents the extent to which this setting occurs, and presents a case not only by which the surveillance-spectacle merger can be understood but also one that can itself be understood against and according to surveillance and spectacle. An example here of the workings of surveillance is the official "monitoring" of testing procedures; an example of spectacle occurs in the media reporting of test scores. Both, in the end, privilege image over authenticity and work as a means of social control, political/economic dominance, and conformity.

Although curriculum standardization represents the dominant, consensus view, and granting its status as a major public policy issue (e.g.,

Johnston & [with] Duffett, 1999), it has not remained without its share of critics (e.g., Kohn, 2000; Ohanian, 1999; Vinson, 1999a, 2001; Vinson, Gibson, & Ross, 2001), most of whom have sought other avenues, including those comprising the notion of *diversity.* In many cases, these critiques have emphasized the nature of SBER as *oppressive* (e.g., drawing on Freire, 1970 and Young, 1992), *antidemocratic* (e.g., drawing on Dewey, 1916/1966), and in contradiction with the demands of the *collective* good (see Vinson, 1999a).

Contextualizing Diversity

The concurrent interest in diversity within the social studies community presents an alternative to the efforts to standardize purpose, curriculum, instruction, and assessment. But as with SBER, it must and can only be understood contextually. It has as its starting point an awareness of U.S. (and global) society as culturally pluralistic rather than monolithic and as grounded in hetero- rather than homogeneity. Its commitments include efforts to rethink and challenge traditional relationships between "center" and "margin," "voiced and voiceless," "dominant" and "subordinate," as well as to uncover and interrogate hierarchical and asymmetric socio-peda-gogical differences—specifically those embedded in relations of power and in privileged constructions of identity, culture, race, ethnicity, gender, language, sexuality, and class (among others)—while simultaneously advocating for the positions of the historically underrepresented (especially in terms of school "achievement" and educational opportunity).[9]

Contextually this perspective rests within a framework based upon taking seriously and critically a number of social developments, including the evolution of U.S. demographics (e.g., increasing diversity vis-à-vis regional hegemony, age, wealth and income, language, race, ethnicity, religion, culture, and so on), the law (e.g., legislation regarding the dynamic status of "ability" and "disability"), state-mandated anti-immigration/anti-bilingual education statutes (e.g., California's Proposition 187), and debates surrounding various aspects of schooling and pedagogy (e.g., privatization schemes such as "vouchers" and "school choice" plans, "whole language" and "phonics," "high-stakes testing" and "authentic assessment," etc.).

Moreover, it exists within and draws upon a setting of recent transformations in educational research, theory, and practice (including the proliferation of qualitative methodologies and discourses, the influence of postmodernism), as well as in other complementary and foundational disciplines (e.g., psychology, sociology, history, and philosophy). Most directly, this orientation among social studies curriculum workers toward diversity springs from the overall ascendancy of "multicultural education" (e.g., Banks, 1994, 1996; McLaren, 1997; Sleeter & Grant, 1999). In social studies, recent works by Cornbleth and Waugh (1996) and Pang (2000), as well as by Banks (e.g., 1995), present a fundamental challenge—indeed a threat—to the essentialist notions of a standardized and standardizing practice with respect to citizenship education and the struggle over social, political, cultural, and historical knowledge.

WHAT NEXT?

Without question, the appearance-of-uniformity-appearance-of-diversity paradox, as understood again within the contemporary context of global, state-sponsored, corporate, infotech capitalism and the ascendancy of the U.S. one-party system, as reflective of and reflected by the evolving convergence of spectacle and surveillance, leaves both standardization and diversity as clear options for the evolution of the social studies curriculum. And yet, given the profoundly problematic effort to blend the two, as well as critical changes and shifts in U.S./global social, scientific, pedagogical, gender, political, ideological, technological, sexual, cultural, linguistic, religious, racial, ethnic, and economic circumstances, social studies educators and curriculum workers must pursue alternative avenues that both advance the field and take seriously new understandings, experiences, and needs— be those academic, theoretical, scholarly, or practical and applied. Social studies curriculum work cannot stand still (or, worse, retreat) in the face of a dynamic world. It must move forward. In perhaps no other field of education is it more important that curriculum and instruction accept the challenges of the day, and recognize that yesterday's citizenship/citizenship education simply (and bluntly) may just not be good enough.

So what do we do? Surprisingly, given the "nature" of social studies content as contested and contestable knowledge (e.g., that surrounding ownership, naming, identity, and meaning vis-à-vis culture, history, politics, economics, etc.), social studies professionals (both academics and practitioners) too often are dishearteningly slow to embrace, critique, and/or interrogate state-of-the-art, progressive approaches relative to curriculum design, development, and reform. As indicated by Wright (2000), describing submissions to a recent academic conference, doing so means understanding and critically interpreting the complexities of contemporary curriculum theory (granted, a difficult task), a field he describes according to six related characteristics:

- That [contemporary curriculum theory] is inherently political, contested, and in a state of productive flux (see also Whitson, 1988; 1991);
- That theoretical frameworks and discourses such as progressivism, phenomenology, hermeneutics, and critical theory, and canonical figures such as John Dewey, Ralph Tyler, Jean Piaget, Jurgen Haber-

mas, and Paulo Freire, while still dominant, appear to have waned (though to different extents) in overall representation;

- [That] curriculum theorizing is increasingly being undertaken within the framework of the "post-discourses" [e.g., postmodernism, postcolonialism, etc.];
- That the politics of social and cultural theory and social difference undergirds and is the dominant premise from which much curriculum theorizing is currently undertaken. Multiculturalism is clearly the predominant discourse in which this is presented, closely followed by critical pedagogy. There is evidence, however, of a cutting-edge shift from multiculturalism and critical pedagogy to cultural studies;
- [That] the supposed struggle between "traditionalist" and "reconceptualization" approaches to curriculum theorizing ... this supposedly highly charged dualism has in fact become passé and we have entered a postdualist ... era in curriculum theorizing [and];
- [That w]hile the mainstream of curriculum theorizing has yet to come to grips with the mainstreaming of the postdiscourses, theorists on the cutting edge have yet to articulate what is to be done about the limits and limitations of the post discourses, and what the combination of the current lull in sociocultural theorizing in general and the related movement "past the last post" into what we might call the "post-post era" will mean for curriculum theorizing (pp. 4–6).

As social studies educators and curriculum professionals we must take on such developments in curriculum theory as we strive for relevance and a meaningful social/citizenship/democratic education. We must consider such approaches as contemporary pragmatism (e.g., Cherryholmes, 1999; Stanley, 1992), postmodernism/poststructuralism (e.g., Doll, 1993; Slattery, 1995; Stanley 1992), feminist theory (postmodern, critical, and multicultural; e.g., Florence, 1998; Hooks, 1994; Lather, 1991), cultural studies (e.g., Giroux, 1999; Giroux & [with] Shannon, 1999; Giroux, Lankshear, McLaren, & Peters, 1996); critical postmodernism (e.g., McLaren, 1995), queer theory (e.g., Pinar, 1998), democratic schooling (e.g., Beane & Apple, 1997), and postcolonialism (e.g., Spivak, 1990), and pursue critically their meaning and relevance not only for the social studies curriculum per se, but also for the lived classroom experiences of teachers and students, community groups, and parents (see also Pinar, Reynolds, Slattery, & Taubman, 1995). Further, we must consider their significance with respect to contemporary (global) democratic citizenship and to key societal issues such as freedom, social justice, equality, and opportunity.

We must, moreover, open up to less traditional approaches to social studies education, such as various and multiple pedagogies of collaboration, contemporary forms of progressive and reconstructivist education, and more authentic (as opposed to high-stakes and standardized) modes of evaluation and assessment (e.g., Hursh & Ross, 2000; Kohn, 1999; Mathison, 2001). Throughout this reconsideration we—whether social studies professionals or not—must take into account the importance of "democratic schools" and their ultimate place within, meaning for, and (desired) influence upon the creation of more authentically democratic societies.

SUMMARY AND CONCLUSIONS

The paradox of appearances implied in the notion of standardization (or uniformity) vs. diversity likely presents the field of social studies—in particular its various curriculum workers—with its most pressing and troubling conflict, a seeming contradiction grounded in a multitude of difficult political, economic, and sociocultural contexts as well as in the current priority of image (especially as established according to the evolving convergence of surveillance and spectacle). The educational implications are clear and yet confusing.

For teachers, they mean daring to challenge traditional and safe mechanisms of instruction, thereby expanding their approaches with respect to their own understandings of society, their students, the contexts of a relevant schooling, and the very meanings of social education. For curriculum workers, they mean taking risks, opening up their efforts in ways that threaten the hegemony of the still largely dominant "Tyler rationale," and perhaps even accepting as good that which at first might seem merely unsettling. And for educational researchers, in terms both of theoretical and empirical studies, they must reprioritize the place of purpose, struggling to take seriously new and evolving curricular understandings, re-emphasizing the importance of the lived and experienced curriculum among members of classroom groups, and addressing the socio-pedagogical role and nature of image (especially in light of the field's commitment to democracy, social justice, equality, anti-oppression, multiculturalism/multicultural education, authenticity, and meaningful citizenship).

But perhaps more important is the extent to which contemporary social studies curriculum work melds with the contemporary goals of social education—democratic citizenship, social justice, and a pedagogy of anti-oppression (e.g., Hursh & Ross, 2000; Kumashiro, 2000). More directly, we must pursue the extent to which such work—generally critical—can indeed make a difference, that is in terms of a social change-oriented schooling dedicated to the needs of the "collective good" and opposed to the dual dominance of the status quo by the economically powerful and the politically well-connected (Apple, 2000; Hursh & Ross, 2000; Vinson, 1999b, 2001). For if nothing else, social studies education—its curriculum as well as its purposes, modes of instruction, and techniques of assessment—is, after all, *social.* Toward these ends, we must continuously interrogate and re-interrogate its goals, aspirations, and aims, continuing the recent work begun by others (e.g., Kohn, 1999, 2000; Postman, 1995; Schrag, 1995), as we ourselves begin our trek into the 21st century—a trek clearly marked by problems, but one replete with promise as well.

NOTES

1.These summaries are drawn from Vinson's (1998) discussion of Barr, Barth, and Shermis (1977) and Martorella (1996).

2. Two points. First, we recognize a certain tension in this rationale between its claim of a social science orientation and its inclusion of disciplines such as geography (both a "social" and a "natural" science) and history (both "social science" and "humanity"). Second, we accept that while the social science rationale provided the "new social studies" with a (perhaps *the*) major component of its curriculum work, one might also argue that such orientations as "discovery learning" and "inquiry" played key and significant roles.

3. As Shulman (1986) argues, "There are many such worlds, perhaps nested within one another, perhaps occupying parallel universes which frequently, albeit unpredictably, intrude on one another. Each of these worlds is occupied by the same people, but in different roles and striving for different purposes simultaneously ... Each has its own set of concepts and principles and, quite inevitably, it own set of facts, for facts are merely those particular phenomena to which our questions and principles direct our attention" (p. 7).

4. Stanley's (e.g., 1992) recent work represents a departure from the more traditional form of "social reconstructionism." His *Curriculum for Utopia*, for example, contains a sustained critique of his earlier (e.g., 1985) views and argues for a significantly revised version of social reconstruction (see also Hursh & Ross, 2000; Stanley, 2000). For as he argues, given the theoretical developments in the areas of postmodernism, poststructuralism, neopragmatism, and cultural theory, the Counts (and Rugg and Brameld) orientation is no longer tenable. In fact, his newer work is quite consistent with many of the positions we take throughout this paper. As *Curriculum for Utopia* indicates, Stanley's critique is constructed against the notion that any apriori "core values" (e.g., social justice) exist upon which to ground curriculum decisions. Instead, using both poststructuralism and neopragmatism, he argues for a focus on *practical reasoning* ("phronesis") as a basis for constructing a social education curriculum for the future.

5. Conflict, of course, is not *necessarily* a bad thing. Rather, it *could* signal a field that is vibrant, dynamic, and dialogical.

6. The specifics of state social studies curriculum standards are available on many state Department of Education websites.

7. See also Apple's (1996) similar analysis of the "neoliberal"/"neoconservative" alliance.

8. Certainly Foucault and Debord do not offer the only ways in which to view image. See also Barthes (1978), Bakhtin (1991), Boorstin (1961/1992), and McLuhan (1964/1998).

9. Necessarily, given space limitations and the multiplicity of perspectives and orientations that make-up what is typically called "multicultural education," this "contextualization" can provide little more than a framing starting point. Needless to say, however, this (these) view(s) do(es) offer a possible counterpoint to the dominant and conformative (and spectacular) effects of SBER. Although it risks being co-opted by the pro-standards movement, its potential to ground a radical revisioning of the social studies remains both exciting and unbounded.

REFERENCES

Adler, M. (1982). *The Paideia proposal.* New York: Macmillan.

Anderson, C., Avery, P.G., Pederson, P.V., Smith, E.S., & Sullivan, J.L. (1997). Divergent perspectives on citizenship education: A Q-method study and survey of social studies teachers. *American Educational Research Journal, 34,* 333–364.

Anyon, J. (1980). Social class and the hidden curriculum of work. *Journal of Education, 162,* 67–92.

Apple, M.W. (1993). *Official knowledge: Democratic education in a conservative age.* New York: Routledge.

Apple, M.W. (1996). *Cultural politics and education.* New York: Teachers College Press.

Apple, M.W. (2000). Can critical pedagogies interrupt rightist policies? *Educational Theory, 50,* 229–254.

Applebee, A., Langer, J., & Mullis, I. (1987). *The nation's report card: Literature and U.S. History.* Princeton, NJ: Educational Testing Service.

Bakhtin, M.M. (1991). *The dialogic imagination* (C. Emerson & M. Holquist, Trans. & Eds.). Austin: University of Texas Press.

Banks, J.A. (1994). *An introduction to multicultural education.* Boston: Allyn and Bacon.

Banks, J.A. (1995). Transformative challenges to the social science disciplines: Implications for social studies teaching and learning. *Theory and Research in Social Education, 23,* 2–20.

Banks, J.A. (Ed.). (1996). *Multicultural education: Transformative knowledge and action: Historical and contemporary perspectives.* New York: Teachers College Press.

Barr, R.D., Barth, J.L., & Shermis, S.S. (1977). *Defining the social studies* (National Council for the Social Studies, Bulletin 51). Arlington, VA: National Council for the Social Studies.

Barthes, R. (1978). *Image, music, text* (S. Heath, Trans.). New York: Noonday Press.

Barton, K.C. (1997). "I just kinda know": Elementary students' ideas about historical evidence. *Theory and Research in Social Education, 25,* 407–430.

Bayles, E.E. (1950). *The theory and practice of teaching.* New York: Harper.

Beane, J.A., & Apple, M.W. (Eds.). (1997). *Democratic schools.* Alexandria, VA: Association for Supervision and Curriculum Development.

Bennett, W.J. (1989). *Our children and our country: Improving America's schools and affirming the common culture.* New York: Touchstone.

Bennett, W.J. (1992). *The de-valuing of America: The fight for our culture and our children.* New York: Summit.

Bloom, A. (1987). *The closing of the American mind.* New York: Simon & Schuster.

Bode, B. (1940). *How we learn.* New York: Heath.

Boorstin, D.J. (1992). *The image: A guide to pseudo-events in America.* New York: Vintage/Random House. (Original work published 1961)

Bowles, S., & Gintis, H. (1976). *Schooling in capitalist America.* New York: Basic Books.

Bracken, L. (1997). *Guy Debord: Revolutionary.* Venice, CA: Feral House.

Brameld, T. (1956). *Toward a reconstructed philosophy of education.* New York: Holt, Rinehart, and Winston.

Brophy, J. (1990). Teaching social studies for understanding and higher order applications. *Elementary School Journal, 90,* 351–417.

Brubaker, D.L., Simon, L.H., & William, J.W. (1977). A conceptual framework for social studies curriculum and instruction. *Social Education, 41*, 201–205.

Bruner, J.S. (1969). Man: A course of study. In M. Feldman & E. Seifman (Eds.), *The social studies: Structure, models, and strategies* (pp. 216–227). Englewood Cliffs, NJ: Prentice-Hall.

Bruner, J.S. (1977). *The process of education* (Rev. ed.). Cambridge, MA: Harvard University Press.

Center for Civic Education. (1991). *CIVITAS: A framework for civic education* (National Council for the Social Studies, Bulletin 86). Calabasas, CA: Author.

Center for Civic Education. (1994). *National standards for civics and government.* Calabasas, CA: Author.

Cherryholmes, C.H. (1980). Social knowledge and citizenship education: Two views of truth and criticism. *Curriculum Inquiry, 10*, 115–141.

Cherryholmes, C.H. (1982). Discourse and criticism in the social studies classroom. *Theory and Research in Social Education, 9*(4), 57–73.

Cherryholmes, C.H. (1999). *Reading pragmatism.* New York and London: Teachers College Press.

Committee on Social Studies of the National Education Association. (1916). *The social studies in secondary education.* Washington, DC: USGPO.

Cornbleth, C., & Waugh, D. (1996). *The great speckled bird: Multicultural politics and education policymaking.* New York: St. Martin's Press.

Cornett, J.W. (1990). Teacher thinking about curriculum and instruction: A case study of a secondary social studies teacher. *Theory and Research in Social Education, 18*, 248–273.

Cornett, J.W., Chase, K.S., Miller, P., Schrock, D., Bennett, B.J., Goins, A., & Hammonds, C. (1992). Insights from the analysis of our own theorizing: The viewpoints of seven teachers. In E.W. Ross, J.W. Cornett, & G. McCutcheon (Eds.), *Teacher personal theorizing: Connecting curriculum practice, theory, and research.* Albany: State University of New York Press.

Counts, G.S. (1932). *Dare the schools build a new social order?* New York: John Day.

Cuban, L. (1991). History of teaching in social studies. In J.P. Shaver (Ed.), *Handbook of research on social studies teaching and learning* (pp. 197–209). New York: Macmillan.

Cuban, L. (1993). *How teachers taught : Constancy and change in American classrooms 1890–1990* (2nd ed.). New York: Teachers College Press.

Debord, G. (1990). *Comments on the society of the spectacle* (M. Imrie, Trans.). London and New York: Verso. (Original work published 1988)

Debord, G. (1994). *The society of the spectacle* (D. Nicholson-Smith, Trans.). New York: Zone Books. (Original work published 1967)

Department of Education. (1991). *America 2000: An education strategy sourcebook.* Washington, DC: USGPO.

Dewey, J. (1933). *How we think* (Rev. ed.). Boston: D.C. Heath.

Dewey, J. (1956). *The child and the curriculum/The school and society.* Chicago: University of Chicago Press.

Dewey, J. (1963). *Experience and education.* New York: Collier. (Original work published 1938)

Dewey, J. (1966). *Democracy and education.* New York: Macmillan. (Originally published in 1916)

Doll, W. (1993). *A post-modern perspective on curriculum.* New York: Teachers College Press.

Egan, K. (1982). Teaching history to young children. *Phi Delta Kappan, 63*, 439–441.

Engle, S.H. (1977). Comments of Shirley H. Engle. In R.D. Barr, J.L. Barth, & S.S. Shermis, *Defining the social studies* (pp. 103–105). Arlington, VA: National Council for the Social Studies.

Engle, S.H. (1987). Decision making: The heart of social studies instruction. In D. Roselle (Ed.), *Voices of social education, 1937–1987* (pp. 74–81). New York: Macmillan. (Reprinted from *Social Education*, 1960, pp. 301–304, 306)

Engle, S.H., & Ochoa, A.S. (1988). *Education for democratic citizenship: Decision making in the social studies.* New York: Teachers College Press.

Evans, R.W., & Saxe, D.W. (Eds.). (1996). *Handbook on teaching social issues.* Washington, DC: National Council for the Social Studies.

Feldman, M., & Seifman, E. (Eds.). (1969). *The social studies: Structure, models, and strategies.* Englewood Cliffs, NJ: Prentice Hall.

Fenstermacher, G.D., & Soltis, J.F. (1992). *Approaches to teaching* (2nd ed.). New York: Teachers College Press.

Fenton, E. (1966). *Teaching the new social studies in secondary schools: An inductive approach.* New York: Holt, Rinehart, & Winston.

Fickle, L.H. (2000). Democracy is messy: Exploring the personal theories of a high school social studies teacher. *Theory and Research in Social Education, 28*, 59–390.

Finn, C.E., Jr., & Petrilli, M.J. (Eds.). (2000). *The state of state standards 2000.* The Thomas B. Fordham Foundation. (Available on-line: http://www.edexcellence.net/library/soss2000/standards%202000.html)

Florence, N. (1998). *bell hooks' engaged pedagogy: A transgressive education for critical consciousness.* Westport, CT: Bergin & Garvey.

Foster, S.J., Hoge, J.D., & Rocsch, R.H. (1999). Thinking aloud about history: Children's and adolescents' responses to historical photographs. *Theory and Research in Social Education, 27*, 179–214.

Foucault, M. (1979). *Discipline and punish: The birth of the prison* (A. Sheridan, Trans.). New York: Vintage. (Original work published 1975)

Freire, P. (1970). *Pedagogy of the oppressed.* New York: Continuum.

Geography Education Standards Project. (1994). *Geography for life: National geography standards: What every young American should know and be able to do in geography.* Washington, DC: National Geographic Research and Exploration.

Gehrke, N.J., Knapp, M.S., & Sirotnik, K.A. (1992). In search of the school curriculum. In G. Grant (Ed.), *Review of Research in Education, 18*, 51–110.

Giroux, H.A. (1999). *The mouse that roared: Disney and the end of innocence.* Lanham, MD: Rowan & Littlefield.

Giroux, H., Lankshear, C., McLaren, P., & Peters, M. (1996). *Counternarratives: Cultural studies and critical pedagogies in postmodern space.* London and New York: Routledge.

Giroux, H.A., & Shannon, P. (Eds.). (1999). *Education and cultural studies: Toward a performative practice.* New York: Routledge.

Goodheart, A. (2000, September 30). Brand-name auctions, cut-rate connoisseurs. *The New York Times*, A 27.

Gore, J.M. (1993). *The struggle for pedagogies: Critical and feminist discourses as regimes of truth.* New York: Routledge.

Haas, M.E., & Laughlin, M.A. (1997). *Meeting the standards: Social studies readings for k-6 educators.* Washington, DC: National Council for the Social Studies.

Hanna, P. (1987). *Assuring quality for the social studies in our schools.* Stanford, CA: Hoover Institution Press, Stanford University.

Hertzberg, H.W. (1981). *Reform in social studies, 1880–1980.* Boulder, CO: Social Science Education Consortium.

Hirsch, E.D., Jr. (1987). *Cultural literacy: What every American needs to know.* Boston: Houghton Mifflin.

Hirsch, E.D., Jr. (1996). *The schools we need and why we don't have them.* New York: Doubleday.

hooks, b. (1994). *Teaching to transgress: Education as the practice of freedom.* New York: Routledge.

Hullfish, H.G., & Smith, P.G. (1961). *Reflective thinking: The method of education.* New York: Dodd, Mead & Company.

Hunt, M.P., & Metcalf, L.E. (1968). *Teaching high school social studies: Problems in reflective thinking and social understanding* (2nd ed.). New York: Harper & Row.

Hursh, D.W., & Ross, E.W. (Eds.). (2000). *Democratic social education: Social studies for social change.* New York: Falmer.

Jappe, A. (1999). *Guy Debord* (D. Nicholson-Smith, Trans.). Berkeley: University of California Press. (Original work published 1993)

Jenne, J.T. (1997). Conserving the status quo in social studies teaching: The case of second career military teachers. *Theory and Research in Social Education, 25,* 446–469.

Johnston, J. [with] Duffett, A. (1999, September 30). *Standards and accountability: Where the public stands: A report from Public Agenda for the 1999 National Education Summit.* New York: Public Agenda.

Joyce, B., & Weil, M. (1992). *Models of teaching* (4th ed.). New York: Harper & Row.

Kanpol, B. (1994). *Critical pedagogy: An introduction.* Westport, CT: Bergin & Garvey.

Kneip, W.M. (1989). Social studies within a global education. *Social Education, 53,* 399–403.

Kohn, A. (1999). *The schools our children deserve: Moving beyond traditional classrooms and "tougher standards."* Boston and New York: Houghton Mifflin.

Kohn, A. (2000). *The case against standardized testing: Raising the scores, ruining the schools.* New York: Heinemann.

Kumashiro, K.K. (2000). Toward a theory of anti-oppressive education. *Review of Educational Research, 70,* 25–53.

Lather, P. (1991). *Getting smart: Feminist research and pedagogy with/in the postmodern.* New York: Routledge.

Leming, J.S. (1989). The two cultures of social studies education. *Social Education, 53,* 404–408.

Leming, J.S. (1992). Ideological perspectives within the social studies profession: An empirical examination of the "two cultures" thesis. *Theory and Research in Social Education, 20,* 293–312.

Leming, J.S. (1994). Past as prologue: A defense of traditional patterns of social studies instruction. In M.R. Nelson (Ed.), *The future of the social studies* (pp. 17–23). Boulder, CO: Social Science Education Consortium.

Lengel, J.G., & Superka, D.P. (1982). Curriculum organization in socials studies. In *The current state of social studies: A report of Project SPAN* (pp. 81–102). Boulder, CO: Social Science Education Consortium.

Levin, H.M. (1998). Educational performance standards and the economy. *Educational Researcher, 27*(4), 4–10.

Loewen, J. (1996). *Lie my teacher told me: Everything your American history textbook got wrong.* New York: New Press.

Marker, G., & Mehlinger, H. (1992). Social studies. In P.W. Jackson (Ed.) *Handbook of research on curriculum* (pp. 830–851). New York: Macmillan.

Martorella, P.H. (1996). *Teaching social studies in middle and secondary schools* (2nd ed.). Englewood Cliffs, NJ: Merrill/Prentice-Hall.

Massialas, B.G. (1992). The "new social studies"—Retrospect and prospect. *The Social Studies, 83,* 120–124.

Mathison, S. (2001). Assessment in social studies: Moving toward authenticity. In E.W. Ross (Ed.), *The social studies curriculum: Purposes, problems, and possibilities.* (Rev. ed.; pp. 217–234). Albany: State University of New York Press.

Mathison, S., Ross, E.W., & Vinson, K.D. (2001). Defining the social studies curriculum: The influence of and resistance to curriculum standards and testing in social studies. In E.W. Ross (Ed.), *The social studies curriculum: Purposes, problems, and possibilities* (Rev. ed., pp. 87–102). Albany: State University of New York Press.

McKee, S.J. (1988). Impediments to implementing critical thinking. *Social Education, 52,* 444–446.

McLaren, P. (1995). Critical pedagogy and the pragmatics of justice. In M. Peters (Ed.), *Education and the postmodern condition* (pp. 87–120). Westport, CT and London: Bergin & Garvey.

McLaren, P. (1997). *Revolutionary multiculturalism: Pedagogies of dissent for the new millennium.* Boulder, CO: Westview Press.

McLaren, P. (1998). *Life in schools* (3rd ed.). New York: Longman.

McLuhan, M. (1998). *Understanding media: The extensions of man.* Cambridge, MA: MIT Press. (Original work published 1964)

McNeil, L. (1986). *Contradictions of control: School structure and school knowledge.* New York: Routledge.

Merryfield, M.M., & Remy, R.C. (1995). *Teaching about international conflict and peace.* Albany: State University of New York Press.

Michaelis, J.U., & Johnston, A.M. (Eds.) (1965). *The social sciences: Foundations of the social studies* (pp. 1–24). Boston: Allyn and Bacon.

Mitsakos, C.L. (1978). A global education program can make a difference. *Theory and Research in Social Education, 6,* 1–15.

Morrissett, I. (1977). Curriculum Information Network sixth report: Preferred approaches to the teaching of social studies. *Social Education, 41,* 206–209.

Morrissett, I., & Hass, J.D. (1982). Rationales, goals, and objectives is social studies. In *The current state of social studies* (pp. 1–79). Boulder, CO: Social Science Education Consortium.

Nash, G.B., Crabtree, C., & Dunn, R.E. (1997). *History on trial: Culture wars and the teaching of the past.* New York: Knopf.

National Assessment of Educational Progress. (1980). *Citizenship and social studies objectives.* Denver, CO: Author.

National Center for History in the Schools. (1994a). *National standards for United States history.* Los Angeles: Author.

National Center for History in the Schools. (1994b). *National standards for world history.* Los Angeles: Author.

National Commission on Excellence in Education. (1983). *A nation at risk: The imperative for educational reform.* Washington, DC: USGPO.

National Council for the Social Studies. (1981). Statement on the essentials of the social studies. *Social Education, 45,* 162–164.

National Council for the Social Studies. (2000). *National standards for teachers.* Washington, DC: Author. [Available on-line: http://www.socialstudies.org/standards/ teachers/home.html]

National Council for the Social Studies Curriculum Standards Task Force. (1994). *Expectations of excellence: Curriculum standards for social studies* (Bulletin 89). Washington, DC: National Council for the Social Studies.

National Council on Economic Education. (1997). *Voluntary national content standards in economics.* New York: Author.

Nelson, J.L. (1985). New criticism and social education. *Social Education, 49,* 368–371.

Nelson, J.L. (1990). Charting a course backwards: A response to the National Commission's nineteenth century social studies program. *Social Education, 54,* 434–437.

Nelson, J.L., & Michaelis, J.U. (1980). *Secondary social studies: Instruction, curriculum, evaluation.* Englewood Cliffs, NJ: Prentice-Hall.

Nelson, J.L., & Ochoa, A.S. (1987). Academic freedom, censorship, and the social studies. *Social Education, 51,* 424–427.

Nelson, J.L., & Pang, V.O. (2001). Racism, prejudice, and the social studies curriculum. In E.W. Ross (Ed.). *The social studies curriculum: Purposes, problems, and possibilities* (Rev. ed., pp. 143–162). Albany: State University of New York Press.

Newmann, F.M. (1985). The radical perspective on social studies: A synthesis and critique. *Theory and Research in Social Education, 13,* 1–18.

Ohanian, S. (1999). *One size fits few: The folly of educational standards.* New York: Heinemann.

Oliner, P. (1983). Putting "community" into citizenship education: The need for prosociality. *Theory and Research in Social Education, 11,* 65–81.

Oliver, D.W., & Shaver, J.P. (1966). *Teaching public issues in the high school.* Boston: Houghton Mifflin.

Pang, V.O. (2000). *Multicultural education: A caring-centered, reflective approach.* New York: McGraw Hill.

Pinar, W. (Ed.). (1998). *Queer theory in education.* Mahwah, NJ: Lawrence Erlbaum Associates.

Pinar, W., Reynolds, W., Slattery, P., & Taubman, P. (Eds.). (1995). *Understanding curriculum.* New York: Peter Lang.

Postman, N. (1995). *The end of education: Redefining the value of school.* New York: Vintage/Random House.

Project SPAN. (1982). *The current state of social studies.* Boulder, CO: Social Science Education Consortium.

Ravitch, D. (1995). *National standards in American education: A citizen's guide.* Washington, DC: Brookings Institution Press.

Ravitch, D. (2000). *Left back: A century of failed school reforms.* New York: Simon and Schuster.

Ravitch, D., & Finn, Jr., C.E. (1987). *What do our 17-year-olds know? A Report of the first national assessment of history and literature.* New York: Harper & Row.

Remy, R.C. (1980). *Handbook of basic citizenship competencies.* Alexandria, VA: Association for Supervision and Curriculum Development.

Ross, E.W. (Ed.). (1994). *Reflective practice in social studies.* Washington, DC: National Council for the Social Studies.

Ross, E.W. (Ed.). (2001a). *The social studies curriculum: Purposes, problems, and possibilities* (2nd ed.). Albany: State University of New York Press.

Ross, E.W. (2001b). The struggle for the social studies curriculum. In E. W. Ross (Ed.), *The social studies curriculum: Purposes, problems, and possibilities* (Rev. ed., pp. 19–41). Albany: State University of New York Press.

Ross, E.W. (2000). Redrawing the lines: The case against traditional social studies instruction. In D.W. Hursh & E.W. Ross (Eds.), *Democratic social education: Social studies for social change* (pp. 43–63). New York: Falmer.

Ross, E.W., Cornett, J.W., & McCutcheon, G. (1992). *Teacher personal theorizing: Connecting curriculum practice, theory, and research.* Albany: State University of New York Press.

Sanders, N.M., & Stone, N.C. (1987). *The California high school curriculum study: Paths through high school.* Sacramento, CA: California Department of Education.

Saxe, D.W. (1997). The unique mission of social studies. In E. W. Ross (Ed.), *The social studies curriculum: Purposes, problems, and possibilities* (pp. 39–55). Albany: State University of New York Press.

Schneider, D.O., & Van Sickle, R.L. (1979). The status of the social studies: The publishers' perspective. *Social Education, 43,* 461–465.

Schrag, F. (1995). *Back to basics: Fundamental educational questions reexamined.* San Francisco: Jossey-Bass.

Schwab, J.J. (1969). The concept of the structure of a discipline. In M. Feldman & E. Seifman (Eds.), *The social studies: Structure, model, and strategies* (pp. 4–12). Englewood Cliffs, NJ: Prentice-Hall.

Seixas, P. (1993). The community of inquiry as a basis for knowledge and learning: The case of history. *American Educational Research Journal, 30,* 302–324.

Seixas, P. (1998). Student teachers thinking historically. *Theory and Research in Social Education, 26,* 310–341.

Shaver, J.P. (1977). The task of rationale-building for citizenship education. In J.P. Shaver (Ed.), *Building rationales for citizenship education* (pp. 96–116). Arlington, VA: National Council for the Social Studies.

Shaver, J.P., Davis, O.L., Jr., Helburn, S.W. (1980). *An interpretive report on the status of precollege social studies education based upon three NSF-funded studies.* Washington, DC: National Council for the Social Studies.

Shor, I., & Freire, P. (1987). *A pedagogy for liberation.* New York: Bergin & Garvey.

Shulman, L.S. (1986). Paradigms and research programs in the study of teaching: A contemporary perspective. In M.C. Wittrock (Ed.), *Handbook of research on teaching* (3rd ed., pp. 3–360. New York: Macmillan.

Slattery, P. (1995). *Curriculum development in the postmodern era.* New York: Garland Press.

Sleeter, C.E., & Grant, C.A. (1999). *Making choices for multicultural education: Five approaches to race, class, and gender* (3rd ed.). New York: John Wiley & Sons.

Slekar, T.D. (1998). Epistemological entanglements: Preservice elementary school teachers' "apprenticeship of observation" and the teaching of history. *Theory and Research in Social Education, 26,* 485–507.

Spectacular Times. (n. d.). Images. (Available on line at http://www.cat.org.au/ spectacular/*images.htm.*

Spivak, G.C. (1990). *The post-colonial critic: Interviews, strategies, dialogue.* New York: Routledge.

Stake, R.E., & Easley, J.A. (1978). *Case studies in science education 2: Design, overview and general findings.* Urbana: Center for Instructional Research and Curriculum Evaluation/University of Illinois.

Stanley, W.B. (1985). Social reconstructionism for today's social education. *Social Education, 49*, 384–389.

Stanley, W.B. (1992). *Curriculum for utopia.* Albany: State University of New York Press.

Stanley, W.B., & Nelson, J.L. (1986). Social education for social transformation. *Social Education, 50*, 528–533.

Stanley, W.B., & Nelson, J.L. (1994). The foundations of social education in historical context. In R. Martusewicz & W. Reynolds (Eds.), *Inside/out: Contemporary critical perspectives in education* (pp. 266–284). New York: St. Martin's.

Stodolsky, S.S. (1988). *The subject matters: Classroom activity in math and social studies.* Chicago: University of Chicago Press.

Stodolsky, S.S., Salk, S., & Glaessner, B. (1991). Students' view about learning math and social studies. *American Educational Research Journal, 28*, 89–116.

Superka, D.P., & Hawke, S. (1982). *Social roles: A focus for social studies in the 1980s.* Boulder, CO: Social Science Education Consortium.

Tabachnick, B.R. (1991). Social studies: Elementary-school programs. In A. Lewy (Ed.), *International encyclopedia of curriculum* (pp. 725–731). Oxford: Pergamon.

Thornton, S.J. (1988). Curriculum consonance in United States history classrooms. *Journal of Curriculum and Supervision, 3*, 308–320.

Thornton, S.J. (1992). How do elementary teachers decide what to teach in social studies? In E.W. Ross, J.W. Cornett, & G. McCutcheon (Eds.), *Teacher personal theorizing: Connecting curriculum practice, theory, and research* (pp. 83–95). Albany: State University of New York Press.

Tucker, M.S., & Codding, J.B. (1998). *Standards for our schools: How to set them, measure them, and reach them.* San Francisco: Jossey-Bass.

Tye, B.B., & Tye, K.A. (1992). *Global education: A study of school change.* Albany: State University of New York Press.

VanSledright, B.A., & Afflerbach, P. (2000). Reconstructing Andrew Jackson: Elementary teachers' readings of revisionist history texts. *Theory and Research in Social Education, 28*, 411–444.

Vinson, K.D. (1998). The "traditions" revisited: Instructional approach and high school social studies teachers. *Theory and Research in Social Education, 23*, 50–82.

Vinson, K.D. (1999a). National curriculum standards and social studies education: Dewey, Freire, Foucault, and the construction of a radical critique. *Theory and Research in Social Education, 27*, 296–328.

Vinson, K.D. (1999b, November). Social education and the collective good: A case against standardization. In E.W. Ross (Chair), *Standards-based reform in social studies education: Defining or undermining the common good?* Paper presented at the annual meeting of the National Council for the Social Studies (NCSSSA), Orlando, FL.

Vinson, K.D. (1999c, November). Spectacle and disciplinarity: Standardization, Foucault, and Debord. In R. Gibson (Chair), *Restraints for brain and body politic:*

Standards for curriculum and instruction: Their theory, history, and practice as spectacles, surveillance, and modes of social control—Which way out? Workshop conducted at the annual meeting of the National Council for the Social Studies (CUFA), Orlando, FL.

Vinson, K.D. (2001). Oppression, anti-oppression, and citizenship education. In E.W. Ross (Ed.), *The social studies curriculum: Purposes, problems, and possibilities* (Rev. ed., pp. 57–84). Albany: State University of New York Press.

Vinson, K.D., Gibson, R., & Ross, E.W. (2001). High-stakes testing and standardization: The threat to authenticity. *Progressive Perspectives, 3*(2). Burlington, VT: John Dewey Project on Progressive Education, University of Vermont. (Available online at: http://www.uvm.edu/~dewey/monographs/ProPer3n2.html)

Wasburn, L. (1997). Accounts of slavery: An analysis of U.S. history textbooks from 1900 to 1992. *Theory and Research in Social Education, 25*, 470–491

Weiss, I.R. (1978). *Report of the 1977 national survey of science, mathematics, and social studies education.* Washington, DC: National Science Foundation/USGPO.

Wesley, E.B., & Wronski, S.P. (1964). *Teaching social studies in high schools* (5th ed.). Boston: D.C. Heath.

Wexler, P. (1985). Social change and the practice of social education. *Social Education, 49*, 390–394.

Whelan, M. (1997). History as the core of social studies curriculum. In E.W. Ross (Ed.), *The social studies curriculum: Purposes, problems, and possibilities* (pp. 21–37). Albany: State University of New York Press.

Whitson, T. (1988). The politics of "non-political" curriculum: Heteroglossia and the discourse of "choice" and "effectiveness. In W. Pinar (Ed.), *Contemporary curriculum discourses* (pp. 279–330). Scottsdale, AZ: Gorsuch Scarisbrick.

Whitson, T. (1991). *Constitution and curriculum: Semiotic analysis of cases and controversies in education, law, and social science.* London: Falmer Press.

Wiley, K.B. (1977). *The status of pre-college science, mathematics, and social science education: 1955–1975.* Washington, DC: National Science Foundation.

Willis, P.E. (1981). *Learning to labor.* New York: Columbia University Press. (Original work published 1977, *Learning to labour: How working class kids get working class jobs)*

Wilson, S.M., & Wineburg, S.S. (1988). Peering at history from different lenses: The role of disciplinary perspectives in the teaching of American history. *Teachers College Record, 89*, 525–539.

Wolf, R.M. (1998). National standards: Do we need them? *Educational Researcher, 27*(4), 22–25.

Wright, H.K. (2000). Nailing jell-o to the wall: Pinpointing aspects of state-of-the-art curriculum theorizing. *Educational Researcher, 29*(5), 4–13.

Wronski, S.P., & Bragaw, D.H. (1986). *Social studies and social sciences: A 50-year perspective* (Bulletin 78). Washington, DC: National Council for the Social Studies.

Young, I.M. (1992). Five faces of oppression. In T.E. Wartenberg (Ed.), *Rethinking power* (pp. 174–195). Albany: State University of New York Press.

CHAPTER 4

CLIMATES OF CONSTRAINT/ RESTRAINT OF TEACHERS AND TEACHING

Catherine Cornbleth

INTRODUCTION

In *Culture Against Man*, anthropologist Jules Henry (1963) argued that the purpose of public elementary and secondary schooling has been to transmit the national culture, not to transform it. Social studies in particular, he observed, teaches students to be stupid, that is, to accept the culture as given, not to question it. A half-century later, it could be argued that little has changed in this regard, even to the extent that the culture being transmitted is at least a decade or two behind the lived culture of teachers and students outside of school. For example, despite various reform efforts, the status of social studies education conveyed by Shaver, Davis, and Helburn (1979) more than 20 years ago appears to be out-of-date in relatively few schools and social studies classrooms across the nation. To understand the holding power of the kind of social studies education portrayed by Henry and by Shaver et al., I critically examine the research evidence regarding external influences, constraints, or controls on teachers and teaching, especially social studies teachers and teaching, and the internal restraints (e.g., self-censorship) felt by teachers with respect to their curriculum practice. Such an examination reveals social and structural obstacles to progressive curriculum and instructional reform, at least some of which presumably could be undermined.

For more than a quarter century, in one way or another, I have been working toward teaching for meaningful learning and critical thinking that incorporates diverse perspectives and students. Evidence from classroom studies indicates that this goal is not all that widely shared within the teaching profession generally or among social studies teachers more particularly (e.g., Cornbleth, 1998; Goodlad, 1984), nor among the general public. Even when it is advocated, it is not widely practiced. Over the years, I have examined teaching and teacher education, curriculum guidelines and the contexts of curriculum practice, and more recently curriculum politics and policy, in an effort to understand what seems to get in the way of—to undermine, discourage, or block—teaching for meaningful learning and critical thinking that incorporates diverse perspectives and students.

A decade ago, in *Curriculum in Context*, (Cornbleth, 1990a), I showed how the setting or conditions of classroom teaching and learning influences what is taught, how and to whom (i.e., curriculum-in-use). Because context powerfully shapes teaching and thus students' opportunities to learn, I have argued that the focus of curriculum reform efforts ought to be on planning *for* the desired curriculum practice. In other words, attention ought to be paid to creating conditions supportive of desired curriculum practice as well as designing the practice itself. And creating supportive conditions involves recognizing and dealing with constraints.[1]

While technical or technocratic approaches to curriculum design and implementation continue to predominate, largely ignoring or attempting to overcome contexts of implementation, there is evidence of increasing attention to context and its effects on curriculum-in-use (e.g., Cornbleth, 2000; McLaughlin, Talbert, & Bascia 1990; Talbert, McLaughlin, & Rowan, 1993). Several researchers have identified context factors that matter including subject area (Grossman & Stodolsky, 1995 Stodolsky & Grossman, 1995), bloated curriculum (Onosko & Newmann, 1994), school administration priorities (McNeil, 1986), social class (Metz, 1990), and policy discourse (Cornbleth & Waugh, 1995, 1999).

Expanding the list of influential context factors may be useful in mapping the territory. A checklist, however, has little explanatory power. It alerts us to what might make a difference in a particular case, what someone interested in a specific school or classroom might look for. It does not tell us which contextual factors are relevant or how the seemingly relevant context factors connect or interact to shape teaching practice and learning opportunities, for example, to constrain or restrain teaching for meaningful learning and critical thinking. In earlier work on hidden curriculum (Cornbleth, 1984) and context (Cornbleth, 1991b), I cautioned against considering context in isolation, against examining either curriculum practice or its social context apart from the other. Rather than inquiry into context *per se*, I suggested contextualized inquiry that explores external relationships as well as internal patterns, recognizing that what is background in one case may be foreground in another. Here, constraining contextual patterns are foregrounded while teaching for meaningful learning and critical thinking that incorporate diverse perspectives and students is background.

In reviewing a range of relevant research, I have tried to cull examples of contextual configurations or climates of constraint and restraint and to illustrate how they operate in particular times and places. Such illustrations are intended to enhance understanding and to be useful primarily in an interpretive sense. Before proceeding to describing and documenting climates of constraint and restraint in teaching, a few words on conceptions and methodology are in order.

Borrowing from meteorology, climate refers to prevailing conditions affecting the life and activity of a place. Sometimes the prevailing conditions are tangible, be they strong winds or the voices of organized interest groups. At other times they are less so as with a "climate of opinion." Without overdrawing the climate metaphor, it seems appropriate to note that climates of constraint and/or restraint appear to be cyclical if not seasonal as well as multifaceted, nested, and fluid. A climate of constraint and/or restraint, like the weather, is neither generic nor fixed.

By meaningful learning, I refer to going beyond memorization at least as far as comprehension and to coherence, both connecting information internally (imagine a diagram rather than a list) and with what one already knows (i.e., elaborating or extending mental schema). Critical thinking refers to raising and pursuing questions about the ideas one encounters (Cornbleth, 1990b). Diverse perspectives refers to different or changing interpretations as well as the voices of various participants in events, movements, and everyday life. So, for example, the kind of teaching and learning I favor might involve students in coming to understand how and why male and female (and/or older and younger) workers tend to have different views of equal employment and advancement opportunities or of a "hostile work environment" and "sexual harassment."

RESEARCH REVIEW METHODOLOGY

After deciding that censorship was too narrow a focus for this project, and that the politics of social studies education was too broad, I settled on constraint/restraint as both manageable and directly relevant to my interest in obstacles to progressive changes in curriculum and teaching. No doubt influenced by my graduate students, many of whom are prospective or new teachers, I have been pursuing their sense of numerous obstacles to the kinds of meaningful learning that "we" favor and consider in class. For the most part, these obstacles are not single factors such as large class size or an ornery principal. Rather, they are broader or larger sets of conditions or something seemingly embedded in the culture of their schools—beyond the typical role demands and material conditions of teaching in U.S. classrooms.

Given my own prior work and conceptual bent, I looked broadly across several fields of education and social science for research about constraints or restraints on curriculum and teaching in elementary and secondary schools both within and beyond social studies. I searched ERIC (RIE and CIJE) and Expanded Academic ASAP databases back to 1980 for relevant research, and I combed my own bookshelves and files. Then, of course, I networked from the reference lists of recent articles and book chapters to previous ones. The resulting stack of research materials to read, analyze, and interpret was not large. The phenomena of interest to me here seem much more often talked about, and perhaps taken-for-granted, than studied systematically.

As I read and thought about the research in relation to my own studies and to my teaching experience in secondary schools and universities, I began to distinguish what I've come to call climates of constraint and/or restraint—the former being external and empirical while the latter include individual and collective perceptions as well as constraints that have been internalized. Of course the two are not always neatly separable, and what is a constraint in one setting may be a restraint in another (or what was a constraint may have become a restraint as when prior parental complaints lead teachers to modify their teaching in future years in the absence of any immediate external challenge). As I continued reading, I modified and refined the apparent climates, noting the research that supported and illustrated each.

So, what are these overlapping climates of constraint and/or restraint, and how do they operate to discourage meaningful teaching and learning? My reading, analysis, and interpretation of the relevant research yielded five climates that I've characterized as:

1. a bureaucratic climate with an administrative emphasis on law and order;
2. a conservative climate intent on maintaining the status quo;
3. a threatening climate of external curriculum challenges and self-censorship;
4. a climate of perceived pupil pathologies and pedagogical pessimism;
5. a competitive climate dominated by student testing and public school ranking.

In each of the following sections, I describe the climate, the research on which it is based, and how it discourages teaching for meaningful learning and critical thinking that incorporates diverse perspectives and students.

CONSTRAINING/RESTRAINING CLIMATES

A Law and Order Climate

A bureaucratic school climate with an administrative emphasis on law and order is primarily an external constraint on meaningful teaching and learning. By "law and order" I mean following the school wide rules (e.g., attendance, dress, homework, grading) and keeping classrooms, bathrooms, and hallways neat, clean, and quiet (i.e., orderly). There is little or no flexibility in application of the rules or tolerance for either questioning or innovation. The underlying assumption seems to be that centralized order is prerequisite to teaching and learning, that learning will occur if teachers and students are orderly, or that learning to be orderly is sufficient. Such an organizational climate can become internalized by teachers and other school personnel as "the way we do things here," which then serves as a climate of restraint in the absence of overt administrative enforcement. The research evidence regarding this climate comes primarily from two sources, sociology of organizations and workplace controls (e.g., Bidwell, Frank, & Quiroz, 1997) and critical studies of social control, classroom curriculum practice, and school knowledge (e.g., McNeil, 1986).

Bidwell et al. (1997) offer a theory of workplace control in U.S. high schools with reference to interview, observation, and questionnaire data from 13 public and private schools in the Chicago area. They posit that workplace controls embedded in the schools' social organization affect teachers' conceptions of teaching purposes and methods and teachers' classroom practice. The nature of these controls differ, according to Bidwell et al., with the size of the faculty and the "power of a school's clientele" (p. 285), that is, the influence of parents and students. In smaller schools, Bidwell et al. expected to find "interpersonal controls, such as collegial consultation or direct supervision by a principal, department chair, or oligarchy of senior teachers" (pp. 286–287) more often than the impersonal controls characteristic of larger schools such as policies and procedures or "the aggregated preferences of parents or students" (p. 287). Client power can work against teacher autonomy, for example when influential parents press their demands directly on teachers. Alternatively, teacher-parent alliances can mitigate administrative or oligarchic controls.

Differences in school size and client power (as measured by students' SES) were hypothesized to yield four types of workplace controls: autocracy-domination (small size, low client power), bureaucracy-rules (large size, low client power), collegium-consultation (small size, high client power), and market-competition (large size, high client power). It is the bureaucracy-rules type of control that is of particular interest here as a form of law and order climate that fosters structured classrooms characterized by teacher lecturing and teacher-dominated recitation. Bidwell et al found that all three of the large schools with low client power in their sample "ranked high on bureaucratic control" (p. 295). However, while the teachers in these schools tended toward the expected teacher-dominated classroom practice, the results were not significant statistically. The authors suggest that the bureaucratic controls in these schools were weak because they were not enforced, thus allowing more teacher variation than was expected. They also noted subject area differences in teaching practices and the possibility of departmental structures as intermediary influences on teacher beliefs and practices. Law and order climates that stifle meaningful teaching and learning may be school-wide or exist as pockets within large schools.

Because bureaucratic controls are not self-enforcing, and direct personal oversight tends to be relatively weak in large schools, it may be that administratively sanctioned technical forms of control play a substantial role in creating and maintaining a law and order climate. Borrowing from Edwards' (1979) analysis of workplace controls, Zeichner, Tabachnick, and Densmore (1987) have shown how technical controls such as scheduling, team-teaching, structured instructional materials, and external exams can shape teachers' beliefs and practice in ways that inhibit teaching for meaningful learning and critical thinking that incorporates diverse perspectives and students. It seems likely that law and order climates are the product of a mix of personal, bureaucratic, and technical controls.

When bureaucratic controls supporting law and order are enforced, with or without personal and technical reinforcement, they can substantially constrain meaningful teaching and learning as vividly portrayed in Linda McNeil's (1986) ethnographic study of social studies classrooms in four Midwest high schools. These seemingly typical schools, all in the same state, were selected for study to represent a range of relations between administration and "curriculum, classrooms, and teacher oversight" (p. 19), including the extent of teacher control over course content. Although McNeil's data are two decades old now, predating the recent and continuing orgy of statewide and other standardized testing and comparison, they are not out-of-date. In what follows, simply substitute "test scores" for "course credits earned," and her account will seem remarkably current.

At all four schools McNeil studied, the social studies teachers saw themselves as professionals and subject matter experts. While required courses (e.g., U.S. history) were specified by the state, their content was not. Only one school had "a curriculum" document to guide classroom practice, and it was developed by the teachers as a starting point, not a mandate. The schools also had similar student populations, resources, and an absence of "new" projects or initiatives. Yet they differed considerably in administrative priorities and the support given teachers (actual and teacher perceived) for meaningful teaching and learning. Only one of the four schools, Nelson, was characterized by an academic reputation and a collegial relationship among teachers and between faculty and administration. A second featured strong department chairs who could moderate administrative controls and a social studies chair who played a key role in shaping his department's positive reputation. The other two schools were marked by distance if not estrangement between controlling administrators and faculty who felt good teaching was neither supported nor rewarded.

While what McNeil dubbed "defensive teaching" was observed at all four schools, it was more common at the latter two schools where administrators distanced themselves from curricular concerns and gave priority to controls on students and, less overtly, on teachers as well. Defensive teaching "cut across differences in teachers' individual political and pedagogical philosophies and across formal definitions of variations in student abilities" (p. 178), suggesting that its occurrence was more a function of the school climate than teacher "style." According to McNeil, when administrators emphasize law and order, teachers choose to simplify content and reduce demands on students in return for classroom order and minimal student compliance on assignments ... they teach 'defensively,' choosing methods of presentation and evaluation that they hope will make their workload more efficient and create as little student resistance as possible (p. 174).

Defensive teaching controls students by controlling classroom knowledge. It is characterized by (a) fragmentation or reducing information, such as New Deal programs, to lists, (b) mystification or presenting a complex or controversial topic, such as the Federal Reserve System or racism, as important but unknowable, (c) omission, for example, of contemporary events in U.S. history, and (d) defensive simplification or seeking "students' compliance on a lesson by promising that it will not be difficult and will not go into any depth" (p. 174), that is, "the ritual of seeming to deal with the topic" (p. 175). Analyzing relationships between an administration-enforced law and order school climate and the occurrence of defensive teaching, McNeil found a parallel between administrators' attempts to gain minimal compliance from teachers and teachers' settling for minimal compliance from students. In those schools where administrators devoted most of the schools' staff time and resources to maintaining order and to attending to such details as course credits, the administrators paid less attention to the academic quality of teaching. The content of the curriculum was clearly secondary to the maintenance of order. Teachers in these schools tended to expend minimal effort in the classroom; frequently this was deliberate and was explained by the teacher as retaliation for or reluctant accommodation to administrative pressure for precision in paperwork, extra hall monitoring, or extended meetings related to such matters as graduation requirements. (p. 177).

In contrast, at Nelson where administrators most supported teaching and provided incentives for quality instruction, teachers responded by demanding more of themselves in the presentation and preparation of lessons. They felt, and demonstrated, less of a wall between their personal knowledge and the 'official' knowledge of the classroom. They developed entire courses, used original handouts and continually collected and redesigned materials. They used fewer lists and provided more extended descriptions, more opportunities for student discussion, more varieties of learning experiences… (p. 177).

The contradiction that McNeil's study and analysis highlight is that efforts to improve schooling (or teaching and learning) by means of regulations, accountability measures, or other controls—what I'm calling a "law and order" climate—have the opposite effect of encouraging defensive teaching and undermining meaningful learning and critical thinking that incorporates diverse perspectives and students. In sum,

> *When the school's organization becomes centered on managing and controlling, teachers and students take school less seriously.* They fall into a ritual of teaching and learning that tends toward minimal standards and minimum effort [or teaching to the test?]. This sets off a vicious cycle. As students disengage from enthusiastic involvement in the learning process, administrators often see the disengagement as a control problem. They then increase their attention to managing students and teachers rather than supporting their instructional purpose. (p. xviii)

And the climate of control continues to constrain/restrain meaningful teaching and learning.

A Conservative Climate

With a conservative climate, the emphasis is less on rules, policies, and procedures and more on community, school, and/or teacher cultures intent on maintaining the status quo by transmitting the prevailing culture to newcomers. New teachers, for example, are initiated into "the way we do things here" and are offered acceptance and support in exchange for not "rocking the boat" (e.g., Lacey, 1977, 1985). The promise of tenure (or the threat of its denial) serves as an implicit or explicit carrot-stick to encourage new teachers to go along. While it is possible that the norms being conserved are supportive of teaching for meaningful learning and critical thinking that incorporates diverse perspectives and students, it is more likely, as Jules Henry reminds us, that the dominant community-school-teacher culture is traditional, oriented toward the acquisition of predetermined information and presumably discrete skills in structured settings that minimize controversy and reward "right answers."

The research evidence regarding this climate comes primarily from studies of new teacher socialization (see Zeichner & Gore, 1990 for a review; and Schempp, Sparkes, & Templin, 1993 as an example of more recent work). Teachers new to teaching or to a particular school do not always go along with socialization pressures. Nor are the pressures always consistent. The existence of more than one teacher culture in a school, or more than one parent culture in a community, can be seen as providing options as well as conflicts to be negotiated. I endorse Zeichner and Gore's (1990, p. 343) "critical view of socialization that depicts the socialization process as contradictory and dialectical, as collective as well as individual, and as situated within the broader context of institutions, society, culture, and history." Influences from this broader context appear to be filtered or mediated by the local school culture and personnel (e.g., Schempp et al., 1993).

Despite long-standing assumptions of teacher individualism and isolation associated with "closing the classroom door" (e.g., Lortie, 1975), Zeichner and Gore (1990, p. 339) find "little question that the influence of colleagues needs to be taken into account in attempts to understand teacher socialization." Further, parental pressures also serve to socialize teachers "into the traditions of a school community" (p. 340; also see Metz, 1990), either directly or indirectly via the school or district administration or through the children (cf. Bidwell et al., 1997). Individual administrators appear to be less influential than colleagues or parents-students.

Unfortunately, most of the research in this area has provided "individual stories of socialization" (Zeichner & Gore, 1990, p. 341) with less attention to the institutional and cultural contexts of that socialization. I concur with Zeichner and Gore on the desirability of more research attention to collective aspects of teacher socialization and to structural issues. The personal accounts of my new teacher-graduate students and my own observations suggest that there is much to be found.

An example of research that does attend to shared teacher socialization experience and the influence of school culture is Schempp et al.'s (1993) study of teacher induction from the perspective of three physical education teachers in three different districts in the same state. It also illustrates the impact of broader societal conditions, specifically how the tight U.S. teacher job market in the early 1990s and the threat of contract nonrenewal served as an incentive to "play it safe" and "fit in."

The three teachers, all white and from the same university, two male and one female, taught in urban, suburban, and rural schools, respectively. All had less than five years of teaching experience and had begun as part-timers. Data came from open-ended interviews and was analyzed to identify common themes and perspectives regarding their induction experience. Schempp et al. identified three "streams of consciousness" shaping the teachers' thought and actions: biography, role demands at the classroom and school levels, and school culture. Here, I focus on school culture.

According to Schempp et al., while "biography served as a starting point in defining our teachers' practices and perspectives, school culture took on an increasingly important role as the inductees attempted to gain veteran status. Cultural codes became particularly pronounced in situations where job security was an important consideration" (1993, p. 462). What the authors call cultural codes or Foucault's (1970) regimes of truth, usually were transmitted informally by insiders (e.g., students, colleagues, administrators), for example, during casual meetings. Similarly, Zeichner et al.

(1987) observed that other teachers were their new teachers' major source of information about the informal school culture and how to interpret "formal school pronouncements" (p. 55). These "*culture lessons*" (Schempp et al., 1993, p. 462) about accepted ways of seeing things, thinking about, and acting on them, informed newcomers about "how things really worked in the school" (p. 462). They often, according to one of the new teachers, took the form of stories.

> I hear stories from students and teachers about teachers who were released the year before. The art teacher, last year, shaved his head and let the kids paint on it. It was something a little too radical for a small town like this, and so he was out the next year. (p. 463)

Such stories clearly if informally communicate expectations for appearance, behavior, and attitude. Yet, neither administrators nor teachers at the three schools paid much attention to the new teachers' pedagogy or classroom practices.

> In the face of apathy, our teachers simply went their own way with little fear of reprisal…. Although our teachers found it important to appease their peers and demonstrate a willingness to conform to institutional norms and standards, colleagues did not seem a particularly powerful socializing agent in terms of pedagogical practice or beliefs. (p. 464).

Teacher acceptance and status in these schools depended on "student control and matters removed from classroom instruction" (p. 469). Other schools may well evidence different cultural codes.

Learning how to present oneself as a newcomer to a school, understanding and accommodating the school culture, does not necessarily encompass learning how to teach. It does mean fitting in, or appearing to fit in, and avoiding violation of major cultural norms or codes, sometimes simply by remaining silent. Imagine, for example, how social studies teachers in these schools or in the schools with law and order climates described by Linda McNeil might respond to a new social studies teacher who talked about his efforts to introduce primary sources and authentic voices into his global history classes and urged colleagues to follow suit. Both law and order and conservative climates discourage widespread or rapid change. A progressive teacher can survive in such climates, however, if s/he is a strong, committed individual and politically savvy. As noted in the Schempp et al. study (1993), a traditional or conservative climate might not extend to classroom practice. Moreover, since the school socialization of new teachers entails adaptation of individuals and the school culture, both to each other and to external conditions, some change is possible over time. Alternatively, newcomers might be intimidated by a conservative climate and wrongly assume that it necessarily encompasses curriculum and classroom practice as well as school corridors and other common areas.

A Climate of Censorship

The indirect or implied influences of law and order and of conservative climates on curriculum and classroom practice are made explicit and direct in a climate of censorship. This is a threatening climate of external curriculum challenges to subject matter, materials, or teaching-learning activities. Over time it can lead to internalization of constraint, that is, self-censorship, in the absence of actual challenge (e.g., Nelson, 1983). Censorship climates wax and wane over time in cycles, waves, or movements, not unlike seasons or cold fronts.

Curriculum generally, and perhaps social studies more than other school subjects, is continually contested as various groups attempt to promote their interests and preferred values, norms, and beliefs. Inclusion in (or exclusion from) school curriculum gives official sanction and legitimacy to one's views and position (see, e.g., Cornbleth & Waugh, 1995, 1999). For example, including women's experience and perspectives in the main story conveyed by history textbooks rather than in special features or not at all communicates that women matter, that women are an integral part of "our" history. Excluding or marginalizing women's experience and perspectives communicates the opposite message. In contrast to mandates that impose the teaching of certain topics and views (e.g., Americanism, national loyalty, the evils of communism, the free enterprise system), censorship efforts aim to limit or prohibit the expression of certain ideas or to control their treatment in schools, often by banning the offensive topic, materials, and activities altogether.[2]

The available evidence indicates that the controversy generated by a censorship attempt, and even the threat of a censorship challenge or the anticipation of such a threat, can have chilling effects on meaningful teaching and learning (see Nelson, 1991 for a review). Administrators, teachers, and other school personnel tend to withdraw to presumably safer, traditional subject matter, materials, and activities in order to avoid controversy.[3] Consequently, it is not necessary that censorship efforts be officially successful in order to be "effective."

Typically, a local censorship challenge begins with an individual or group representative raising a question or voicing objection to a topic, materials, or activity with the teacher or librarian or with a school or district administrator. What happens next depends in large part upon whether the school district has a policy for dealing fairly with such complaints (i.e., providing procedural due process) and, if so, whether the policy is followed by school personnel.[4] Actual or potential censorship challenges provide alluring grist for local rumor mills, and soon "everybody knows" about the incident. What everybody knows usually has become embellished in the retelling, which may make resolving the matter calmly, fairly, and constructively much more difficult. Just about everyone in and around schools has heard such a story. Most recently in western New

York, the stories have concerned use of the Harry Potter books in suburban elementary and middle schools.

I describe this rumor mill phenomenon because it exacerbates the effects of censorship challenges and encourages self-censorship on the part of teachers and other school personnel, both within the district and in neighboring ones. Based on a 1993 survey of California school districts, Adler (1993) reports that 93 percent of the responding administrators indicated that they had read or heard about curriculum challenges in other districts (down slightly from 95 percent two years earlier), and only 12 percent recalled that the incidents "were handled routinely with little controversy" (p. 20). About half of the respondents recalled the incidents as being "somewhat contentious and disruptive" while about a third characterized them as "very disruptive" and/or causing the community "wide controversy" (p. 20).

Asked how they were influenced by what they heard about experiences in other districts, only 13 percent of respondents "said they were not influenced at all" (p. 20). While most said that they plan curriculum and materials adoption processes carefully so as to avoid controversies and then make independent judgments, 9 percent reported that "(a) they would be less likely to adopt material challenged elsewhere, (b) might not consider items known to have caused contentious challenges, or (c) would not consider such materials" (p. 20). Adler (1993, p. 20) provides clear evidence for what she terms an "echo effect" of curriculum challenges.

Most educators, particularly administrators, abhor controversy and avoid conflict, in part because of their political vulnerability "along with the paucity of incentives for risk-taking" (Boyd, 1979, p. 15). Consequently, censorship incidents threaten meaningful teaching and learning not only in the specific case of critical thinking or incorporation of diverse perspectives being challenged within a school or district, but also insofar as the targeted teachers are blamed by administrators (and sometimes their colleagues as well) for stirring things up or causing trouble. For example, "if you hadn't angered those parents by asking your students to analyze that far-out literature, we wouldn't have them looking over our shoulders now." Wanting the acceptance of one's colleagues, and tenure if one is a newcomer, few teachers totally eschew self-censorship. It is in this way that a censorship climate hinders teaching for meaningful learning which more than occasionally in social studies involves controversy of one sort or another (e.g., changing gender roles worldwide).

Nelson (1991, p. 337) observes that teacher self-censorship "results from the teacher's acceptance of community norms, the conformist traditions of schooling, and the chilling effects that notoriety for dealing with controversy can bring to a teacher and faculty." Here, the blurring of boundaries between conservative and censorship climates and their effects is evident. Miller and Trzyna (2000) provide vivid examples of teachers trying to use multicultural literature "safely," in order to avoid racial issues and racism close to home. Students in these classes who raised questions or voiced dissenting views were silenced by their teachers (and sometimes their classmates as well) and considered troublemakers. The books that sparked the "uncomfortable" student comments, such as Claude Brown's *Manchild in the Promised Land,* might not be used again.

Finally, observable trends in censorship challenges merit attention. They can be seen as a censorship version of global warming including its unanticipated side-effects. Throughout the 1980s and into the 1990s, school (curriculum and library) censorship efforts or incidents nationwide were on the rise (Adler, 1992–93; People for the American Way, 1988), and the success rate of censorship challenges was growing (McCarthy, 1989). More recently, the number of reported incidents appears to be stable or declining slightly.[5] It may be, however, that curriculum challenges are merely receiving less notice as attention has turned to standards and assessment and to school alternatives such as magnets, charters, and vouchers. Another possibility is that censorship is being masked in some cases as "parental rights."

During the mid 1980s an estimated 2000 groups—national, state, and local—were "involved in efforts to restrict the public school curriculum" (Jenkinson, 1986 cited in McCarthy, 1989, p. 28). While the would-be censors and targets of censorship span the political spectrum, religious fundamentalists and conservative parent-family groups have held center stage in recent years, displacing the ultra-nationalists and traditional Americanizers of previous eras (Adler, 1992–93; McCarthy, 1989; Provenzo, 1990; also, see People for the American Way's "Attacks on the Freedom to Learn Online," at www.pfaw.org/issues/education/aflo).

Significant recent shifts in censorship challenges serve to more directly discourage teaching for meaningful learning and critical thinking that incorporates diverse perspectives and students. These include the moves (a) from requests/demands that *library* books be banned to requests/demands to remove *classroom* curriculum materials, and (b) from requests/demands that individual students be accommodated (e.g., exempted from activities seen to interfere with religious beliefs) to requests/demands that classroom practice be changed for all students. These are moves from claiming your own rights to demanding that others live according to your beliefs—as well as toward direct intrusion into classroom practice.

From a position endorsing critical literacy—social and scientific as well as reading, writing, and thinking—Tony Whitson cautions against tacit acceptance of censors' conceptions of education, learning, and knowledge. He points out that teaching as selective information transmission and learning as the acquisition of "authoritative bits of factual and procedural knowledge" (1994, p. 22) are sought by religious and right-wing censors such as the Eagle Forum who do not want children thinking critically or questioning what the censors take to be absolute truth. Also suspect is the notion of "balance," which appears to resonate with democratic notions of equity and fairness but can have anti-intellectual and undemocratic effects. Should equal school time be given to all sides regardless of their warrant? to creationism and evolutionary theory? to pro- and anti-slavery arguments? to Holocaust deniers? If not, on what basis are decisions to be made? Not, I hope, by the squeakiest wheel.

A broader understanding of censorship is necessary, Whitson (1994) concludes, to avoid limited conceptions of literacy and education where curriculum becomes trivialized. The broader understanding that Whitson advocates avoids the pitfalls of "balance" and "bits of knowledge" as well as efforts to ban specific information and activities altogether. He understands censorship as any effort to limit literacy by pre- or proscribing what is to be learned and how it is to be learned in ways that minimize critical thinking and questioning, and/or contradict democratic values and processes. This is a high standard that I strongly endorse.

The challenge to social education was well put by Jack Nelson and Anna Ochoa more than a decade ago in their introduction to a special issue of *Social Education* entitled "Freedom to Teach, Freedom to Learn:" "The challenge that censorship poses is how to assure that education in a democracy will be open to conflicting ideas and controversial topics, while assuring that individual rights of parents, teachers, and students to their own beliefs and practices are not abrogated" (1987, p. 426).

A Climate of Pathology and Pessimism

Pathology and pessimism refers to a teacher or school wide climate where students are perceived to have numerous problems along with limited abilities, motivation, and/or future prospects. The students so pathologized are more often poor, limited-English proficient, and/or of color than middle class, native speakers of English, and white. Because of the "problems" that these students bring with them to the school, teachers and other school personnel do not expect much of them and do not try to teach them much. Pedagogical pessimism tends to be self-fulling. Students are offered "basics" and drill, but they are not considered "ready" for more meaningful learning or critical thinking. Ironically, a more inclusive, challenging curriculum might well be more engaging and effective (e.g., Stevenson 1990). Instead, students' lack of involvement in and "progress" through dreary, routine activities is taken as evidence of their pathology and grounds for continued pessimism. This climate thus sustains itself.[6]

Most studies of teachers' thinking and classroom practice that have involved asking teachers why they teach specific topics or use particular approaches have found that teachers rank their students high on the list of influences or reasons for what they do (e.g., Cornbleth, 1991a; Sparapani, 1998). In their review of research on teacher socialization, Zeichner and Gore (1990, p. 339) conclude that "teachers' perceptions of pupils' characteristics, expectations, and behaviors" shape their practice. Important here is the emphasis on teacher *perceptions*. Different teachers might perceive the same student behavior differently—or perceive the same behavior differently depending on the student who exhibits it. For example, a student pause in responding to a teacher question might be interpreted as "taking time to think it through" if the student is considered bright or as "she probably doesn't know the answer" if the student is considered slow. The teacher might wait longer for a response or offer encouragement in the first case and move on in the second. While it is a truism in education that taking one's students into account is a good thing, it is not at all good to deny students opportunities for meaningful academic learning, perhaps especially those students who have fewer such opportunities outside of school.

In a study of curriculum knowledge-in-use with 22 elementary and secondary, urban and suburban teachers working with a university teacher education program (Cornbleth, 1991a), we asked teachers about specific classroom segments that we had observed. We asked (a) why they taught what they did the way they did it, and (b) what influenced them to do it that way. Inductive analysis of interview transcripts and field notes was the major means of data analysis. Overall, teachers emphasized that their perceptions shaped their practice, particularly perceptions of their students, but also their past experience. Other frequently cited categories of influence were physical conditions and syllabi and exams, especially state syllabi and exams. Asked what was most influential or important, teachers most often mentioned their past experience and the nature of their students. But they interpreted and responded differently to their students' perceived "nature." Some teachers who saw their students as lacking prerequisite knowledge, skill, or motivation tried to encourage and support these students and bring them "up to speed" while others simplified things so students could handle them without major difficulty.

Among secondary teachers, homework provides a clear-cut example of teacher differences. Neither the urban nor the suburban students, it appeared to their teachers, were particularly fond of doing homework. Urban secondary teachers tended not to assign homework because many or most students, even higher track students, were unwilling to do it. One teacher had assigned more homework in the past and spent considerable time hassling students who didn't turn it in and calling their parents. Now, she said, her time and energy are better used in the classroom, doing "as much as you can while they're there" (Cornbleth, 1991a, pp. 15–16). In contrast, suburban teachers were more likely to insist on homework. "I do not leave it to their willingness," (p. 16) one teacher told us, and went on to describe a stringent homework routine that she establishes early in the year.

Overall, urban and secondary teachers talked more about the nature of their students influencing their classroom practice than did other teachers. They talked about how their students have changed over time, describing current students as less motivated and capable than they used to be.

While none of these teachers spoke in more extreme terms of pathology and pessimism, the influence of their perceptions of students is clear: some teachers simplified, taught less, and expected less of their students. When several teachers in a school or department share such perceptions and practices, a climate is created that discourages teaching for meaningful learning and critical thinking for most if not all students.

Again, the phenomenon here is not merely an individual one where a teacher or a few teachers hold and act on low expectations for individual students. It is a pervasive climate of opinion and practice. As in the case of teacher socialization into particular school settings, it is collective as well as individual, shaped by beliefs and practices in the larger community and culture.

The more extreme case is illustrated, for example, by Ryan in *Blaming the Victim* (1976) and in what Popkewitz, Tabachnick, and Wehlage (1982) dubbed "illusory schooling" in their field study of six elementary schools identified as model implementors of the IGE (Individually Guided Education) curriculum management reform.[7] All six schools adapted IGE in ways that maintained existing conditions including prevailing beliefs about students and perceptions of parents/community lifestyles, occupations, and values. In the two illusory schools, there was little evidence of teaching and learning academic or subject matter knowledge. Instead,

> children and teachers engage in the rituals and ceremonies of reading, writing, and arithmetic, but in practice the lessons contain many instances in which the substance of teaching is not carried through. What occurs is an emphasis on form *as* substance.... the discourse of schooling emphasizes co-operation, hard work, respect for property, and delay of gratification—qualities that teachers in illusory schools believe are not taught at home and have to be built into the school before any 'real academic' learning can take place. (Popkewitz, 1981, p. 194)

For example, students might recite the Pledge of Allegiance daily without ever being asked to examine the concepts of republic, liberty, or justice. Or, students might read aloud from their textbooks, corrected by the teacher but not asked to talk or write about what they have just read.

Located in poor communities, one mainly white and one mainly black, the illusory schools reflected school personnel's belief in "community pathology, pedagogy as therapy, and ritual" (Popkewitz et al., 1982, p. 122), that is, a belief that the problems that students brought to school made substantive teaching and learning impossible. Instead or first, students needed to learn appropriate behavior, attitudes, and morality such as self-control and obedience to school authority. According to Popkewitz et al. (1982), illusory school personnel "made frequent references to the unstable and unsupportive home lives of their pupils," and teachers were doubtful that students could overcome their perceived "learning deficiencies" and "social deficits" (p. 127).

While "pathology" may sound strong, it is consistent with seeing student "problems" such as poverty, uncooperativeness, or communication difficulties as individual or in the person, not in the situation or structurally conditioned. The individual student is pathologized insofar as s/he is viewed as responsible for the apparent problem(s). Pessimism about students' capabilities, in contrast, sounds much more benign.

A Competitive Climate

This school climate is dominated by student testing and public school ranking based on standardized, usually statewide, test results. Test scores are given priority, and other goals are secondary at best. Such a competitive climate can be seen as parallel to a law and order climate insofar as a single goal predominates and is imposed by administrators on teachers who, in turn, focus their efforts on gaining students' acquiescence (in this case, higher test scores). Students, teachers, administrators, schools, and districts may come to be judged as more or less meritorious or desirable depending on their ranking in local, state, or national comparisons. New York, for example, is among the states making such school and district data available (e.g., at www.nysed.gov/). In western New York, a business newspaper publishes its own annual rankings of school districts based in large part on test scores, which are reputed to affect real estate values in the suburbs. The stakes become economic as well as status and bragging rights. The pressure on teachers to raise students' scores has become intense in some schools and districts as evidenced by newspaper reports including instances of various forms of teacher cheating (e.g., Campagna & Vogel, 1999).

If these state-mandated, standardized tests assessed meaningful learning and critical thinking that incorporates diverse perspectives, teaching to them might be worthwhile. But that is not the case. Even New York State's highly touted DBQs (document-based questions) on new Regents exams in secondary social studies, which supposedly encourage and tap different viewpoints and higher order thinking, are disappointing. According to an analysis of the scoring "rubric" by one of my experienced teacher-graduate students earlier this year, only one-quarter of the allocated points on the global history DBQs required more than description or literal interpretation of individual documents. The incentives for teaching for synthesis, evaluation, or taking and supporting a position in a well-organized essay are meager.

While published research regarding separate effects of the public accountability or competitive pressures associated with the current testing movement is scarce, testing effects on curriculum and teaching have received research attention. The claims that testing shapes curriculum and teaching receives empirical support, but the evidence is not unequivocal. For a sound review of earlier work still relevant today, see Madaus (1988, 1999).

Madaus (1988, 1999, pp. 78–88) summarizes the literature through the mid-1980s, very little of which was data-based, on the impact of testing on curriculum, teaching, and learning in the form of seven principles, modestly paraphrased as follows.

1. The power of tests to affect individuals, institutions, curriculum, or teaching is a perceptual phenomenon, that is, if students, teachers, administrators, or others believe that exam results are important, whether this is true or false matters very little inasmuch as the effect is a consequence of what people perceive to be the case.

2. The more a quantitative indicator is used for social decision making, the more apt it is to distort and corrupt the social processes it is intended to monitor.

3. If important decisions are thought to be linked to test results, then teachers will teach to the test.

4. Wherever a high-stakes test is used, a tradition of past exams emerges and eventually comes to define the curriculum.

5. Teachers pay particular attention to the form of questions on high-stakes tests (e.g., short answer, multiple-choice, essay), and adjust their teaching accordingly.

6. When test results are a partial or the sole arbiter of future education or life options, they tend to be treated as the major goal of schooling instead of as a useful but fallible indicator of student achievement.

7. High-stakes tests transfer control over curriculum to the agency which sets or controls the exam.

Using testing to shape classroom instruction has a not insignificant history, dating at least to the 1960s (to the late nineteenth century in New York State) when state boards and legislatures began to mandate exams and link students' scores to rewards and/or sanctions. For example, about two decades ago, in Pittsburgh, the highly regarded superintendent and a university faculty member well known in measurement circles worked together toward what they called "assessment-driven instructional improvement." A "critical thinking" project was launched in social studies with a focus on essay-writing to explicit criteria or standards that were taken as evidence of critical thought. Not surprisingly, classroom observation revealed little discussion or critical thinking in teacher-student interaction. Rather, there was an emphasis on writing "critical thinking essays" similar to those that constituted the tests (see, e.g., Cornbleth, 1990b).

In terms of climates of con/restraint, my concern is that, in the current testing milieu, teaching for meaningful learning not be held hostage to the technology of testing or to education politics. To date, the measurement experts have not constructed reliable and valid means of assessing meaningful learning and critical thinking that incorporates diverse perspectives which education policymakers find cost-effective and otherwise politically palatable. And the misuses to which class, teacher, school, and district tests scores are being put in the name of accountability and competitive rating or ranking (market-driven reform?) only exacerbate the situation.

In a review of more recent research on the effects of state-mandated testing on teacher practice, Cimbricz (2000) found only a handful of relevant studies, all of which "consistently confirmed" the existence of "a relationship between state testing and teachers' thinking and practice" (p. 5). However, the nature and extent of the relationship is less clear and apparently context-dependent. Influences of state-mandated testing germane to a climate of constraint include the focusing or narrowing of curriculum and teaching to what is tested and the loss of instructional time to test preparation and testing (an estimated 100 hours per year in one elementary school study). For example, Brown (1992) conducted open-ended interviews with 30 fifth and sixth-grade teachers and twelve principals from three states with high stakes testing and found that "teachers reported altering the scope and sequence of the curriculum and eliminating concepts that were not covered on the state tests" (p. 13, cited in Cimbricz, 2000, p. 6). Moreover, these teachers and principals

> reported a reluctance to use innovative instructional strategies (e.g., whole language approach, cooperative learning, high order thinking activities) and mentioned the use of more traditional instructional methods (e.g., lecture, recitation) due to the belief that these strategies would better prepare students for state tests. (p. 14, cited in Cimbricz, 2000, p. 6).

Devoting more time to "basic skills" or information acquisition leaves less time for other learning. Brown's teachers also expressed concern that too much emphasis was being given to test scores by parents, the media, and others outside the schools. Elementary teachers in another study "reported pressure stemming from the publishing of test results in newspapers and on television and the subsequent comparison of scores among schools and school districts" (Cimbricz, 2000, p. 7).

Overall, this competitive climate of student testing and public school ranking appears to influence what is taught more than how it is taught (although the distinction is not always clear) and to be stronger (a) in secondary than elementary schools, (b) in high than low stakes arenas, (c) in subject areas and grades directly tested, (d) in higher status or reputation schools and districts (because of the press to maintain or increase one's rank), and (e) among teachers with less established positions in a school. Encompassing individual (teacher, administrator, school, district, state) variations, this too is a collective climate and one that appears nationwide at the present time.

CONCLUDING COMMENT

Con/restraints on teachers and teaching are not merely singular or individual as in a single factor affecting an individual teacher. Rather, to understand obstacles to meaningful teaching and learning, attention is directed to recurring patterns of contextual con/restraints that I call climates and to how these climates are collectively and interactively created and maintained. Based on the analysis of research presented above, contextual climates have had, by and large, a negative impact on social studies curriculum and instruction.

The existence of an unfavorable climate need not doom teaching social studies for meaningful learning and critical thinking that incorporates diverse perspectives and students. These are socially constructed climates that can be modified if not deconstructed and reconstituted, albeit not without sustained, collective effort. Alternatively, pragmatic accommodations can be made, and committed teachers can always don the pedagogical equivalent of sunglasses or a warm sweater.

NOTES

1.   I am less interested here in teachers' coping or survival strategies, critically important as these are, than in the circumstances they must deal with, purposefully (and preferably reflectively) or by default. On such strategies see Lacey (1985) with secondary teachers and Zeichner et al. (1987) with elementary teachers. Also instructive are accounts of overcoming constraints to teaching science well in elementary schools (e.g., Abell & Roth, 1994; Eiriksson, 1997; Tobin, Briscoe, & Holman, 1990).

2.   Parents or groups of parents requesting that their children not read a book or participate in a specific activity is much different than requesting/demanding that no students be allowed to read a book in question under the school's auspices. The latter is my concern here.

3.   Textbook publishers also appear to engage in pre-emptive or self-censorship in order to sell more books, especially in conservative adoption-states such as Texas (see, e.g., Beall, 1987; Loewen, 1995).

4.   I continue to be dismayed that more districts do not have and use written policies for dealing with curriculum challenges. See, for example, Adler (1992–93) and Jamieson (1987).

5.   This inference is drawn from the paucity of 1990s journal articles on the subject and People For the American Way's decision to suspend publication of its annual report on censorship incidents and provide a website featuring selected incidents (which had not been updated for several months as of this writing).

6.   I use quotation marks to set off "problems," "ready," and "progress" to encourage questioning of their conventional meanings and usage.

7.   Jonathan Kozol's popular books also illustrate this phenomenon (e.g., his *Death at an Early Age*).

REFERENCES

Abell, S.K., & Roth, M. (1994). Constructing science teaching in the elementary school: The socialization of a science enthusiast student teacher. *Journal of Research in Science Teaching, 31*(1), 77–90.

Adler, L. (1992–3). School board policy as a control mechanism in curriculum challenges. *Journal of Research for School Executives, 2*, 101–110. (ED375500)

Adler, L. (1993). *Curriculum challenges in California: Third statewide survey of challenges to curriculum materials and services.* Fullerton: California State University (for The Educational Congress of California). (ED375475)

Beall, M.L. (1987). Censorship and self-censorship: A problem in the schools. *Communication Education, 36*(4), 313–316.

Bidwell, C.E., Frank, K.A., and Quiroz, P.A. (1997). Teacher types, workplace controls, and the organization of schools. *Sociology of Education, 70*(4), 285–308.

Boyd, W.L. (1979). The politics of curriculum change and stability. *Educational Researcher, 8*(2), 12–18.

Brown, D.F. (1992, April). *Altering curricula through state testing: Perceptions of teachers and principals.* Paper presented at the annual meeting of the American Educational Research Association, San Francisco (cited in Cimbricz, 2000).

Campagna, D., & Vogel, C. (1999, August 29). Teachers under pressure. *The Buffalo News,* A1, 10.

Cimbricz, S. (2000). *State-mandated testing and teachers' thinking and practice.* Unpublished manuscript, University at Buffalo Graduate School of Education.

Cornbleth, C. (1984). Beyond hidden curriculum? *Journal of Curriculum Studies, 16*(1), 29–36.

Cornbleth, C. (1990a). *Curriculum in context.* London: Falmer Press.

Cornbleth, C. (1990b). Reforming curriculum reform. In L. Weis, C. Cornbleth, K.M. Zeichner, & M.W. Apple (Eds.), *Curriculum for tomorrow's schools* (pp. 1–31). Buffalo, NY: University at Buffalo Graduate School of Education Publications, Special Studies in Teaching and Teacher Education, No. 3.

Cornbleth, C. (1991a). Capturing contexts of curriculum knowledge-in-use. In C. Cornbleth, J. Ellsworth, R. Forni, S.E. Noffke, & L. Pfalzer (Eds.), *Understanding teacher knowledge-in-use* (pp. 1–23). Buffalo, NY: University at Buffalo Graduate School of Education Publications, Special Studies in Teaching and Teacher Education, No. 6.

Cornbleth, C. (1991b). Research on context, research in context. In J.P. Shaver (Ed.), *Handbook of research on social studies teaching and learning* (pp. 265–275). New York: Macmillan.

Cornbleth, C. (1998). An America curriculum? *Teachers College Record, 99*(4), 622–646.

Cornbleth, C. (Ed.) (2000). *Curriculum politics, policy, practice: Cases in comparative context.* Albany: State University of New York Press.

Cornbleth, C., & Waugh, D. (1995, 1999). *The great speckled bird: Multicultural politics and education policymaking.* Mahwah, NJ: Erlbaum (originally published by St. Martin's).

Edwards, R. (1979). *Contested terrain: The transformation of the American workplace in the 20th century.* New York: Basic Books.

Eriksson, S. (1997). Preservice teachers' perceived constraints of teaching science in the elementary classroom. *Journal of Elementary Science Education, 9*(2), 18–27.

Foucault, M. (1970). *The order of things: An archaeology of the human sciences.* New York: Pantheon.

Goodlad, J.I. (1984). *A place called school.* New York: McGraw-Hill.

Grossman, P.L., & Stodolsky, S.S. (1995). Content as context: The role of school subjects in secondary school teaching. *Educational Researcher, 24*(8), 5–11.

Henry, J. (1963). *Culture against man.* New York: Random House.

Jamieson, K.H. (1987). Protection from censorship. *Communication Education, 36,* 402.

Jenkinson, E. (1986). *The schoolbook protest movement.* Bloomingtron, IN: Phi Delta Kappa.

Kozol, J. (1967). *Death at an early age.* Boston: Houghton Mifflin.

Lacey, C. (1977). *The socialization of teachers.* London: Methuen.

Lacey, C. (1985). Professional socialization of teachers. In T. Husen & T.N. Postleth-waite (Eds.), *The international encyclopedia of education* (pp. 4073–4084). Oxford: Pergamon.

Loewen, J.W. (1995). *Lies my teacher told me: Everything your American history textbook got wrong.* New York: New Press.

Lortie, D.C. (1975). *Schoolteacher.* Chicago: University of Chicago Press.

Madaus, G.F. (1988, 1999). The influence of testing on the curriculum. In M.J. Early & K.J. Rehage (Eds.), *Issues in curriculum: A selection of chapters from past NSSE yearbooks* (Part II, pp. 73–111). Chicago: University of Chicago Press.

McCarthy, M.M. (1989). Curriculum censorship: Values in conflict. *Educational Horizons, 67*(1–2), 26–34.

McLaughlin, M.W., Talbert, J.E., & Bascia, N. (Eds.) (1990). *The contexts of teaching in secondary schools: Teachers' realities.* New York: Teachers College Press.

McNeil, L.M. (1986). *Contradictions of control: School structure and school knowledge.* New York & London: Routledge & Kegan Paul.

Metz, M.H. (1990). How social class differences shape teachers' work. In M.W. McLaughlin, J.E. Talbert, & N. Bascia (Eds.), *The contexts of teaching in secondary schools: Teachers' realities* (pp. 40–107). New York: Teachers College Press.

Miller, S., & Trzyna, G.D. (2000). 'They don't want to hear it': Ways of talking and habits of the heart in multicultural literature classrooms. In C. Cornbleth (Ed.), *Curriculum politics, policy, practice: Cases in comparative context* (pp. 139–174). Albany: State University of New York Press.

Nelson, J.L. (1983, Sept.). Teacher self-censorship and academic freedom. *The Social Studies Professional,* pp. 1,2.

Nelson, J.L. (1991). Communities, local to national, as influences on social studies education. In J.P. Shaver (Ed.), *Handbook of research on social studies teaching and learning* (pp. 332–341). New York: Macmillan.

Nelson, J.L., & Ochoa, A. (1987). Academic freedom, censorship, and the social studies. *Social Education, 51,* 424–427.

Onosko, J., & Newmann, F. (1994). Creating more thoughtful learning environments. In J. Mangieri & C. Collins-Block (Eds.), *Creating powerful thinking in teachers and students: Diverse perspectives.* Fort Worth, TX: Harcourt Brace.

People for the American Way. (1988). *Attacks on the freedom to learn, 1987–88.* Washington, DC: Author.

Popkewitz, T.S. (1981). The social contexts of schooling, change, and educational research. *Journal of Curriuclum Studies, 13,* 189–206.

Popkewitz, T.S., Tabachnick, B.R., & Wehlage, G. (1982). *The myth of educational reform.* Madison: University of Wisconsin Press.

Provenzo, E.F., Jr. (1990). *Religious fundamentalism and American education.* Albany: State University of New York Press.

Ryan, W. (1976). *Blaming the victim.* New York: Vintage.

Schempp, P.G., Sparkes, A.C., & Templin, T.J. (1993). The micropolitics of teacher induction. *American Educational Research Journal, 30*(3), 447–472.

Shaver, J.P., Davis, O.L., Jr., & Helburn, S.W. (1979). The status of social studies education: Impressions from three NSF studies. *Social Education, 43*(2), 150–153.

Sparapani, E.F. (1998). Encouraging thinking in high school and middle school: Constraints and possibilities. *Clearing House, 71*(5), 274–276.

Stevenson, R.B. (1990). Engagement and cognitive challenge in thoughtful social studies classes: A study of student perspectives. *Journal of Curriculum Studies, 22*(4), 329–341.

Stodolsky, S.S., & Grossman, P.L. (1995). The impact of subject matter on curricular activity: An analysis of five academic subjects. *American Educational Research Journal, 32*(2), 227–251.

Talbert, J.W., McLaughlin, M.W., & Rowan, B. (1993). Understanding context effects on secondary school teaching. *Teachers College Record, 95*(1), 45–68.

Tobin, K., Briscoe, C., & Holman, J.R. (1990). Overcoming constraints to effective elementary science teaching. *Science Education, 74*(4), 409–420.

Whitson, J.A. (1994). Critical literacy versus censorship across the curriculum. In J.S. Simmons (Ed.), *Censorship: A threat to reading, learning, thinking* (pp. 13–28). Newark, DE: International Reading Association.

Zeichner, K.M., & Gore, J.M. (1990). Teacher socialization. In W.R. Houston (Ed.), *Handbook of research on teacher education* (pp. 329–348). New York: Macmillan.

Zeichner, K.M., Tabachnick, B.R., & Densmore, K. (1987). Individual, institutional, and cultural influences on the development of teachers' craft knowledge. In J. Calderhead (Ed.), *Exploring teachers' thinking* (pp. 21–59). London: Cassell.

CHAPTER 5

TOWARD ENLIGHTENED POLITICAL ENGAGEMENT

Walter C. Parker

INTRODUCTION

Current interest in the concept and activity of *citizenship* is strong. Events, and our inability to explain them, appear to have forced the issue. Each day more and more social theorists "are drawn to reflect on the many-layered crises that are rendering citizenship ever more problematical," writes Canadian political scientist Ronald Beiner (1995, p. 1). These "crises" center on the resurgence of nationalism and identity politics simultaneously with the creation of new political unities and coalitions. Examples of the former are the Quebec separatist movement, the Tibetan struggle for autonomy, the Serbian and Rwandan debacles, and the gay-lesbian and linguistic rights campaigns in the United States. Examples of the latter are the unification of Germany, the creation of the European Economic Union (EEU), and the attempt among disparate groups in South Africa to cooperate under a post apartheid political community. This sometimes contradictory activity—seeking recognition with separation (Quebec), seeking recognition with inclusion (gay-lesbian rights)—has brought the problem of citizenship once again to the forefront of social theory. The "problem of citizenship" is the problem of what causes otherwise diverse individuals and groups to draw together into an overarching political community, or what causes them to seek separation from one such community and to unite under another. At the heart of this activity are the enduring needs to reconcile liberty with belonging, recognition with equality.

The problem of citizenship raises, in turn, the problem of *citizenship education.* Here the problem is how to affirm liberty and diversity on the one hand, protecting both freedom and inclusion, while, on the other, shaping individuals into the particular kinds of citizen required by the norms and ideals of the overarching political community. Citizenship education is not a completely neutral project in any society, of course. Everywhere, it seeks to predispose citizens to particular ways of knowing, relating, and being that are deemed appropriate to the political culture at hand. If limited government is an ideal of the political community, as in most democracies, then citizens must understand separation of powers, the rule of law, the inalienable rights of people, and so forth. Particular forms of political involvement will be required as well, such as the ability to deliberate shared problems across cultural differences. If cultural differences are valued, then tolerance not only of political dissent but also of deeper ethnic and linguistic differences must be nurtured as an integral part of the citizen identity. Beyond tolerance, genuine appreciation of diversity as a cornerstone of democracy and of individual development must be had on a wide scale. In summary, the norms and ideals of a political community will require citizens suited to them, and the formation of these citizens is the goal of citizenship education.

I hope in this chapter to accomplish three things. First, I will specify and clarify the primary goal of citizenship education as *Enlightened Political Engagement.* Second, I will examine two means to this end—two realms of citizenship education, each of which to some extent predicts Enlightened Political Engagement. One is the impact of going to school, regardless of what goes on inside school, and the other is what goes on inside schools: curriculum, instruction, and school climate and governance. I will suggest that citizenship educators, who typically concern themselves with the latter realm only, and then only a small portion of it, might enlarge their focus to incorporate more of the territory of democratic citizenship education. Third, I will examine a gap that bears on education for Enlightened Political Engagement. It is the gap between multicultural education and citizenship education. Here, I will suggest that citizenship educators and multicultural educators have skirted one another's projects, and that this is miseducative. Citizenship educators generally have concentrated on the principles, institutions, and practices that constitute democratic political community while multicultural educators generally have concentrated on inclusion. Multicultural educators ask "Who is included?" while citizenship educators ask "Included in what?" Neither is remotely coherent without the other.

This is a lot of ground to cover in one chapter, but doing so has advantages. One is to achieve a broad understanding of the field of citizenship education rather than a partial view from the vantage point of one corner or camp. Another is to suggest an array of action arenas in which citizenship educators need to work, from increasing the school-retention rate to involving students in the governance of the school.

ENLIGHTENED POLITICAL ENGAGEMENT

Let me begin by specifying the desired outcome of education for democracy as Enlightened Political Engagement. This term names a concept that is well established in the literature on citizenship and citizenship education.[1] The concept has two dimensions—democratic enlightenment and political engagement—and together they suggest something like *wise participation* or *reflective involvement* in civic affairs. Political Engagement refers to the action or participatory domain of citizenship, from voting and contacting public officials to deliberating public problems, campaigning, and engaging in civil disobedience, boycotts, strikes, rebellions, and other forms of direct action. Democratic Enlightenment refers to the moral-cognitive knowledge, norms, and commitments that shape this engagement: knowledge of the ideals of democratic living, the commitment to freedom and justice, and so forth. Without Democratic Enlightenment, Political Engagement has nowhere to go in particular. The freedom marchers of the Civil Rights Movement "participated," but so did Hitler's thugs and so did (and does) the Klan. Put differently, knowledge, attitudes, and moral principles constitute the ballast that a liberally educated citizen brings to civic activities from elections and jury deliberations to discussions of public issues, protests, and community service.

I will elaborate the meaning of Enlightened Political Engagement in the following sections. With this rough definition in hand, however, we are ready to look at two realms of citizenship education: school attendance itself and, inside the school, curricular and extracurricular programs.

SCHOOLS AND ENLIGHTENED POLITICAL ENGAGEMENT

Schools are potentially rich sites for citizenship education. They present both the formal curriculum—a planned scope and sequence of teaching and learning that can be aimed directly at the development of Enlightened Political Engagement—along with daily situations of living together "in public" outside the family. Schools, then, are both curricular and civic spaces, and both can be marshaled toward the education of democrats. But before peering inside schools, let us look at something that educators interested in curriculum and school climate typically overlook: the effect of simple school attendance on the development of Enlightened Political Engagement.

School Attendance

By simple school attendance I mean nothing more than *years* of school attendance, ignoring what goes inside schools and all the attendant variability.[2] Political scientists who are interested in citizen development call this independent variable "educational attainment" or "level of schooling." Using mainly surveys, they find again and again that years of schooling is the chief predictive variable of citizenship knowledge, attitudes, and behavior—in other words, Enlightened Political Engagement. In fact, there is probably no single variable in the survey research literature that generates as substantial correlations in such a variety of directions in political understanding and behavior as years of schooling. It is *"everywhere the universal solvent,"* political scientist Philip Converse writes, *"and the relationship is always in the same direction"* (1972, p. 324, emphasis in original). As for the outcomes used in this body of research, there are five associated with Political Engagement and five associated with Democratic Enlightenment.

The first set of five outcomes enables citizens to participate in popular sovereignty—to engage in politics and influence public policy. These five are knowledge of current political leaders, knowledge of current political facts, political attentiveness, participation in difficult political activities, and frequency of voting. The citizen who pays attention to public issues and knows the names and addresses of her current elected and appointed officials and contacts them now and then is better positioned to influence public policy than the citizen whose engagement begins and ends with watching political spectacles on television and/or voting. The second set of outcomes (there is some overlap) helps citizens understand and support the norms and ideals of democratic political community. These five are knowledge of principles of democracy, knowledge of current political facts, political attentiveness, frequency of voting, and tolerance. The citizen who knows that tolerance of diversity is crucial to making a democracy work possesses knowledge that is directly consequential for living together cooperatively in a pluralist society. This knowledge should, for example, restrain her from advocating a state religion or the incarceration of dissidents. This knowledge should help her to argue not only for her own rights but for the rights of others, especially those with whom she disagrees or whose cultural life she finds repugnant. What could otherwise be a kind of political engagement dedicated to self-aggrandizement at the expense of the common good (what the ancient Greeks called "idiocy") is moderated by a grasp of democratic principles and one's obligations to the political community.[3]

Table 1 displays correlations between years of schooling and these two sets of citizenship outcomes based on data from the 1990 Citizen Participation Study (Nie et al., 1996). They reveal a positive and consistent relationship between school attendance and the seven citizen outcomes. This is survey research, recall, so let me give examples of the questions used. The first citizen characteristic, "knowledge of principles of democracy," was measured by three questions: One asked respondents to identify a constitutional guarantee dealing with the Fifth Amendment, another asked them to distinguish between democracy and dictatorship, and the third to give

Table 1.   Correlations between citizenship outcomes and years of formal education completed.

Citizenship Outcome	Correlation	Dimension
Knowledge of principles of democracy	.38	Democratic enlightenment
Knowledge of current political leaders	.29	Political engagement
Knowledge of other current political facts	.37	both
Political attentiveness	.39	both
Participation in difficult political activities	.29	Political engagement
Frequency of voting	.25	both
Tolerance	.35	Democratic enlightenment

Source: Nie, Junn and Stehlik-Barry, 1996

the meaning of "civil liberties." The seventh citizen characteristic, political tolerance, was defined as "a willingness to permit the expression of ideas or interests one opposes." There were four questions: Respondents were asked if they would allow someone to make a speech in their community who called for letting the military rule the country or who was against all churches and religions, and they were asked whether books should be removed from the library when they advocate homosexuality or argue that blacks are genetically inferior to whites.

To be sure, these seven characteristics of Enlightened Political Engagement do not capture the full range of desired citizenship outcomes. Deliberative competence, for example, is not addressed nor is the commitment beyond "tolerance" to fight for inclusion of groups historically marginalized. Still, they certainly are headed in the right direction, and I suspect that none would be excluded from a more complete list.

Why does school attendance predict Enlightened Political Engagement? Norman Nie and his colleagues (1996) conducted a path analysis to develop an explanatory model, and they reached the following conclusions: First, school attendance influences Political Engagement by allocating access to political resources. Citizens with more schooling get more access; citizens with less schooling get less. This is because schooling positions a citizen in the sociopolitical network. If we liken this network to a giant stadium with a stage at the front, those persons with more schooling generally are placed closer to the stage where it is easier to hear and be heard and to become a player oneself.

What about the Democratic Enlightenment a citizen will or won't bring to his or her place in the stadium? (Recall, participation alone is not necessarily pro-democratic.) A high-school or college graduate may have won a seat close to the civic stage but lacks the liberal understanding of democratic community needed to use that position for the common good rather than as a power base from which to launch his or her private agenda. As with the engagement dimension, enlightenment is also correlated positively with school attendance, but the path now, according to Nie and his colleagues, is cognitive rather than positional. Knowledge of principles of democracy and the disposition to tolerate dissent are explained by formal schooling's positive impact on political knowledge and attitude. (When kids are taught these things, they stand a better chance of learning them than when they're not.) There are two explanatory paths, then, in this attempt to reason why educational attainment has its well-established positive ties to citizenship outcomes: social network positionality and intellectual attainment. Schooling is important for democracy because it gives one relatively more power *and* gives one ideas about how to use it.

Educators who labor to shape school curricula and climate toward critical and democratic ends may find this school-attendance data annoying. Perhaps they *presume* school attendance, for that battle seems largely to have been won thanks to the long struggle to integrate public schools (see Franklin and McNeil, 1995). Accordingly, educators concentrate on practices internal to school buildings, on inequalities between affluent and impoverished schools (and between high and low tracks in the same school), on the effects of teaching quality, building leadership, materials availability, funding, the local policy context, and on the battle against racist and sexist practices embedded deeply within the school culture. Yet, were educators to take a broader view of democratic citizenship education, they would not dismiss the role of school attendance in positioning citizens to exercise power and to shape how that power is exercised, and they would take seriously two social reform movements that have been eclipsed in recent decades: increasing the school-retention (high-school graduation) rate and making higher education available to all, either free of charge or on a sliding scale.

Inside Schools

Asked why they ignore the phenomena to which teachers and students devote their days and educational researchers devote their careers—namely what goes on *inside* schools—political scientists could respond, "We don't need to look inside schools; attending them is what matters, and we have data that supports this claim." But there exists also a conceptual habit that might help to explain how they manage not to peer inside at curriculum, instruction, and the quality of school life. These political scientists operate within a discipline that subsumes education within the concept *political socialization,* and political socialization studies generally are concerned with *unconscious* social reproduction. They are grounded in a descriptive-explanatory aim, whereas the aim of educators is conscious social reproduction and transformation. The currency of educators' realm is not description so much as prescription: reform, renewal, amelioration. They (we) are concerned to intervene in history and intentionally shape society's future—increasing the literacy rate, strengthening citizens' ability to analyze social issues, deepening their grasp of constitutional principles, creating equal access where there has been only limited access, and so forth. When citizenship education is assimilated into political socialization, it is easy, as Amy Gutmann (1999) observes, "to lose sight of the distinctive virtue of a democratic society, that it authorizes citizens to influence *how* their society reproduces itself" (p. 15).

Democratic citizenship educators of all stripes act on this virtue and prescribe an array of interventions toward increasing some aspect or other of Enlightened Political Engagement. There are a good number of empirical studies among this work,[4] but probably the bulk of it is theoretical and philosophical. Underlying debates (e.g., Which should be emphasized: enlightenment or engagement?) fuel ever more literature on what *ought* to be done to educate democrats, and it is this amelioration-oriented literature that I want to explore in this section.

It is a sprawling literature, and I am certainly not the first to organize it. Two prominent reviews are by Barr, Barth, and Shermis (1977) and Cherryholmes (1980). Barr, Barth, and Shermis described three traditions of citizenship education inside schools: citizenship transmission, social science, and reflective inquiry. The first affirms existing political institutions and ideals (e.g., the rule of law, civil liberties, tolerance) and seeks to deploy education in their service, intentionally passing them to succeeding generations. The second and third are reform initiatives that endeavor to replace the transmission model. The social science tradition aims to help young people acquire the knowledge and methods of inquiry esteemed by the several social science disciplines. The desired citizen can form and test hypotheses about social and political life; she can evaluate data, reason historically, and she has appropriated some of the central concepts of each discipline. This model is exemplified by Edwin Fenton's (1967) work and others in the New Social Studies movement. The third tradition seeks to develop citizens capable of rational decision making in sociopolitical contexts. It is exemplified by Shirley Engle's (1960) famous article, "Decision making: The heart of social studies instruction," and Hunt and Metcalf's (1968) curriculum that focused on those social problems that have been closed off from open and critical discussion (society's "closed areas").

Cleo Cherryholmes (1980) reviewed largely the same literature but from a different epistemological standpoint. He argued that *each* tradition described by Barr et al. was epistemologically naïve—the third (reflective inquiry) as much as the first (citizenship transmission), and the second (social sciences) more so than the other two. All three assume positivism; they endorse the fact-value dichotomy without examination and ignore the relationship of knowledge to biography—to interests and ideology. Reflective inquiry gets the bulk of Cherryholmes' criticism, for while it admirably educates students to grapple with society's problems, it fails to work out a methodological stance that would allow citizens "to gain a critical perspective on solutions for which they and others strive" (p. 136). In other words, it engages students in social problem solving without enabling them to think about which problems are worth solving, according to whom, to what ends, and in whose favor. Cherryholmes thus delineates two basic approaches to citizenship education inside schools: critical and noncritical.

These two analyses of inside-school citizenship education are helpful as far as they go, but I want to supplement them by highlighting a set of tensions that speak more directly to the content of educators' current debates—feminist critiques of traditional citizenship education, for example, and the tension between teaching about democracy and teaching democratically. My organization of this literature can be summarized as follows: There are both curricular and extracurricular approaches, and within each is a central tension. This makes four basic clusters of approaches to democratic citizenship education within the schools (see Figure 1). Let us begin with the curricular approaches, looking at both their common characteristic and the central opposition that divides them, then move to the two extracurricular approaches, again looking at the common characteristic and the central opposition.[5]

Curricular Approaches

Curricular approaches to citizenship education focus on intentional (conscious) curriculum and instruction in schools—on what educators have planned for students to learn in school and how students are to be helped (instructed, coached) to achieve those objectives. These include the three traditions described by Barr et al. (1977) and they cut across the

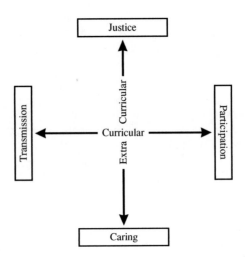

Figure 1.   Curricular and Extra-Curricular Approaches

critical/noncritical distinction described by Cherryholmes. There can be both critical and noncritical treatments of a reflective inquiry curriculum, for example. One need only compare Engle's (noncritical, 1960) to Apple's (critical, 1975) work.

The central opposition within the curricular cluster today is *participation* versus *transmission.* Participation approaches seek to engage students in the actual activity of democratic politics rather than, as is the case with transmission approaches, preparing them for it. Participation advocates ask incredulously: How can young people possibly learn to be democratic citizens in nondemocratic schools? On the participation end of the curricular dimension is involvement *in* democracy; on the transmission side is learning *about* democracy. The work of Shirley Engle (1960), Fred Newmann (1975), and Richard Pratte (1988), among others, suggest the participation approach; the work of Paul Gagnon (1996) and the committee that produced the *National Standards for Civics and Government* (Center for Civic Education, 1994), among others, suggest the latter.

Gagnon's main concern is that children should know the past because "historical knowledge is the precondition for political intelligence" (1996, p. 243). He urges teachers to "leap at (Thomas) Jefferson's argument" that the general education of citizens should be chiefly historical. Quoting Jefferson,

> History, by apprising them (citizens) of the past, will enable them to judge of the future; it will avail them of the experience of other times and other nations; it will qualify them as judges ... and enable them to know ambition under every disguise it may assume; and knowing it, to defeat its views. (in Gagnon, 1996, p. 242)

Transmission advocates are not found only among conservative educators. Transmission is alive and well among critical educators who focus on multicultural and prolabor curricula. For example, the problem with an Anglocentric curriculum is that one perspective is uncritically transmitted rather than multiple perspectives being transmitted critically. The problem with a curriculum that celebrates generals and entrepreneurs but says nothing about the labor or civil rights struggles or economic democracy is not that a set of information is being transmitted but that it is the wrong set or that it privileges a single perspective (one that uncritically advantages the status quo) rather than multiple, competing perspectives that open up the inquiry to other possibilities (see Stanley, 1992). The popular Canadian socialist educator, Ken Osborne (1995), wrote a devastating review of a new book on democratic education. He observed that many authors in the collection held forth on "democracy" and "democratic education" without defining it substantively, instead viewing it as a procedure or set of activities. One contributor to the book wrote: "We believe democracy is best taught as a process and best learned through active participation in decision-making..." Osborne responds:

There is, of course, a certain truth to this notion of democracy as process, but it takes us only so far. It is obviously true that a richer and more powerful democratic life will depend on a higher level of civic engagement than now exists. However, it is equally true that democracy involves more than simply "empowerment" and "participation," for fascists, racists, and assorted other anti-democrats can, and often do, feel highly empowered and participative, and also feel highly committed to a certain sense of community. The fundamental question must be this: once students are empowered and are ready to participate, what will they use their skills and powers to do? What will ensure that they will use them in the interests of democracy? (1995, p. 122)

There is considerable overlap between the transmission and participation camps, it should be noted. Participation advocates typically want liberal values (e.g., liberty, tolerance, equality, justice) and institutions (e.g., rule of law, separation of church and state) transmitted somehow from one generation to the next. Yet, inside the school, they don't want this transmission to eat up so much instructional time that none is left for deliberation, service learning, and direct political action (three kinds of participation) on real social problems both inside and outside the schoolhouse. Conversely, transmission advocates typically want students to participate in political activity, but they worry that without reasoned understandings of democratic principles this activity will be impulsive and unwise. Using the terms established earlier, we could say that at one pole of this curricular tension is Political Engagement, and at the opposite pole is Democratic Enlightenment.

Extracurricular Approaches

Extracurricular approaches involve the implicit or informal curriculum of the school. They focus not on what students should be learning directly from classroom instruction but on what they should be learning indirectly from the governance and climate of the classroom and the school. The common characteristic of extracurricular approaches is a concentration on the norms by which adults and young people in the school relate to one another and by which decisions on school and classroom policies are made. Toward the goal of cultivating democratic citizens, egalitarian and caring relations are prescribed over authoritarian and formalistic relations; cultural pluralism over assimilation; classroom and school climates that are open to the free expression of opinions and controversy over climates that encourage conformity and agreement; and student engagement in school and classroom governance over exclusion from such decision making.[6] The rallying cry here, similar to the participation end of the curriculum dimension, is that it is absurd to teach about democracy without practicing it.

What would divide this apparently cozy group into opposing camps? Plenty. The central opposition among the extracurricular approaches today is between two social goods: caring and justice. The work of Nel Noddings (1992) and Donna Kerr (1997) suggests the former; the work of

Lawrence Kohlberg (Power, Higgins, and Kohlberg, 1989) and Myra and David Sadker (1994) suggests the latter. Kohlberg, recall, delineated a conception of morality as just (fair; principled) reasoning, which he specified as the ability to imagine oneself in another's shoes—to take the perspective of others with empathic understanding. Students can develop in their ability to reason justly, Kohlberg found, given the right kinds of classroom and school support which are exemplified in the pedagogic setting he created and studied in his later work, following his sociological turn, called the "just community."[7]

For Noddings and Kerr, a keen sense of fairness is not the central moral requirement of democratic citizens; there is more importantly a realm of care, which is relational, responsive, and concrete versus intellectual, imaginative, and abstract. Donna Kerr writes,

> (T)he democratic psyche, formed in human relationships, is both receptive of the other and self-expressive. Genuine hope for democracy is grounded in this circuit of recognition. To jump over this reality in favor of talk of civil society and the requirements of political life is to fail to acknowledge the psychic and social realities in which democratic relations take root, when they do.... If democracy is to have substance [rather than being superimposed upon human relationships], it can come only through the development of relations of mutual recognition and regard. (1997, pp. 81–82)

This opposition among the extracurricular approaches is not a simple feminist/non-feminist one. Feminists are found on both sides of the justice/caring debate. For example, the Noddings/Kerr strand of feminist analysis is "maternalist"—grounded in the virtues of mothering—according to feminist political theorists like Mary Dietz (1992), Nancy Fraser (1995), and Anne Phillips (1991). By contrast, the latter articulate a strand of feminism that does not shy from reason, argument, and politics. "There are crucial distinctions between being a citizen and being a nice caring person," Phillips writes (p.160). An ethic of care can lead (and historically *has* led) care givers to neglect their own welfare.

The main tension on the extracurricular dimension, then, is between a worry on the one hand that the moral and political struggle for social justice and inclusion has edged out an ethic of care, and, on the other, a worry that social justice will not be won, nor institutionalized repression dismantled, by caring people.[8]

To summarize, four sets of inside-school approaches are formed by intersecting two dimensions of inside-school democratic citizenship education: curricular and extracurricular activity. The resulting four quadrants should be helpful for making sense of several contemporary debates within the educator community about how best to nurture democrats. While I am aware that I have not exemplified the four quadrants fully nor reviewed the empirical work in each,[9] I want to stop here so that I can take up another related issue. If I may make just one more point first, however, about where this effort to conceptualize the inside-school approaches could go next it would be to add a *third* dimension to the matrix: the critical/non-critical dimension that was mentioned earlier (e.g., Cherryholmes, 1980). Imagine Figure 1 now becoming a three-dimensional representation of the four quadrants. Doing so would create a near and a far version of each of the four quadrants for a total of eight. We would have then a critical and a non-critical variation of each of the four quadrants. For example: In the non-critical variant of the upper right quadrant (see Figure 1), we might place Shirley Engle's (1960) seminal work on decision making; in the critical variant of the same quadrant, we could place Michael Apple's (1975) seminal work on conflict. In the noncritical variant of the lower-right quadrant, we might place community service programs that help children perform good deeds, such as canned food drives for the hungry; in the critical variant of the same quadrant we could place service programs with social justice goals (Wade, 2000). Related to this, on the critical side of the upper-left quadrant, we would hope to see serious study of the economic system that assures the need for food drives generation after generation.

When compared to the citizenship effects of simply attending school, we see in the inside-school quadrants a multifaceted array of *intentional* educational activity the combined effect of which ought to supplement school-attendance effects, maybe even overtake them. This is not only a conceptual but also an empirical matter, of course, and the necessary research question would go something like this: Can a multifaceted citizenship education program inside schools add something more to the development of Enlightened Political Engagement than what already is contributed by school attendance alone?

INTO THE BREACH

Let us turn our attention now to the chasm between democratic citizenship education and multicultural education. Not to include this gap in the present chapter would only perpetuate the blind spot that citizenship educators busy in one or more of the four corners represented in the preceding section have been perpetuating for decades. Indeed, citizenship education and multicultural education have become distinct literatures, professional organizations, and social movements. Education for and about racial and ethnic diversity has been relegated largely to the multicultural education field where little attention is paid to the construction of the overarching political community that is needed to secure and nurture this diversity. Meanwhile, the citizenship education field attends to the overarching political community but pays little attention to diversity and inequality. Sadly, both fields have assumed a defensive posture in relation to the other and continue to believe they have little in common.

The resulting gap between multicultural education and citizenship education is not only miseducative but incoherent. The *interdependence* of pluralism and democratic unity is one of the most important understandings that culturally diverse democratic citizens can construct. Enlightened Political Engagement in a diverse democracy is simply impossible without it. Clinging exclusively and defensively to the citizen identity while ignoring, denying, or trying to "melt" away (as in the "melting pot" metaphor) our other identities avoids one of the tensions on which democracies have been rising and falling for millennia. Doing the opposite has the same effect: By attending exclusively and defensively to our diverse cultural identities, we ignore the shared political framework upon which we rely, in diverse societies, to secure and nurture this diversity.

I hope in this third section to shed some light on this gap. Because space is limited, I will concentrate on just one aspect of it, which I believe is crucial for both citizenship and multicultural educators to consider: *Why, generally speaking, have democratic citizenship educators circumvented racial and ethnic (including religious) diversity?* My response falls into four parts: The first points to the misunderstanding of democracy as an accomplishment rather than an aspiration, the second to another misunderstanding—of democratic citizenship itself. The third points to ethnocentrism (particularly Eurocentrism) among democratic theorists and citizenship educators, and the fourth looks at the failure to grasp the interdependence of diversity and unity. Each of these is a failure on the enlightenment side of Enlightened Political Engagement and, therefore, each might respond to education.[10]

Aspiration or Accomplishment?

Reading the current landscape of democratic citizenship education in the United States (texts, policy, curriculum standards, classroom practice, research), I find that democracy is viewed and taught mainly as an accomplishment.[11] It was achieved with the ratification of the Constitution and Bill of Rights. Checks and balances, federalism, representation, civil rights, the amendment process—the formula has been struck and nothing more needs to be done about it. Like baked bread, there's really nothing left to do but eat it. In this way, an accomplishment is substituted for what actually is an aspiration: an ongoing, creative struggle to work out a way of living together fairly, freely, and equally; and to work out a relationship between culture and politics—between communities of heart, language, and memory, on the one hand, and, on the other, a larger civic realm (a polity or commonwealth) that binds these groups together in some sort of democratic political community.

Dewey (1916) called this *creative democracy,* by which he meant that democracy is a way of living with others, a way of being. It has no end other than the "way" itself. It follows that there is no period or place, either in the past or today, that can serve as a definitive model of democracy. Viewed as a creative, constructive process, democracy is not already achieved, needing only protection and maintenance, but a path that citizens in a pluralist society try to walk together. It is this trek—this commitment—that unites them, not ethnicity, language, race, or religion. The ratification of the Constitution and the several democratic struggles that followed it hardly closed the book on democracy in the United States. Democracy is not now "done" like so much baked bread. The "miracle of Philadelphia" was an important step on the path, the Emancipation Proclamation another, the widening of suffrage another, the Civil Rights Movement another, the homosexual rights campaign another, but the work continues.

Democratic Citizenship

A revolutionary moment in history came after centuries of religious wars in Europe. A peace was achieved thanks to a new *idea*: a social agreement to live with a deep difference, a diversity that goes all the way down: religious diversity. With the Treaty of Westphalia in 1648, ratified largely because no side could "win" the religious wars, it was agreed that religion would be treated as one's personal affair—private—rather than a public affair of the political community.[12] With this treaty an important precedent was set by which today we recognize that "democratic citizenship" by definition excludes the category of culture. To the contrary, it is, so to speak, culturally neutral.[13] As a citizen, one is an *it*, an abstraction with inalienable rights. This "it-ness," if awkward, is worth it, for it demands the protection of citizens from what had been the norm: unbridled tyranny by the power elite (monarchs, clerics, aristocrats, men, etc.). When residing in the citizen role, one is an abstraction or an idea; one is of indifferent religion, first language, national origin, gender, social class, race, ethnicity, and, in some political communities, sexual orientation. One is, in this identity, devoid of racial or ethnic identity, historical tradition, or geographic setting. One is, therefore, equal to all other citizens. When residing in our cultural identities, however, we are defined by our cultural memberships. These tend to be warmer (greater feelings of shared-ness, belonging-ness, we-ness) and thicker (these relationships "go way back"; "blood is thicker than water"). These are communities of the heart and blood, of faith and language and origin.

The institutional analog to the citizen identity is the democratic state or republic; just as the citizen is a zero, so too is the democratic state, ideally; it is color-blind, gender-blind, religion-blind and so on. In other words, it is neutral. At least, that's the metaphor that seems best to capture the aspiration of a state created in part to secure liberty, including cultural difference. Citizenship educators need to understand that the larger democratic civic framework is an overarching *political* association, not an ethnic or familial one. Indeed, an overarching ethnic or familial association is impossible in a diverse society without discrimination and repression. It is a democratic civic virtue, therefore, to keep oneself from seeking it—to give up that yearning for warmth and similarity *on a broad scale.* When individuals long for it, or when elites use their power to force it into existence, is to act on a fascistic impulse to make the nation into a tightly knit group—one big family; a "fatherland." It is to conflate culture and politics, ethnic identity and citizen identity. Being a modern democrat means being *politically* one (here is our citizenship identity) while *culturally* many (here are our other identifications). That political unity is the larger civic realm created to secure individual liberty and group difference while at the same time allowing citizens to conjoin to solve common, public problems. A democrat's sentiments, meanwhile, his or her feelings of cozy belonging and warm rushes of we-ness, will need to come from his or her cultural associations—families, friendships, churches, temples, ethnic communities, and other deep wells of intimacy.[14]

This is the aspiration, paradoxically, to which people *excluded* from the larger civic realm have again and again returned the attention of those who are comfortably included (so comfortably as to be taken for granted). The democratic struggle in this nation has relied fundamentally upon those barred from the unum to deepen and extend the democracy that the brethren founded. It was from the outskirts of the public square, from the "corners of American society," that Martin Luther King, Jr. came to Washington, DC in 1963 to say, "When the architects of our republic wrote the magnificent words of the Constitution and the Declaration of Independence, they were signing a promissory note to which every American was to fall heir ... We have come to cash this check..." (1963a, p. 1). And it was from the Birmingham city jail that he wrote "We know from painful experience that freedom is never voluntarily given by the oppressor; it must be demanded by the oppressed" (1963b, p. 80). Similarly, Gary Okihiro writes: "The core values and ideals of the nation emanate not from the mainstream but from the margins—from among Asian and African Americans, Latinos, and American Indians, women, and gays and lesbians. In their struggles for equality, these groups have helped preserve and advance the principles and ideals of democracy..." (1994, p. ix). The "founders" may have been the birth parents of democracy, American style, but those who were excluded (then and now) became the adoptive, nurturing parents.

Ethnocentrism

That "larger civic realm" (state; polity; commonwealth; overarching political community) referred to above is believed by many who should know better to be neutral *already.* This in turn reflects the aspiration/accomplishment misunderstanding. The "larger civic realm" in the United

States has not in fact been sufficiently neutral. Instead, it has been the province, more or less, of a particular ethnic group. To wit: John Jay wrote in *The Federalist No. 2* that "Providence" gave this land "to one united people—a people descended from the same ancestors, speaking the same language, professing the same religion..." They were indeed, he asserted, a "band of brethren." In order to assert this social cohesion, Jay had to ignore (and this was not unusual) native peoples, blacks, women, and others who were not figured into "we the people." Years later, performing the same feat, Arthur Schlesinger (1992) feared the "disuniting" of the brethren. He regarded *e pluribus unum* as a more-or-less established fact (from the many have come the one) which now will be undone if multiculturalism isn't constrained. Both men perceived a neutrality that wasn't, and both spoke from a tribal vantage point. These are related. The effect was to conceal existing power and status imbalances. Once concealed, they were more easily ignored while attention conveniently was diverted to the supposed deficits of those without power or status.[15]

There is another way of looking at this neutrality problem. The "neutrality" of the state, which I have been reading as a democratic aspiration, is not actually a culture-free, neutral zone but another culture—a democratic political culture. I use the term *neutrality*, then, as a metaphor for a particular political culture (Dewey's "way of living") that values diversity under the terms "rights," "tolerance," "equality," "pluralism," "justice," "separation of church and state," "live and let live," "tapestry," and "humanity." Who practices this way of life? Any of us do when occupying the role of democratic citizen. The citizens who practice this way of life belong to various other cultures, of course, referring now to religion, ethnicity, first language, sexual orientation, and so forth. But it is the democratic political culture that is responsible for safeguarding and nurturing these other cultures. It is a unique culture then, one I have thus far been calling an overarching political community, and it is not to be confused with ethnicity, religion, kinship, fatherland, and the like. It is a "cooler" kind of culture, to use Michael Walzer's metaphor (1992), because it asks one temporarily to set aside, in principle if not in fact, one's "warmer" cultural-ethnic identities of home and kinship. In the citizen role, then, one is not actually an "abstraction with inalienable rights," a "zero," as I said above, but this does suggest the proper connotation. Similarly, the term "neutrality," just like the term "blind justice," connotes a political community capable of protecting, even nurturing, diversity. Its consequences are democratic progress and democratic hope—progress toward and, in the absence of progress, hope for such democratic aspirations as the nondiscriminatory "neutral" state (e.g., separation of church and state) and "blind" justice (e.g., equality before the law).

Diversity and Liberty

Only when differences (diversity) are taken seriously does there arise in the larger political community the desire to either repress or protect them. Why have modern liberal democrats generally (with notable exceptions) sought to protect them? There are several reasons, but I'll offer just three. The most basic and far reaching is that diversity protects liberty and, thereby, is causal in reproducing it. This was Machiavelli's insight[16] and it is in James Madison's arguments in favor of the U.S. Constitution. In *The Federalist No. 10,* Madison wrote of diversity using the term "factions," by which he means groups of citizens "united and actuated by some common impulse of passion or of interest" that is adverse to the rights of other citizens or to the "aggregate interests of the community"—the common good (1937, p. 17). Factions are, in at least this way, a threat to liberty. Simultaneously, however, factions help prevent the tyranny of the majority or of the government. The advantage of a large nation like the United States, as far as liberty is concerned, is that because it includes more people it includes more factions, more diversity. In this way, wrote Madison, "you make it less probable that a majority of the whole will have a common motive to invade the rights of other citizens; or if such a common motive exists, it will be more difficult for all who feel it to discover their own strength and to act in union with each other" (p. 22). Were it not for diversity, today's Christian Right, could not exist. Yet, it is the same diversity that prevents this faction from implementing its anti-democratic, anti-pluralist, theocratic platform. Where pluralism is actual and vigorous and protected by law, the danger posed against democracy by a majority or minority faction—the very danger that has doomed most democracies from ancient Athens to the Weimar republic in prewar Germany—is mitigated. Differences are mediated politically through "neutral" public institutions and shared citizenship, and in this way all manner of differences—liberty—are assured. Liberty and diversity are in this way interdependent.

There is another way in which diversity "causes" liberty: It assures critique of dominant norms and practices. Thanks to the multiplicity of Madison's "factions" or what today more broadly and inclusively is called "cultural diversity," not only is the majority kept relatively small (smaller than it otherwise might be) and relatively ineffectual (less effective than if there were no factional contestation), but the primary sources of criticism of established conventions of thought and action are kept alive. On this view, to reduce diversity is dangerously anti-democratic because doing so removes from public spaces much of the lively debate, boycotts, protests and so forth that contest an entrenched status quo. As Carole Gould (1996) puts it, to reduce diversity is to undercut "the creativity that issues forth in imaginative critique and rejection of existing agreement and in the generation of new and unexpected frameworks for agreement" (p. 173). This is known especially well, again, by peoples who are excluded from the mainstream culture where many of the norms of social life are made. These subordinated groups often create rebellious underground factions. These have been called "free spaces" (Evans & Boyte, 1992) because of their potential for unrepressed, creative discourse. Historically, writes David Trend, they have been "key staging grounds for interventionist politics—from the small group meetings of the early women's movement, to the 'free pulpits' of black churches in the Deep South during the civil rights era, to the 'liberated zones' of independence movements in the third world" (1995, p. 10). The point here is that without diverse viewpoints there can hardly be constructive or deconstructive criticism of the dominant viewpoint, and without this there can be nothing of the creative problem-solving needed to deal with the actual problems and always-changing circumstances of life.

A third way that diversity supports liberty, and another reason why diversity itself must be nurtured, is that it brings to individual life a sense of the possible. We can benefit from the full range of human flowering and capacity only if we are fortunate enough to live in close association with others who are different, who embody that range. As Charles Taylor writes, "To attempt to impose uniformity is to condemn ourselves to a narrower and poorer life" (Taylor, 1998, p. 153).

CONCLUSION

History gives democracy no advantages. All democracies are weak and their incumbencies brief. And, no actually-existing democracy is an ideal democracy. Most are minimalist democracies: most adults are allowed to vote in elections that are more-or-less fair, by which representatives, most of them rich, win their seats in media performances. Attempting in the face of this to educate for principled democratic involvement—for Enlightened Political Engagement—is ambitious (to say the least), yet a moral necessity.

How to do it? That was the subject of this chapter. School attendance itself goes a long way by positioning citizens closer to the political stage and helping them to behave in principled ways whenever and however they climb on. What might be done *inside* schools to contribute to the school-attendance effect? Four kinds of inside-school initiatives were drawn by intersecting two dimensions of school life: curricular and extracurricular activity. But what about discrimination, repression, and the persistence of racism? How can *differential* access to the political stage and to curriculum and climate within schools be squared with the goals of citizenship education? That was the subject of the final section, where I considered the gap between multicultural education and citizenship education. I suggested four reasons why citizenship educators traditionally have circumvented both cultural diversity and the problem of exclusion. First, citizenship educators generally have reflected the broader social tendency to treat democracy as an accomplishment rather than an aspiration, as a fact rather than an ideal. Second, we have tended to conflate the cultural with the political rather than accepting parallel identities: the political (citizen) alongside the cultural (e.g., white, female, Southerner, Baptist). Third, we have been ethnocentric, claiming that the overarching political community is already neutral—color blind and culture blind—when it is not, when actually it expresses a tribal vantage point, that of the male WASP. Fourth, just as we have been unclear about the proper relationship of the citizen identity to the ethnic-cultural identity, confusing the two, so have we been unclear about the relationship of diversity to liberty. Fearing diversity as a threat to liberty, many citizenship educators have taken up the assimilationist cause and overlooked a curious thing: diversity "causes" liberty. Liberty cannot be protected without diversity.

Across the array of efforts to cultivate Enlightened Political Engagement, where should educators focus their attention? "All of the above" seems to me the best course: Strive to keep students in school through high school and college, provide a multidimensional citizenship education inside schools, fight for equal access to education, and, rather than shying from diversity, support it vigorously as a democratic force and a necessary condition for freedom.

ACKNOWLEDGMENT

My thanks go to Patricia Avery, Gene Edgar, and William Stanley for helpful feedback on earlier drafts of this chapter.

NOTES

1. The term is from Nie et al. (1996).
2. I acknowledge that school attendance is no "simple" matter for students or their parents, particularly disabled or challenged students and students in poor city schools (see Anyon, 1997). I use the term "simple" to distinguish this variable from the more complex matters of what goes on *inside* schools and the variability *between* schools.
3. Toqueville saw that unenlightened citizens act too often in what they believe to be their own "self-interest" but that the idea of self-interest they entertain "is a very crude one; and the more they look after what they call their own business, they neglect their chief business, which is to remain their own masters" (1969, p. 540).
4. Among the best: Torney-Purta et al. (1999) gathered case studies of civic education in twenty-four nations; Niemi & Junn (1998) analyzed the effects of civics courses using data from the 1988 NAEP civics assessment; Hahn (1998) compared student political attitudes and school civics curriculum and instruction across five established democracies; Avery et al. (1992) explored adolescents' political tolerance; Kohlberg and his colleagues created and studied "just communities" in schools (Power, Higgins, & Kohlberg, 1989). Also, see the reviews by Patrick (1999), Patrick & Hoge (1991), Hahn (1996) and Youniss et al. (1997).
5. The following section builds on Parker (2001).

6.   See Hahn (1998).
7.   See Cogan and Derricott (1998) and Parker, Ninomiya, and Cogan (1999) for a multinational project aimed at achieving a global "just community."
8.   See the analyses of justice *and* caring in Katz, Noddings, and Strike (1999). This volume tries, in some chapters, to venture beyond the justice/caring dualism. See also the symposium on caring in *Hypatia*, 1990, vol. 5, pp. 101–126.
9.   See note 4.
10.   Portions of the following section draw on Parker (1996, 1997).
11.   Support for this claim is found in Hahn (1999).
12.   See Gellner (1994).
13.   In the next section I will deal with the myth of cultural neutrality. For now, the connotative meaning of "neutrality" is helpful.
14.   See Michael Walzer's (1992) treatment of this idea in *What it means to be an American.*
15.   I elaborate this misunderstanding in "'Advanced' Ideas about Democracy" (1996).
16.   See Isaiah Berlin (1998) on Machiavelli's original contribution to radical pluralism.

REFERENCES

Anyon, J. (1997). *Ghetto schooling: A political economy of urban educational reform.* New York: Teachers College Press.

Apple, M. W. (1975). The hidden curriculum and the nature of conflict. In W. Pinar (Ed.), *Curriculum theorizing: The reconceptualists* (pp. 95–119). Berkeley, CA: McCutchan.

Avery, P.G., Bird, K., Johnstone, S., Sullivan, J.L., & Thalhammer, K. (1992). Exploring political tolerance with adolescents. *Theory and Research in Social Education, 20,* 386–420.

Barr, R., Barth, J., & Shermis, S. (1977). *Defining the social studies.* Washington, DC: National Council for the Social Studies.

Beiner, R. (Ed.). (1995). *Theorizing citizenship.* Albany: State University of New York Press.

Berlin, I. (1998). *The proper study of mankind.* New York: Farrar, Straus and Giroux.

Center for Civic Education. (1994). *National Standards for Civics and Government.* Calabasas, CA: author.

Cherryholmes, C. H. (1980). Social knowledge and citizenship education: Two views of truth and criticism. *Curriculum Inquiry, 10,* 115–151.

Cogan, J., & Derricott, R. (Eds.). (1998). *Citizenship for the 21st century: An international perspective on education.* London: Kogan-Page.

Converse, P.E. (1972). Change in the American electorate. In A. Campbell & P.E. Converse (Eds.), *The human meaning of social change.* New York: Russell Sage Foundation.

Dewey, J. (1916). *Democracy and education.* New York: Macmillan.

Dietz, M.G. (1992). Feminism and theories of citizenship. In C. Mouffe (Ed.), *Dimensions of radical democracy: Pluralism, citizenship, community* (pp. 63–85). London: Verso.

Engle, S.H. (1960). Decision making: The heart of social studies instruction. *Social Education, 24,* 301–304, 306.

Evans, S.M., & Boyte, H.C. (1992). *Free spaces: the sources of democratic change in America.* Chicago: University of Chicago Press.

Fenton, E. (1967). *The new social studies.* New York: Holt, Rinehart and Winston.

Franklin, J.H., & McNeil, G.R. (Eds.). (1995). *African Americans and the living Constitution.* Washington DC: Smithsonian Institution Press.

Fraser, N. (1995). Politics, culture, and the public space: Toward a post-modern conception. In L. Nicholson & S. Seidman (Eds.), *Social postmodernism: Beyond identity politics* (pp. 287–312). Cambridge: Cambridge University Press.

Gagnon, P. (1996). History's role in civic education. In W.C. Parker (Ed.), *Educating the democratic mind* (pp. 241–62). Albany: State University of New York Press.

Gellner, E. (1994). *Conditions of liberty: Civil society and its rivals.* London: Hamish Hamilton.

Gould, C.C. (1996). Diversity and democracy: Representing differences. In S. Benhabib (Ed.), *Democracy and difference* (pp. 171–186). Princeton, NJ: Princeton University Press.

Gutmann, A. (1999). *Democratic education* (2nd ed.). Princeton, NJ: Princeton University Press.

Hahn, C.L. (1996). Research on issues-centered social studies. In R.W. Evans & D.W. Saxe (Eds.), *Handbook on teaching social issues* (pp. 25–41). Washington, DC: National Council for the Social Studies.

Hahn, C.L. (1998). *Becoming political.* Albany: State University of New York Press.

Hahn, C.L. (1999). Challenges to civic education in the United States. In J. Torney-Purta, J. Schwille, & J. Amadeo (Eds.), *Civic education across countries: Twenty-four national case studies from the IEA civic education project* (pp. 583–607). Amsterdam: International Association for the Evaluation of Educational Achievement.

Hunt, M.P., & Metcalf, L.E. (1968). *Teaching high school social studies: Problems in reflective thinking and social understanding.* New York: HarperCollins.

Katz, M.S., Noddings, N., & Strike, K.A. (Eds.). (1999). *Justice and caring: The search for common ground in education.* New York: Teachers College Press.

Kerr, D. (1997). Toward a democratic rhetoric of schooling. In J.I. Goodlad & T.J. McMannon (Eds.), *The public purpose of education and schooling* (pp. 73–83). San Francisco: Jossey-Bass.

King, M.L., Jr. (1963a, August). *I have a dream* (address). The Martin Luther King, Jr. Papers Project, Stanford University, http://www.stanford.edu/group/King/speeches/.

King, M.L. (1963b). Letter from Birmingham Jail. In *Why we can't wait* (pp. 76–95). New York: Mentor.

Madison, J. (1937). *The Federalist, No. 10.* New York: Modern Library. (Originally published in 1787.)

Newmann, F.M. (1975). *Education for citizen action: Challenge for the secondary curriculum.* Berkeley, CA: McCutchan.

Nie, N.H., Junn, J., & Stehlik-Barry, K. (1996). *Education and democratic citizenship in America.* Chicago: University of Chicago Press.

Niemi, R.G., & Junn, J. (1998). *Civic education: What makes students learn?* New Haven, CT: Yale University Press.

Noddings, N. (1992). *The challenge to care in schools.* New York: Teachers College Press.

Okihiro, G.Y. (1994). *Margins and mainstream: Asians in American history and culture.* Seattle: University of Washington Press.

Osborne, K. (1995). [Review of the book *Democratic teacher education: Programs, processes, problems, and prospects*]. *The Canadian Journal of Higher Education, 25,* 119–123.

Parker, W.C. (1996). "Advanced" ideas about democracy: Toward a pluralist conception of citizen education. *Teachers College Record, 98,* 104–125.

Parker, W.C. (1997). Democracy and difference. *Theory and Research in Social Education, 25,* 220–234.

Parker, W.C., Ninomiya, A., & Cogan, J. (1999). Educating "world citizens": Toward multinational curriculum development. *American Educational Research Journal, 36,* 117–145.

Parker, W.C. (2001). Educating democratic citizens: A broad view. *Theory Into Practice, 40,* 6–13.

Patrick, J. J. (1999). Education for constructive engagement of citizens in democratic civil society and government. In C.F. Bahmueller and J.J. Patrick (Eds.), *Principles and practices of education for democratic citizenship: International perspectives and projects* (pp. 41–60). Bloomington, IN: ERIC Clearinghouse for Social Studies/Social Science Education.

Patrick, J.J., & Hoge, J.D. (1991). Teaching government, civics, and law. In J.P. Shaver (Ed.), *Handbook of research on social studies teaching and learning* (pp. 427–8–436). New York: Macmillan.

Phillips, A. (1991). *Democracy and difference.* University Park: Pennsylvania State University Press.

Power, F.C., Higgins, A., & Kohlberg, L. (1989). *Lawrence Kohlberg's approach to moral education.* New York: Columbia University Press.

Pratte, R. (1988). *The civic imperative: Examining the need for civic education.* New York: Teachers College Press.

Sadker, M.P., & Sadker, D.M. (1994). *Failing at fairness: How America's schools cheat girls.* New York: Scribner.

Schlesinger, A.M., Jr. (1992). *The disuniting of America: Reflections on a multicultural society.* Yew York: Norton.

Stanley, W.B. (1992). *Curriculum for utopia.* Albany: State University of New York Press.

Taylor, C. (1998). The dynamics of democratic exclusion. *Journal of Democracy, 9,* 143–156.

de Tocqueville, A. (1969). *Democracy in America* (J.P. Mayer, Ed., G. Lawrence, Trans.). Garden City, NY: Doubleday.

Torney-Purta, J., Schwille, J., & Amadeo, J. (Eds.). (1999). *Civic education across countries: Twenty-four national case studies from the IEA civic education project.* Amsterdam: International Association for the Evaluation of Educational Achievement.

Trend, D. (1995). *The crisis of meaning: Contexts of meaning in culture and education.* Minneapolis: University of Minneapolis Press.

Wade, R.C. (2000). Beyond charity: Service learning for social justice. *Social Studies and the Young Learner, 12,* 6–9.

Walzer, M. (1992). *What it means to be an American.* New York: Marsilio.

Youniss, J. McLellan, J.A., & Yates, M. (1997). What we know about engendering civic identity. *American Behavioral Scientist, 40,* 620–631.

CHAPTER 6

COMMITTING ACTS OF HISTORY: MEDIATED ACTION, HUMANISTIC EDUCATION, AND PARTICIPATORY DEMOCRACY

Linda S. Levstik and Keith C. Barton

INTRODUCTION

Over the last quarter-century, research into the development of children's understanding of mathematics, literacy, and science has revolutionized ideas about the nature of teaching and learning in those subject areas; although much work remains to be done in translating that research into practice, most teachers—and practically all teacher-educators—have at least a basic familiarity with research-based ideas about emergent literacy, children's constructions of mathematical knowledge, and their experience-based conceptions in science. In history education, however, research into children's thinking has remained largely the preserve of a small body of scholars: Dissemination of the empirical research in the field over the last decade has not been widespread, and many teachers continue to ground curricular and instructional practices in outdated or anecdotal ideas about children's historical understanding. Traditionally, this has led to a doubly dysfunctional pattern: A near absence of history in the early elementary grades and a reliance on fact-based "coverage" in the upper elementary and middle school years.

Ironically, educators who try to break out of this pattern are hampered by a lack of agreement on what is meant by *history*. Too often discussions about teaching and learning proceed as if history were a single thing—a set of agreed-upon practices, employed for an agreed-upon purpose. Other perspectives on the past quickly become denigrated as "unhistoric" or non-disciplinary—merely popular uses of the past that have no place in the academy. In consequence, discussion bogs down in yet another foray into identifying which practices or which sets of facts count as "authentic" history and which do not. Not only do such dichotomies misrepresent the various ways in which history operates in schools and in the larger society, they tend to limit teachers' ability to make connections among the various histories to which they and their students have access (Barton, 1998).

Students' and teachers' ideas are shaped by a variety of public uses of the past—both "official" representations found in textbooks, curriculum guides, or standards documents and "vernacular" histories that provide alternative explanations of social realities (Barton & Levstik 1998; Bodnar, 1992; Holt, 1990; Levstik, in press; Levstik & Barton, 1996; VanSledright, 1997). We suggest in this chapter that these differing perspectives can most usefully be thought of as distinct *stances* toward history. Grounded in theories of mediated action, our description of historical stances centers on the specific acts in which students (and adults) engage when they "do" history. Although there may be any number of such stances, four exert a particularly strong influence on education in contemporary Western society: the rationalistic stance (analyzing relationships among historical events, patterns, or evidence), the identification stance (identifying with local or national communities), the moral response stance (judging the morality of historical actions), and the exhibition stance (displaying information about the past). Each of these is valued by adults in our society. Each can contribute to the education of students. And, realistically, each will continue to exert a powerful impact on the history curriculum. The difficulty occurs when the differences among them—and their sometimes conflicting demands—go unacknowledged and unanalyzed. Indeed, ignoring the differences between stances sometimes results in a disconnect between the official curriculum and the students who are expected to master it—a rupture that makes it less likely that students will either learn or care about history at school (Seixas, 1993; Epstein, 1997).

But although we recognize and accept the diversity of historical stances that characterize contemporary society—and although we refuse to sanction any set of practices or any body of knowledge as "authentic" history—we are unwilling to accept that one use of history is as good as another. Each of the four stances can be characterized by multiple purposes, and not all of these are equally appropriate for educational settings; decisions must be made about what history should, and should not, be taught. We suggest that the difference between appropriate and inappropriate history education lies not in the "disciplinary" status of a given topic, approach, or activity, but in the extent to which historical study contributes to education for democratic citizenship. In the United States, where precollegiate history education is a segment of the larger field of social studies—whose very reason for being is the development of citizenship (National Council for the Social Studies, 1994)—this may not seem like a very radical proposition. But we hope to move beyond dominant notions of citizenship education by grounding our ideas in a different vision, one derived from a concept of participatory and pluralist democracy such as that advanced by Parker (1996). In the following pages, we explain the theoretical underpinning of our attempt to distinguish among historical stances, we describe the role played by humanistic study in creating a pluralist, participatory democracy, and we detail how each of the four stances may contribute—or fail to contribute—to such study.

FOUNDATIONS OF HISTORICAL THINKING AND LEARNING

Mediated Action

Our analysis of children's historical thinking is grounded in theories of mediated action. This perspective is rooted in the work of Russian cultural-historical psychologists such as Vygotsky and his successors, and it has been articulated more recently by Wertsch (1985, 1991, 1998). This approach rejects both the assumption that cognitive processes exist solely within individuals—as though knowledge were a stable property of mind or the outcome of a course of neurological development—and the idea that knowledge resides in objects external to individuals. Rather, *knowing* is conceptualized as something one *does* while engaged in goal-directed activity. In the course of formal and informal activity and interaction in a variety of settings, "history" is enacted, transmitted, resisted, and transformed (Levstik & Barton, 1996; Rogoff, 1990; Wertsch, Del Rio, & Alvarez, 1995). Working within this framework, then, means identifying the specific acts people engage in when "thinking historically" or "doing history," as well as establishing the socially defined purposes that guide those acts.

This perspective has the potential to advance our understanding of historical understanding in a number of ways. First, it provides a direct link between individuals and their environment; although most approaches to human thought recognize the importance of both "inside the head" cognition and larger contexts, the theory of mediated action focuses attention specifically on instances in which those two constructs come into contact. Rather than analyzing one pole of the cognition-context continuum and simply making inferences about the other, it promises to shed light on the specific interactions that shape thought and behavior by examining how people go about acting on their world. Second, this perspective allows us to resist the temptation to define historical understanding in normative terms. Instead of establishing a priori definitions of what it means to "think historically" or "do history"—and then detailing the extent to which children or teachers conform to those definitions—a mediated action approach seeks to establish what people actually do with the past. It thus expands our ability to make sense of the kinds of historical thinking that go on among children and adults. And, in a related way, emphasizing mediated action allows us to consider the determinative role of human purposes—it acknowledges that people draw from a range of goals sanctioned by their culture, and that when they engage in any activity they do so with the intent of achieving one or more such goals. In essence, it treats them as agents, rather than as passive objects of instructional policies or as pawns of broad social forces. Historical thinking, then, becomes a matter of "committing acts of history."

Two other characteristics of mediated action should be kept in mind. First, the "mediational" component of such theories refers to the use of cultural tools or artifacts; people do not simply *act*—they *use tools to act*, and these tools have arisen in particular social contexts that shape their function as mediational means. A complete analysis of historical thinking, then, would involve a consideration of what tools are available to people as they engage in activities related to history, and that project is one of the most pressing needs in current theory and research in the field. In this chapter, however, we attempt no such "complete" analysis—we have chosen to focus only on acts of history, not on the tools used in those acts. That focus, however, should not obscure the fact that cultural tools are invariably involved in the process and exert an important influence on how historical acts take place.

A second point to keep in mind is that activities typically are not determined by single, clearly-defined goals. Indeed, any activity can be guided by multiple, overlapping, simultaneous, and even conflicting purposes. It is never enough simply to know what people are doing; analysis must also focus on the range of ends they may be attempting to accomplish. As a result, we have chosen to use the term "stance" to categorize the varieties of historical thinking. Although each stance focuses on a single activity—identification, analysis, exhibition, or moral response—a variety of goals may characterize any one of them. We believe that this kind of analysis is useful in helping educators think about the interdependence of children and their social partners in cultural contexts, including the classroom. Focusing on children as historical agents provides insights into the multiple and sometimes contradictory influences on their historical understanding. It can also help us recognize the roots of conflict in the different stances taken toward history and historical thinking. Short of this sort of attention, neither children's responses to history nor their teachers' difficulties in effecting change can be fully understood. But this kind of analysis cannot be the sole guide to classroom practice. It may describe the sociocultural settings within which the act of historical thinking develops, but it cannot suggest which of the multiple aims of history teaching and learning are most appropriate for schools. This requires attention to the purposes, not just of history, but of social education in schools.

Participatory Democracy

One problem with sociocultural perspectives on learning is that they may fail to discriminate between better and worse educational purposes. Recognizing the situated nature of all learning provides no direct guidance for educators: Children and adults may engage in a variety of contextually bound activities, in a variety of settings, but how should formal educational institutions—schools and museums, for example—*direct* children's learning? Surely not all educative activities are equally prized by society, and surely there are some that are more appropriate in formal settings than elsewhere. Otherwise, history education could be left in the care of those informal influences in which children are already immersed—families, communities, and the media. To justify its position as the object of formal study in schools or other institutions, history must have a clearly defined purpose; it must do something that history in these other settings does not do, or that it does only haphazardly or unsystematically. Following in a long tradition of social educators, we suggest that history's purpose lies in its ability to contribute to democratic citizenship. But the potential for such a statement to be misunderstood—or passed over as a glib generalization—requires a fuller explanation of our understanding of citizenship. In this, our ideas are close to those of Parker (1996) and other advocates of a more participatory, more pluralist democracy.

Parker (1996) argues for a reconceptualization of education for citizenship. The current model, he argues, derives from a "mainstream civics" orientation biased in favor of learning about the mechanisms of government. This orientation is consistent with the orthodox liberalism that underlies representative, republican forms of government, an orientation in which the citizen valued most is the one who participates least. Political action is seen as the responsibility of politicians and government officials, and the remainder of the population are turned into spectators, with little more to do than vote. Parker criticizes this conception of citizenship for its preoccupation with individual rights, its limited tolerance for direct political participation, and its devaluation of social, cultural, and political diversity. Drawing on a rich tradition of political philosophy—articulated most recently by theorists of "radical democracy" (e.g., Mouffe, 1992) "strong democracy" (e.g., Barber, 1984), and the "public sphere" (e.g., Arendt, 1958; Habermas, 1989, Calhoun, 1992)—as well as a long line of social educators, Parker calls for a more direct form of citizenship. This alternative does not reject the achievements of liberal democracy, but it recognizes the need to deepen and extend the quest to achieve democracy's foundational values of freedom and equality (cf. Mouffe, 1992).

Toward that end, Parker argues for a more pluralist and participatory form of citizenship, one that revolves around "public agency": the ability to engage in practical reasoning in pursuit of the common good (Boyte, 1992). Rather than remaining content with the promotion of individual interests and the protection of individual rights—the central concerns of liberal democracy—citizens in a more participatory framework would conceive of themselves as participants in a collective undertaking (Mouffe, 1992), one in which they must envision "a common world in which every member of the community can live" (Barber, 1984, p. 201). The term *participatory democracy* is a particularly apt characterization of this perspective, because it focuses especially on the need to establish active participation by the greatest number of citizens in determining the affairs of the community (Dietz, 1992; Benhabib, 1992).

Advocates of a more participatory form of democracy conceive of politics not in terms of a given endpoint of development, but as a path or journey—a way of living with others and engaging in public debate (Parker, 1996). Citizens come together to make decisions in the interest of the common good, but there is no single, pre-existing, determinative vision of what the common good might be; such a vision is forged, instead, through participation in the hard work of common discourse. Citizenship thus involves a never-ending process of deliberation, decision, and action (Barber, 1984). Habermas' theories of "communicative rationality" and the public sphere are particularly relevant to this conception of citizenship, for (along with his many interpreters and critics), he has sought to establish the conditions under which rational and critical discourse can be brought to bear on political matters, and the means by which reason can be advanced by public debate itself (Calhoun, 1992). Participation in the public sphere, on the other hand, is not an inherently equal undertaking: status differences among participants are unlikely simply to be set aside, and as Parker (1996) notes, those with more power can impose their own meanings on the less powerful without debate or negotiation. Moreover, within social systems riddled with inequalities based on ethnicity, gender, and class, the liberal ideal of neutral, rational debate—in which the identities and concerns of particular groups are considered "private" and thus irrelevant to the public sphere—usually works to the advantage of dominant groups and serves to silence the voices of women, minorities, and others less able to impose their will on public discourse (Fraser, 1992). Democratic politics that takes seriously the need for pluralistic debate, then, would respond to these inequities precisely by making them the object of common talk and action; the role of conflict, division, and antagonism would become an acknowledged part of advancing democratic aims (Mouffe, 1992). Far from being destructive of democratic politics, negotiation around individual and group differences would represent the cornerstone of an inclusive political community.

This is the form of democratic citizenship we have in mind—one characterized by an engaged and active citizenry, dense and diverse networks of associational life, public discourse and action centered on the common good, and a conscious, sustained effort to expand the range of voices that make up the debate. What contribution can the study of history make to this kind of citizenship? We do not believe that learning about the past will somehow magically bring about these lofty goals. Indeed, the entire field of social studies—or even schooling more generally—will not be sufficient to overcome the distorting effects of social systems that promote the individualistic pursuit of material self-interest and that rely for their maintenance on social and economic inequality. On the contrary, progress toward a more participatory, democratic society will require the concerted action of people in many realms of social life—in their homes, spiritual communities, neighborhoods, jobs, and so on. But we do believe that education has an important role to play in developing citizens who are committed to, and capable of taking part in, the kind of society we envision; moreover, we believe that history can justify its position in the curriculum *only* if it contributes to such citizenship.

The Humanistic Study of History

We suggest that in order for history education to contribute to participatory democracy, it must take on a very traditional focus—that of humanistic study. Words like *humanism, humanistic,* and *humanities* are likely to call forth a range of meanings, some of which may not be compatible either with each other or with the goals of participatory citizenship. John Dewey suggested that humanism is a "portmanteau word" (cited in Kliebard, 1984, p. 7), and Kliebard notes that by the end of the nineteenth century the concept of humanistic study had already developed two very different meanings. One perspective, long the dominant one, justified the study of certain school subjects (including history) by reference to their ability to develop innate human mental capacities—in essence, their ability to teach people to think. With the demise of the faculty psychology upon which such assumptions were based, educators had to turn to other reasons to justify the position afforded Latin, Greek, history, and other subjects whose study had no clear technical or vocational utility. This new perspective emphasized the role of the humanities in passing on the "vital core of the Western cultural heritage," and came to be associated with an elitist view that true education required familiarity with "the finest expressions of [Western] civilization" (Kliebard, 1984, pp. 24–25).

Kliebard argues that it is this second justification—the preservation of cultural heritage—that dominates the attenuated remains of humanistic study today, but we find that this conception exists alongside remnants of the belief that the humanities should accomplish something more meaningful. The idea that there exists a canon of artistic or literary works whose value can be objectively established and then passed on to each new generation has been so problematized that it can no longer be taken at face value, and such assertions have been at the center of numerous scholarly debates in recent years. We would side with those who maintain that in a world of multiple voices and perspectives, no single cultural tradition can be singled out to represent the "finest" achievements of humanity. But the idea that something can be learned from the past—whether through art, literature, or history—still has a great deal of appeal: The suggestion that the disciplined study of history can develop important intellectual abilities seems so self-evident (even if its precise implications remain to be worked out) that outright rejection of such a position seems unlikely. As Kliebard (1984) notes, the idea that studying certain subjects can enhance thinking is still plausible, but not the antiquated belief that such study *in itself* has that effect—"the key lies in *how* the subjects are studied" (p. 27; emphasis in original).

How then, can history be studied humanistically? And more important, how could such humanistic study contribute to participatory democracy? In the next sections we suggest how each of the four stances toward history might assist in that endeavor, but here we sketch out three general requirements of such study. The first characteristic of a humanistic study of history is that it *develops judgment*. The humanities have long been associated with developing powers of critical appraisal; as Eisner (1984) notes, there is no precise yardstick for measuring intellectual or artistic value, and thus such judgments require "attention and sensitivity to nuance, they require appreciation for context, they require the ability to deliberate and judge" (p. 115). The development of this kind of judgment is also a key requirement for participatory democracy. Because there is no independent ground for political knowledge—no certain truths upon which decisions can be made—action depends on careful reasoning and consideration of evidence (Barber, 1984, Parker, 1996). Citizens do not merely choose, they judge options and possibilities. Eisner's synopsis of humanism could as easily have been written by a proponent of participatory democracy: "Humanists place premium on the human's ability to be critically rational, that is, to reason deeply and sensitively about important human matters" (Eisner, 1984, p. 116). The study of history should be able to contribute to this kind of critical rationality, this deep and sensitive reasoning.

The second characteristic of a humanistic study of history is that it *promotes an expanded view of humanity*. The humanities, at their best, take us beyond the narrow confines of our present circumstances and help us understand the cares, the concerns, and the ways of thinking of people different than ourselves—as Eisner (1984) notes, "There is a shared agreement that humanistic studies shed light on what it means to be a human being" (p. 115). Humanistic study, that is, can help us move beyond the belief that our own lives are the natural or universal way of being in the world, and can inspire our appreciation of the lives of those in other times and places—including those of a different ethnicity, class, gender, sexual orientation, or physical ability. This ability to recognize, respect, and even embrace the range of human diversity is critical to participatory democracy. As Parker (1996) notes, one of the chief obstacles to a pluralist political community is the refusal by some to "walk with others" along the path of democratic action. This path of democratic talk, Barber (1984) points out, entails listening—receiving, hearing, empathizing with others. Such listening is possible only if we truly believe that the views of others are potentially as sensible as our own—if we understand that there are ways of being human other than those to which we are accustomed. History can help provide this expanded perspective on humanity.

The third and final characteristic of the humanistic study of history is that it *provides experience in public discourse*. Ladner (1984) argues that "it is the special task of the humanities to sustain a community of discourse that fosters thinking not only as an isolated, private activity but also as convivial, collective, public deliberation" (p. 5) This aspect of the humanities unifies and brings meaning to the first two. It is not enough simply to be able to reason carefully, nor to recognize the humanity of others. Humanistic study draws on these two capacities in order to bring people together—to engage them in common discussion. This public deliberation is also a defining characteristic of participatory democracy, and Parker, Cogan, and Ninomiya (1999) argue that such deliberation should form the core of the school curriculum. We should note, though, that providing experience in discourse does not mean simply practicing debate—the competitive scoring of points that seems to be synonymous with much public talk in contemporary society (Barber, 1984). Rather, experience in public discourse must also develop students' ability to withstand the imposition of meanings, values, and interpretations by others, and must help them learn to communicate equitably. Discourse in humanistic education must aim to overcome—not reproduce—social inequality, and this is a goal toward which the study of history can aspire.

FOUR STANCES TOWARD HISTORY

In this section we describe each of the four stances that affect historical study in educational contexts, both formal and informal. We identify the central activity associated with each stance and describe the range of purposes that typically accompany that activity, and we suggest how these may contribute—or fail to contribute—to the kind of humanistic study necessary for participatory democracy.

The Identification Stance

In every society there are efforts to make use of the past in the service of present interests. One of the most common—and problematic—of these is the stance we call *identification*. In this stance the purpose of history is to anchor our present lives in the past through three interrelated acts: (1) Celebrating historical origins as a means of establishing "who we are;" (2) Extolling the virtues of past members of a community as a way of providing examples for those in the present; and (3) Using the past as a "charter" or justification for present actions or societal arrangements. These purposes exert a powerful influence on historical understanding, and indeed, this is probably the most commonly held and publicly endorsed stance toward history (Rosenzweig & Thelen, 1998). Holidays across the world recall historical events in order to remind people of their common attachment to nation, region, or community; historical sites, markers, and museum exhibits commemorate events in ways calculated to encourage identification with some aspect of the past (Loewen, 1998); and school history is often premised on pride in national identity. Identification, in fact, often provides the explicit basis for curricular and instructional patterns in history. As an early New Zealand advocate of this stance argued, historical study in his country should develop "worthy citizens of a great empire." Students and teachers in the United States, meanwhile, regularly describe "finding out about our past" as a major reason for studying history; in their view, certain historical events take on importance because they define communities of identification (Barton & Levstik, 1998; Holt, 1990; Levstik, 2000; Levstik & Barton, 1997; VanSledright, 1999).

At its most basic level, the identification stance involves interactions among family members; it includes identifying family characteristics, passing on of family heirlooms and artifacts, sharing stories and jointly reconstructing reminiscences. But in many countries—and certainly in the United States—the identification stance also pervades the school curriculum and other "official" public representations of history. From an early age, for example, children begin to learn stories of the origin and development of the U.S. national community, and many of these continue to form the foundation for historical study through the years of early adolescence and beyond—Columbus' "discovery" of the New World, the arrival of the Pilgrims, the American Revolution, and so on. Such topics dominate presentations of history not only—or even primarily—because of their impact on contemporary life, but because they provide a way of establishing where "we" began as a national community; indeed, many of these stories were developed during the eighteenth century as a way of providing just this kind of identification for an otherwise disparate populace. This stance also involves selecting historic individuals as representative of the values that good citizens should imitate; thus the images of leaders such as Washington and Lincoln developed as national icons in the nineteenth century

(Schwartz, 1990, 2000) and became staples of children's exposure to history; Martin Luther King, Jr., has fulfilled a similar role more recently.

Such historical stories and symbols are not just neutral attempts at developing shared feelings among a community; rather, they typically assert the moral rightness of that community (Malinowski, 1948; Shils, 1971). People want to identify with an enlightened—or at least benign—history. As academic historians pay increasing attention to the complexities and moral ambiguities of the past, much of the public turns to other, more comforting renditions of history (Brinkley, 1994). Disney's romantic vision of Pocahontas, rather than Jean Fritz's more ambiguous history, captures children's imaginations; a monument and historical markers commemorate Nathan Bedford Forrest as a Confederate war hero, but fail to mention that he helped found the Ku Klux Klan; and a docent at an antebellum Southern home mentions that "servants" lived on the plantation grounds (Loewen, 1998). Textbooks, meanwhile, adhere to a story of progress, one in which social relations and material prosperity have steadily improved over time (Loewen, 1995). Children have internalized the belief that the historical development of the United States as a land of freedom and prosperity makes it the envy of the world (Barton & Levstik, 1998).

The need to assert the moral rightness of the community points toward ways in which the identification stance toward history can lead to abuses, for stories of "who we are" can also become stories of "who we aren't." Students and teachers alike separate history into "ours" and "theirs," depending on varying group identities. Thus girls and women may talk about women's history as "ours" while boys and men identify it as "theirs." Similarly, European American students may perceive the civil rights movement as someone else's history, while African American students think of it as their own. Similar patterns occur in other nations with significantly marginalized populations. In response, these groups—left off the markers and monuments or confined to glib asides in textbooks and classrooms—develop alternative or vernacular histories of identification. They then call for *their* history's inclusion in the curriculum and in public memorials—thus Native American perspectives become part of the Little Big Horn historical site, the role of African Americans becomes a focus of attention at Colonial Williamsburg, and the treatment of women and minorities is expanded (at least in token ways) in history textbooks and curriculum guides. Again, these stories are not meant to be merely neutral or "academic" attempts at inclusion, nor to simply extend the community of identification; perceiving themselves to be the "missing subjects" of history, marginalized groups seek alternative narratives—rooted in stories of the hardships and accomplishments of forebears—that can sustain and empower them in contemporary struggles. The image of Malcolm X, for example, is not a neutral figure to be included in textbooks along with George Washington Carver, but a basis for pride, affirmation, imitation, or resistance; similarly, Afrocentric approaches to history are not meant to be dispassionate chronologies, but to inspire the kind of community pride that has always accompanied Eurocentric histories.

As one advocate of a more pluralist history notes in regard to the tendency of mainstream histories to "forget" past oppressions, "exactly because the past is forgotten, it rules unchallenged; to be transcended it must first be remembered." This, of course, is exactly what those most empowered by traditional national histories most resist. Groups and individuals empowered by official histories often recoil from attempts to revise standard historical narratives. Recall, for instance, the disputes in the United States over the Enola Gay exhibit at the Smithsonian. The exhibition attempted to represent differing perspectives on the decision to use the atomic bomb on a civilian population. Veterans' groups objected to representations of "ground zero"—the human impact of the bomb on Japanese as well as American citizens. They wanted viewers to identify with veterans—and by extension, with the United States—not vilify either the U.S. soldiers or U.S. policy (Kohn, 1995). As Representative Peter I. Blute (Mass.) commented, "I don't want sixteen-year-olds walking out of there thinking badly of the U.S." Similarly, when school history in the United States moved—quite modestly—away from traditional forms of national identification to include some attention to such issues as the rise and persistence of the KKK, a virulent rebuke followed (Nash, Crabtree, & Dunn, 1997). A similar backlash greeted curricular reform in New Zealand, where critics of reform warned of social disintegration if all New Zealanders did not identify first and foremost with the nation (Openshaw, 1998). Traditional history generally has the advantage here, because its perspective is promoted through the unexamined repetition that comes with monopoly control. So ubiquitous is this control that traditional history is perceived as "objective" and alternative histories are immediately suspect—signaled by their very difference from the orthodox (Parenti, 1999). Faced with the complexities of the present, groups and individuals long for the perceived comfort and clarity of tradition. They seek a history that preserves their social prerogatives, provides them with a sense of communal safety, and justifies present inequities (Lowenthal, 1998). Clearly, focusing on history as a source of communal identification can be the basis for exclusivity and social conservatism. At the same time, varnacular histories aimed at producing an admirable past for marginalized people too often become replacement orthodoxies—substituting one set of misrepresentations for another. At its worst, then the identification stance can set one community against another, undergird various oppressions and misperceptions, and even drive the murderous impulse to genocide.

But the identification stance constitutes an important component of the humanistic study of history, for it recognizes the fundamental human desire to be connected in time as well as place—to tell ourselves, as Lowenthal suggests, "who we are, where we came from, and to what we belong" (p. xvii). This view can provide "a sense of perspective about our own lives and encourage us to transcend the finite span of one lifetime by identifying with the generations that came before us and measuring our own actions against the generations that will follow" (Lerner, 1998, p. 201). In this sense, history becomes a fundamental aspect of our sense of self, the foundation for envisioning a future, a "coherent narrative which gives shape and order to our existence" (Lerner, p. 201). This sense of identification is the foundation for concern with the common good—only if we feel connected to others are we likely to act in their interests as well as our own. By contributing to students' sense of group membership, historical study may help them understand and appreciate the rationale for participatory democracy.

This need not be a call to exclusive or exclusionary membership. Indeed, from a sociocultural perspective we can conceive of individuals as having multiple identities—chosen, as well as ascribed. We live within and among these identities, change them over time, and interact with groups and individuals who may participate in quite different communities. This is an inevitable part of living almost anywhere, but is particularly true of multicultural societies. *How* we interact, however, is not inevitable. We can choose to cut off dialogue with some groups or treat them with disdain or derision. We can refuse to hear their historical narratives or act on their historical concerns. Participation in the ongoing development of the kind of pluralist democracy we have already described suggests a different kind of interaction and a different kind of preparation for that interaction. To begin with, a pluralist democracy requires some recognition that identities are socially constructed—that groups and individuals fashion their history out of the residue of the past for constantly shifting purposes. These histories must be continually interrogated and revised as time, evidence, and new questions about the past outdate their claims—and this should be one of the functions of historical study. History cannot be allowed simply to preserve one group's power and prestige or satisfy another group's need for heroic forebears. Instead, historical study should focus attention on how histories—and people's attachments to those histories—not only develop over time but come either to support existing social arrangements or challenge them. In a democracy the people are supposed to learn about and think about these things (Parenti, 1999). Rather than *telling* us who we are then, history might be more appropriately thought of as helping us *think about* who we are—and who we might become.

The Rationalistic Stance

When historians and history educators articulate the reasons for studying history, they most often advocate some form of what we refer to as the *rationalistic* stance. This stance revolves around the act of analysis: Students are expected to analyze information in order to identify relationships among people and events in the past. That might include examining long-term patterns of historical continuity and change, looking for the factors that caused historical events, or considering the forces that have motivated groups and individuals. Proponents of this stance—the intellectual descendants of von Ranke, whose goal was to write history "as it actually was"—aim toward the historian's "noble dream" of objectivity (Novick, 1988); even while recognizing that pure disinterest is impossible, they strive for a dispassionate analysis that avoids the narrow interests of nationalism or politics. This goal, however, implies no particular instructional method: Students may be asked to analyze by extracting information from didactic presentations, by collecting information to answer questions they find personally meaningful, or by engaging in the process of historical interpretation.

At least three versions of the rationalistic stance have had a major impact on the school curriculum and on teachers' and students' conceptions of what history is for. The first involves learning how society has developed. In this, students are expected to study how societies have grown and changed over the course of human history, particularly as that development relates to the evolution of the contemporary world. By analyzing "enduring patterns and critical turning points" in history (McNeill, Kamman, & Craig, 1989, p. 107) or "what decisions of the past account for present circumstances" (National Center for History in the Schools, 1994, p. 1), students are expected to gain a better understanding of the world in which they live. In the United States, this version of the rationalistic stance has most often focused on the development of national institutions and social patterns—the evolution of the political structure of the country and, more recently, change and continuity in patterns of interaction among Americans of differing ethnicities, social classes, or genders. Students are well aware of this perspective, and a number of studies have shown that they often explain the purpose of history by pointing to the need to understand how the world came to be the way it is today (Barton, 1999, 2001; Barton & Levstik, 1998; Evans, 1989, 1990; VanSledright, 1997).

The second version of the rationalistic stance is more explicitly pragmatic. In this perspective, learning about the past—including the development of contemporary life—is important insofar as it aids in the solution of present problems. Becker's "Everyman His Own Historian" (1932) is one of the most famous articulations of this perspective; Becker argues that history expands the range of experience upon which people (and societies) can draw in order to solve practical problems. Although this pragmatic version of the rationalistic stance is especially associated with Becker and other "New Historians" of the 1910s and 1920s (Novick, 1988), it both predates the Progressive Era's concern with social progress and endures into more recent formulations of history's role in schools. Developers of national standards in history and contributors to the Bradley Commission's *Historical Literacy*, for example, approvingly quote Thomas Jefferson's suggestion that history avails people of "the experiences of other times and other nations; it will qualify them as judges of the actions and designs of men" (cited in McNeill, Kammen, & Craig, 1989, p. 112; National Center for History in the Schools, 1992, p. 3). Knowing history, in this view, provides lessons—not simplistic aphorisms or invariant principles, but analogies, examples, and evidence that enrich our understanding and that can guide action in the present. The idea that lessons can be learned from the past is one of the most prevalent understandings of the purpose of history expressed by students in the United States (Barton, 2001; Barton & Levstik, 1998; Evans, 1989, 1990; VanSledright, 1997).

A final version of the rationalistic stance has gained popularity in the United States over the last decade and has been influential in other countries for an even longer period. In this view, the aim of history education is not for students to learn a body of specific content (either particular narratives or concepts such as *feudalism* or *industrialization*) but to learn about historical investigation and interpretation. In order for students to understand how historical knowledge is constructed, they must understand the procedures historians engage in as they investigate the past—such as how they identify questions, evaluate evidence, and draw conclusions. The popularity of this perspective is closely tied to recent concerns with engaging students in authentic investigations, not only in history but throughout their school studies. As Seixas (1993) notes, expecting students simply to assimilate the products of historical inquiry—to treat the accounts of historians as undisputed fact, for example—fundamentally misportrays the nature of historical knowledge (cf. Segall, 1999). To develop an understanding of history, then, students must understand the analytic procedures as historians—developing meaningful questions, using a variety of sources to investigate their questions, and reaching conclusions based on evidence (Levstik & Barton, 1997). This conception of history education is much less prevalent among students than the first two versions of the rationalistic stance, however, and even in classrooms in which students take part in such investigations, they do not explain the *purpose* of history in terms of understanding the process of historical inquiry.

The rationalistic stance constitutes an important component of the humanistic study of history and has the potential to contribute a great deal toward participatory democracy. One of the chief benefits of this stance is that it can illustrate the socially constructed nature of society—that is, it can show how contemporary institutions arose in the past. If democracy requires that people work together to make decisions about their collective future, they must recognize their own ability to undertake and implement such decisions. This ability is by no means obvious. The institutions, beliefs, and social relations of modern society—whether the rules of the capitalist economy, the shape of national boundaries, the content of religious beliefs, or the antagonisms among groups—often are regarded as timeless and universal, as though the way things *are* is the way they *must* be. But by analyzing the development of society, students can see more clearly the human decisions that led to current circumstances. By recognizing that the world today is the product of collective human decisions in the past, students may come to understand that they can work together to make decisions that shape the present and the future.

A second contribution of the rationalistic stance derives from its concern with illustrating the range of ways people have coped with the common problems of humanity. Focusing on the development of societies—not simply a single group or nation—may help students understand that there are a variety of meaningful ways of thinking, working, believing, deciding, or interacting. Broadening students' knowledge in this way has two potential benefits. First, it may help them recognize the possibility that alternatives exist to current social arrangements: Other societies have done things differently, so perhaps we can as well. Second, it may contribute to the fundamental humanistic goal of understanding and working together with those who are different than ourselves. If students think there is only one sensible way of arranging the affairs of the world, they can hardly avoid coming to the conclusion that anyone who disagrees must be crazy. But if they understand that people in other times and other places have had different ideas, attitudes, and beliefs—and if they see that those are as reasonable as their own—then they may be better able to accept the legitimacy of differing perspectives among their contemporaries.

Developing skills in the collection and interpretation of evidence also has the potential to contribute to the humanistic study of history in at least two important ways. First, the judgments demanded in humanistic study (and in participatory democracy) depend on the analysis of evidence. Students who passively accept the conclusions of others—particularly if they do not even understand the process of developing those conclusions—are liable to fall prey to any number of ill-advised manipulations. Those who have experience finding information, evaluating reliability, and developing interpretations should be better able to use those skills in making decisions for the common good, and they may be more likely to recognize flaws in the conclusions of others. Just as important, students who are skilled in historical inquiry may better be able to engage with those who would use history to justify their own dominance in relations of power. In a society in which access to knowledge is not always free and equal, the democratization of historical interpretation can help those who have not traditionally wielded such power to formulate effective counterarguments grounded in a solid and convincing foundation of evidence.

But the rationalistic stance is also subject to a variety of problems that limit its contribution to a humanistic study of history; indeed, some approaches within this stance may stand directly in the way of a more participatory, more democratic society. First, analyzing the development of society can be done in a way that makes the present state of affairs appear inevitable. Although rationalistic study might highlight the socially constructed nature of society, that is, it could just as easily be used to demonstrate the opposite: If people's individual and collective agency is ignored, then the way past events occurred may appear to be the only possibility, and the present state of society the only conceivable arrangement. As we noted in the previous section, history is often used to justify contemporary social arrangements, and a story of development that avoids considering alternatives is an effective way of legitimating the status quo. Unless students recognize the agency of people involved in the events of the past—their ability to make choices and to influence their world, for good or ill—they may think of history as providing only limitations, not possibilities.

Second, if analysis of history simply becomes the repetition of other people's ideas—through acquaintance with a canonical set of issues and conclusions found in a standardized curriculum—it is unlikely to contribute to meaningful political judgment. If analysis of the Vietnam War, for example, means studying someone else's list of "lessons learned," or if the analysis of evidence means applying a set of procedures in lockstep fashion as in a high school chemistry lab, students are unlikely to become more adept at working toward the common good. This drawback will be particularly debilitating if the topics themselves bear no relevance to contemporary issues—if students' study of the past never quite connects to their understanding of the present, then the irrelevance of their analytical activities will become all too apparent. If the rationalistic stance toward history is to contribute the humanistic study necessary for participatory democracy, the curriculum will have to address questions of importance for society, and students will have to play a role in developing those questions (Seixas, 1993).

The Exhibition Stance

One of the most common acts of history students are expected to perform is the *exhibition of information*. In the routine discourse of instruction, through homework assignments and classroom evaluations, and on standardized tests at state and national levels, students are required to show what they know—to demonstrate that they have retained a specific body of content knowledge. Information also plays a part in each of the other acts of history, but here we are concerned only with those instances in which students are asked to exhibit information in and of itself, apart from its role in any analysis, identification, or moral response. As currently constituted, such exhibition rarely makes a significant contribution to the humanistic study of history, yet certain kinds of instruction might elevate this activity to a more meaningful role in preparation for participatory democracy.

The exhibition of historical information is a long-established tradition in the classroom. Although recommendations of each of the early U.S. commissions on the teaching of history and social studies railed against having students simply memorize and display historical facts (American

Historical Association, 1899, 1909, 1912; National Education Association, 1894, 1916), recitation—the public exhibition of knowledge—nonetheless became a staple of the methods recommended for history teaching (Tryon, 1921). Memorization may have given way to more instructionally sound procedures for developing knowledge, and the term *recitation* has passed from the active vocabulary of most educators, but the display of knowledge remains a central component of the teaching and learning of history. A clear purpose of history in many (if not most) classrooms is for students to exhibit information when called upon to do so—in response to oral questioning by the teacher, on written assignments or classroom tests, or as part of external examinations such as state achievement tests and the National Assessment of Educational Progress (NAEP).

Recent NAEP history assessments—as well as many state tests—go beyond measuring simple factual information and focus instead on students' proficiency in historical analysis; indeed, such tests often include all required information in the question prompts themselves. But many teachers appear to be unaware of this deemphasis on the retention of historical information and continue to expect that their students will be called upon to display discrete pieces of knowledge—and they predictably orient their classroom practices accordingly. The belief that students will be asked to exhibit information on these tests is well founded in recent history, for analysis of students' performance on the 1986 NAEP U.S. history assessment was part of the rationale for "reviving" history in the schools in the 1980s. Proponents of increased attention to the subject (e.g., Hirsch, 1987; Ravitch and Finn, 1987) attacked students' lack of historical knowledge—not the underdevelopment of their analytical abilities, nor their inadequately formulated historical judgments, nor even their failure to identify with the national community, but rather their inability to exhibit the amount of information some authors considered necessary. The publicity generated by these episodes demonstrates how highly valued this historical activity is in our society, and when schools are subject to repeated criticism for failing to prepare students to engage in it, they understandably will gear instruction to avoid such charges.

But schools are not the only contexts in which historical information is exhibited, and testing is only an extreme and artificial manifestation of a much more widespread phenomenon. Perhaps the most visible settings for this activity are museums—widespread, popular, and well-funded institutions whose primary goal is to exhibit information. Individuals also engage in historical exhibition in a number of other settings—through collecting and displaying antiques and other historical memorabilia, restoring historic homes or furniture, creating family trees, or taking part in reenactments of historic settings or events. These popular hobbies may also include varying amounts of analysis, or identification, or moral response, but their primary focus is exhibition: People aim to show what they know about aspects of history they find particularly interesting. Game shows like

Jeopardy present this kind of historical activity at its most basic level: Success depends solely upon the ability to exhibit information on demand, without any suggestion that such knowledge plays a part in more significant undertakings. Children are well aware that exhibition is a valued historical activity, and they sometimes conclude that the purpose of studying history at school is to prepare them for just such exhibition—including the possibility of appearing on game shows (Barton, 1994; VanSledright, 1997).

Information clearly plays a role in a humanistic education and in preparing students for participatory democracy; information is the foundation of debate, discourse, and judgment. No decision about the common good would be meaningful if it were not based on a solid foundation of information. But does the activity of *exhibiting* information contribute to the humanistic study of history? Being able to stand up in class and recite the details of historical events clearly has little or no importance for a democratic society—*knowing* those details may be important, but *displaying* them on demand for a teacher does nothing to inspire commitment to the common good or to enhance students' ability to engage in critical discourse. Similarly, performance on a standardized test is irrelevant to students' ability to use history in meaningful ways—such performance amounts to little more than a parlor trick, unrelated to the demands of democracy. Nor do parallel activities outside school provide a compelling rationale for requiring students to exhibit information: Displaying antiques, restoring historic homes, or taking part in living history reenactments may be worthwhile and fulfilling pastimes, but personal fulfillment provides little justification for a curriculum centered around the development of participatory democracy.

But some aspects of the exhibition stance point toward a more compelling rationale for such activities. One Civil War battle reenactor, when asked why he participated in these displays, explained that he did so because people need to see just how horrible war can be—they need to see the cruelty, pain, suffering, and death up close. It is too easy, he thought, for people to distance themselves from these unpleasant realities, or to romanticize them and thus shield themselves from the horrors of war. Living reenactments, he hoped, would give people information they otherwise lacked. Museums, we would point out, can fulfill much the same purpose: Although their displays may also attempt to present analysis, inspire identification, or promote remembrance, one of their chief goals is to exhibit information that others may use in thinking about history; museums exist, in part, so that historical information is public and available—not hidden, nor secret, nor obscure. In this function of museums (as in the words of the reenactor) lies the justification for a humanistic use of exhibition: providing others the information they need. Public discourse and political judgment can proceed meaningfully only when access to information is equitably distributed, and this often means the sharing of information that some have and others do not.

Children themselves recognize the importance of this aspect of history—passing on information other people need to know. A consistent finding of our work with elementary and secondary students, both in the United States and internationally, is that they are accustomed to listening to older people tell them about the past—whether about their own direct experiences or information they have learned elsewhere. Grandparents explain what life was like when they were younger, parents talk about historical topics or time periods that interest them, and older siblings recount details of the subjects they are studying in school. Moreover, children consciously expect one day to fulfill the same role themselves: They anticipate that when they are older their children, their grandchildren, and perhaps their students will need to learn what they already know—they will come to them to ask what life was like when they were young, or to inquire after their knowledge of more distant times and places. Although children do not frame this process within the context of education for participatory democracy, they are nonetheless aware that one reason for learning history is that they will be able to exhibit historical information for others who need it (Barton, 2001).

A humanistic history education, then, would give students practice displaying information that others need to know; such an education would involve experiences in which students present their learning to authentic audiences. Literacy educators have long stressed the importance of creating an audience beyond the teacher; doing so may motivate students, improve their performance, and lead to transfer of skills beyond the classroom. Indeed, some students have difficulty at school precisely because they are expected to exhibit information unrelated to the genuine needs of others (Heath, 1983). Yet the display of historical information in schools rarely involves authentic audiences. Reciting before the teacher does not do so—the teacher already knows the content, else she would not be asking students to repeat it. Answering questions on an achievement test has even less connection to the needs of others: It involves simple accountability, unconnected to the reasons for teaching history in the schools. To prepare for participatory democracy, a different kind of practice is called for. This might involve students working in small groups to become experts on one aspect of a topic and then sharing their findings with other groups or with students from other classrooms (Levstik & Barton, 1997); older students teaching history to younger children would also involve authentic exhibitions of information, and would correspond to students' expectation that part of the reason for learning history is to pass the knowledge on to others. These are not just pedagogically sound practices—instructional methods that effectively promote retention and transfer of knowledge—they are practices that prepare students to use historical information in socially valuable ways.

The Moral Response Stance

Sometimes history calls up strong moral and emotional responses: Lincoln is admirable, Hitler reprehensible, slavery is evil, human rights essential, and so forth. People have always regarded some aspects of the past with admiration, others with condemnation, and still others with simple remembrance. In response to these feelings we erect memorials and monuments, dedicate plaques, and set aside days for remembrance and celebration. In addition, books, plays, films, and artwork express differing moral responses to history. Spike Lee recalls civil rights leader Malcolm X on film, Picasso paints the horror of war in *Guernica*, Kathryn Sklar uses biography to help make sense of Florence Kelley's passionate commitment to reform. Historical interest is often sparked by our need to understand the best and worst of human activity. Children especially explain their interest in the past in terms of needing to "know the truth" or "what really happened" about morally charged events (Bardige, 1988; Levstik 1986, 1993, 1995). A sixth grader expresses outrage at Nazi atrocities and declares that she would like to "punch Hitler in the nose!" An eighth grader ponders the "fairness" of nineteenth century marital property laws while a classmate declares the conditions in nineteenth century mills "horrible ... they treated the machines better than the children. The owners knew what was happening, too." Indeed, we are often drawn to the study of history precisely because it involves vital moral and ethical issues. And, it is our interest in these issues that propels us to consider what constitutes the common good—the kind of humanistic deliberation that prepares students for participatory democracy.

We characterize these acts of admiration, condemnation, and remembrance as the *moral response* stance. This stance is especially common in schools. Curriculum often focuses first on the "good" things people did in the past, then on things people are expected to perceive as "wrong" or "bad," and finally (though less often) on remembering people who unfairly were made to suffer or who gave their lives for a cause. Thus students are invited to celebrate the lives of important people not only because they are symbols of national identity but because the larger society recognizes them as morally admirable examples: Students are exhorted to be as honest as Abe Lincoln or to make King's dream of better relations between the races come true, and so on. In some classrooms, for instance, young children study King's "I Have a Dream" speech and are asked, in response, to write their own dreams for a better future (Levstik, 1994). At the opposite end of the moral spectrum, students are expected to condemn Hitler, to regard slavery as abhorrent, and (sometimes) to denounce Europeans' treatment of Native Americans.

There is little evidence that students consider learning to admire (or condemn) historic individuals a particularly important part of history, but they do say that one of the reasons for studying the topic is to avoid the mistakes of the past, particularly when these involve highly charged moral issues (Barton & Levstik, 1998; Levstik & Barton, 1996, VanSledright, 1997). As Banks (1982) suggests, one of the most important human characteristics is our ability to create cultures that regard human life as precious and that promote human dignity and creativity. Yet threats to human life and dignity often appear intractable and overwhelming. Not surprisingly, human beings often respond with moral indignation to these threats. Students are especially quick to express outrage over human rights violations, to condemn the perpetrators of what they perceive to be historical wrongs, and, sometimes, to call for retaliation or redress (Bardige, 1988; Levstik, 1995). In this they are not unlike many adults. Calling up moral indignation—particularly in order to incite retaliation—has long been the recourse of politicians, demagogues, and terrorists. At one time or another people have been called upon to remember the Maine or the Alamo, the Battle of Kosovo or Bloody Sunday and countless other massacres, real and imagined. The powerful emotions attached to these memories are evoked to foment war, perpetuate interethnic hatreds and sway political opinions. An alternative moral response—taking social responsibility for injustices— is a more slowly evolving reaction to history. Sometimes victims demand redress—land for displaced peoples, compensation for those interned, or simple acknowledgment of fault. In other cases, leaders apologize for historical wrongs—the Pope asks for forgiveness for the Catholic church's intolerance of non-Catholics, the South African Truth Commission seeks acknowledgment of wrongdoing in the wake of generations of apartheid, and the United States and Canada pay reparations to Japanese internees.

Sometimes the moral response stance elicits neither admiration nor condemnation so much as simple remembrance of people who suffered unfairly, or gave their lives. Thus the victims of natural disasters, of holocausts and terrorist attacks, as well as veterans of innumerable wars are memorialized and recalled with great emotion. Communities and nations build memorials, observe holidays, and hold religious services (Loewen, 1998). The mall in Washington, DC bears powerful witness to the strength of this response to history. As visitors pass by the Vietnam Wall they may gently touch a name, leave a memento, or weep. They are not necessarily there to admire or condemn. Rather, they simply want to recognize and remember the individuals involved in a historic moment. In the same way, the Korean War memorial focuses on remembering the sacrifices of individuals—tired soldiers slogging up a hill, heading to another battle. In other places, the victims of the terrorist bombing in Oklahoma City are recalled with a memorial park, the masses of immigrants who came through New York Harbor are recalled at the Ellis Island memorial, and the experiences of Japanese internees are documented at Gila River, Manzanar, and Tule Lake. Similar memorials and monuments dot the landscape in countries around the world. Apart from any historical lessons that might be learned from the experiences of the people commemorated in these ways, they are recalled because it is perceived as somehow *right* to recognize their suffering. Although schools in the United States observe some holidays associated with remembrance, this is not a major feature of the history curriculum, nor is there any evidence that children in the United States attach much significance to this aspect of historical thinking (Barton & Levstik, 1998). In other countries, though, remembrance constitutes an important component of children's understanding of why history is a subject worth studying (Barton, 1998; Levstik, 2000).

Each aspect of the moral response stance—admiration, condemnation, and remembrance—is vital in developing the humanistic study of history and preparing students for participatory democracy. Without them there would be little ground for establishing a "common good" based on human dignity and respect (Branson & Torney-Purta, 1982). Educators, after all, are charged with preparing their students both to resist threats to human rights and dignity and to take some responsibility for improving the human condition (Banks, 1995; Ministry of Education, 1997; National Council for the Social Studies, 1994; Stone, 1994; Woyshner & Gelfond, 1998). A rationalistic stance attends to how people lived in the past and why they made the decisions they did, but not whether they *should have* made the choices they did. It is the *should haves* that distinguish the moral response stance from the rationalistic stance. Too often, students are asked to study other human beings as if they were mere objects or pawns in a cosmic game of chess. Human particularity disappears. In consequence, neither the choices people made nor the uncertainties they faced seem compelling. In such a curriculum human suffering appears both banal and inevitable—nothing that could be prevented by individual or collective action, nothing particularly worthy of concern (Greene, 1995). But in a humanistic study of history, our ideas about what constitutes human dignity may be drawn, in part, from our response to the past.

Bardige (1988) suggests that recognizing and accepting students' moral responses are crucial if we are ever to prepare them to take action against evil. She argues that pushing students to rationalistic analysis without attention to their moral response leaves them unable to take any kind of stand because they perceive all perspectives as equally good—or, as one sixth grader explained, as "just a matter of opinion." Allowing for—even encouraging—students' moral and emotional responses to history recognizes that human beings are not coldly rationalistic. None of us—historians included—approach the past in a neutral or value-free fashion, nor do we abstain from making moral judgments about the past. Of course, an emotional response is not sufficient in itself to impel intelligent participation in the kind of participatory democracy we have in mind—at its best, the moral response stance suggests action as well as emotion. What might be done in response to the good and evil inherited from the past? What should be done to enhance the common good? Much of the current interest in service learning rests on similar premises—calling upon students to respond humanely to the experiences of people now and in the past, jointly consider how those experiences might inform their understanding of the common good, and take action to promote that (Wade, 1997).

One difficulty with this stance, though, is that moral responses often become hopelessly conflated with rational analysis. In some places, for example, study of the Irish Famine is directed less at analyzing the relationships among economic relations, societal institutions, and demographic changes than at condemning the British. Similarly, the study of the Columbian encounter may have less to do with understanding what happens when three worlds meet than with berating Columbus for torturing Native Americans. If moral responses are established in advance ("the British were attempting genocide"), then empirical evidence will likely be included only to the extent that it supports those responses. This stance is fraught with problems of manipulation. Too often, complex historical events are oversimplified in order to present students with heroes or villains. In addition, teachers may impose moral responses rather than give students opportunities to develop their own. For example, we know of one elementary classroom—one we fear is no exception—in which students were presented with an oversimplified and one-sided view of Cuban history designed to prompt a particular response to the Elian Gonzalez dispute. Sometimes, too, when students are offered bland platitudes or inspirational lessons rather than serious attention to their moral concerns, their response is anger, uncritical "hero" worship, or unsubstantiated judgments (Epstein, 1997). The empirical relationship between students' moral responses and their ability to analyze historical connections await more extensive research and theorizing, but clearly the biggest danger with the moral response stance is that it can be used to turn history into a set of simplistic moral "lessons" that are little more than propaganda. Just as with each of the other stances described in this paper, this one can be used to support the humanistic goals of education or subvert them, to prepare students for participatory democracy or handicap them in their interactions with others.

CONCLUSION

In this chapter we have tried to lay the groundwork for curricular decisions in history. Despite the attention afforded the subject over the last decade, educators have been given little realistic guidance in thinking through the issues surrounding what history should be taught, or why. National standards, state objectives, and local curriculum documents often present lists of topics, facts, or concepts with little explicit consideration of why they have been chosen or how they might contribute to the broader purposes of social education. Historians, educational researchers, and other scholars, meanwhile, frequently equate the study of history in schools with some notion (real or imagined) of the university-based discipline of history, and they are prone to make grand claims—largely unsubstantiated—about the contribution of such academic study to students' personal and political judgment. We find that these approaches fail to account for the multiple, even contradictory, purposes of history in contemporary society. Schools are expected to engage students in a range of activities—not only the analysis favored by most academics, but also identification, exhibition, and moral response—and to the extent that curricular formulations ignore this variety of historical stances, they are unlikely to have an enduring impact on educators. The expectation that history will provide a foundation for community identification, for example, is unlikely to disappear simply because "that's not what historians do." Any attempt at reforming the history curriculum must be grounded in the recognition that schools and other educational institutions have a mandate that is broader—and more significant—than replicating a rarified ideal of academic study.

And the history curriculum must, indeed, be reformed. At present, the subject—in the United States, at least—is bogged down in a morass of narrow topics, mythical stories, and unexamined instructional practices. But we have argued that decisions about what to teach—and ultimately, how to teach—cannot be grounded in simplistic oppositions between popular and academic history. Instead, the historical activities in which students are expected to engage must be examined in light of their potential contribution to participatory democracy in a pluralistic society. It is not the activity itself that determines the utility of a given stance toward history, but rather the purposes that guide it. When those purposes revolve around the goals of humanistic education—developing students' judgment, expanding their view of humanity, and committing them to discourse about the common good—then they deserve a place in the curriculum. But when historical study contradicts these goals, or when it remains irrelevant to them, it cannot justify its inclusion in educational settings. Out intent is to provide some foundation for sorting out these distinctions.

REFERENCES

American Historical Association (1899). *The study of history in schools: Report to the American Historical Association by the Committee of Seven.* New York: Macmillan.

American Historical Association. (1909). *The study of history in the elementary schools: Report to the American Historical Association by the Committee of Eight.* New York: Charles Scribner's Sons.

American Historical Association. (1912). *The study of history in secondary schools: Report to the American Historical Association by a Committee of Five.* New York: Macmillan.

Arendt, H. (1958). *The human condition.* Chicago: University of Chicago Press.

Banks, J.A. (1982). Foreword. In M.S. Branson & J. Torney-Purta (Eds.) *International human rights, society, and the schools* (pp. viii-x). Bulletin No. 68 of the

National Council for the Social Studies. Washington, DC: National Council for the Social Studies.

Banks, J.A. (1995). The transformative challenges to the social science disciplines: implications for social studies teaching and learning. *Theory and Research in Social Education, 23,* 2–20.

Barber, B.R. (1984). *Strong democracy: Participatory politics for a new age.* Berkeley: University of California Press.

Bardige, B. (1988). Things so finely human: Moral sensibilities at risk in adolescence. In C. Gilligan, J.V. Ward, & J.M. Taylor (Eds.), *Mapping the moral domain: A contribution of women's thinking to psychological theory and education* (pp. 87–110). Cambridge, MA: Harvard University Press.

Barton, K.C. (1994). *Historical understanding among elementary children.* Unpublished doctoral dissertation, University of Kentucky, Lexington.

Barton, K.C. (1999, April). *"Best not to forget them:" Positionality and students' ideas about significance in Northern Ireland.* Paper presented at the Annual Meeting of the American Educational Research Association, Montreal.

Barton, K.C. (2001). "You'd be wanting to know about the past:" Social contexts of children's historical understanding in Northern Ireland and the United States. *Comparative Education 39,* 87–106.

Barton, K.C., & Levstik, L.S. (1998). "It wasn't a good part of history:" National identity and students' explanations of historical significance. *Teachers College Record, 99,* 478–513.

Becker, C. (1932). Everyman his own historian. *American Historical Review, 37,* 221–236.

Benhabib, S. (1992). Models of public space: Hannah Arendt, the liberal tradition, and Jürgen Habermas. In C. Calhoun (Ed.), *Habermas and the public sphere* (pp. 73–98). Cambridge, MA: MIT Press.

Bodnar, J.E. (1992). *Remaking America: Public memory, commemoration, and patriotism in the twentieth century.* Princeton, NJ: Princeton University Press.

Boyte, H.C. (1992). In C. Calhoun (Ed.), *Habermas and the public sphere* (pp. 340–355). Cambridge, MA: MIT Press.

Branson, M.S., & Torney-Purta, J. (Eds.). (1982). *International human rights, society, and the schools.* Bulletin No. 68 of the National Council for the Social Studies. Washington, DC: National Council for the Social Studies.

Brinkley, A. (1994). Historians and their Publics. *Journal of American History, 81,* 1027–1030.

Calhoun, C. (1992). Introduction: Habermas and the public sphere. In C. Calhoun (Ed.), *Habermas and the public sphere* (pp. 1–48). Cambridge, MA: MIT Press.

Dietz, M. (1992). Context is all: Feminism and theories of citizenship. In C. Mouffe (Ed.), *Dimensions of radical democracy: Pluralism, citizenship, community* (pp. 63–85). New York: Verso.

Eisner, E. (1984). Can the humanities be taught in American public schools? In B. Ladner (Ed.), *The humanities in precollegiate education* (pp. 119–129). Eighty-third yearbook of the National Society for the Study of Education, Part II. Chicago: University of Chicago Press.

Epstein, T.L. (1997). Sociocultural approaches to young people's historical understanding. *Social Education, 61,* 28–31.

Evans, R.W. (1989). Teacher conceptions of history. *Theory and Research in Social Education, 17,* 210–240.

Evans, R.W. (1990). Teacher conceptions of history revisited: Ideology, curriculum, and student belief. *Theory and Research in Social Education, 18,* 101–138.

Fraser, N. (1992). Rethinking the public sphere: A contribution to the critique of actually existing democracy. In C. Calhoun (Ed.), *Habermas and the public sphere* (pp. 109–142). Cambridge, MA: MIT Press.

Greene, M. (1995). *Releasing the Imagination: Essays on education the arts and social change.* New York: Teachers College Press.

Habermas, J. (1989). *The structural transformation of the public sphere: An inquiry into a category of bourgeois society.* Cambridge, MA: MIT Press.

Heath, S.B. (1983). *Ways with words: Language, life, and work in communities and classrooms.* New York: Cambridge University Press.

Hirsch, E.D., Jr. (1987). *Cultural literacy: What every American needs to know.* New York: Houghton Mifflin.

Holt, T.C. (1990). *Thinking historically: Narrative, imagination, and understanding.* New Yoek: College Entrance Examination Boards.

Kliebard, H.M. (1984). The decline of humanistic studies in the American school curriculum. In B. Ladner (Ed.), *The humanities in precollegiate education* (pp. 7–30). Eighty-third yearbook of the National Society for the Study of Education, Part II. Chicago: University of Chicago Press.

Kohn, R. (1995). History and the culture wars. *Journal of American History, 82,* 1036–1063.

Ladner, B. (1984). Introduction: The humanities and the schools. In B. Ladner (Ed.), *The humanities in precollegiate education* (pp. 1–6). Eighty-third yearbook of the National Society for the Study of Education, Part II. Chicago: University of Chicago Press.

Lerner, G. (1998). *Why history matters.* New York: Oxford University Press.

Levstik, L. (1986). The relationship between historical response and narrative in a sixth-grade classroom. *Theory and Research in Social Education, 28,* 114–119.

Levstik, L.S. (1993). Making the past come to life. In B. Cullinan (Ed.), *Fact and faction: Literature across the curriculum.* Newark, DE: International Reading Association.

Levstik, L.S. (1994). Building a sense of history in a first grade classroom. In J. Brophy (Ed.), *Research in elementary social studies.* Greenwich, CT: JAI.

Levstik, L.S. (1995). Narrative constructions: Cultural frames for history. *The Social Studies, 86,* 113–116.

Levstik, L.S. (2000). Articulating the silences: Teachers' and students' conceptions of historical significance. In P. Stearns, P. Seixas, & S. Wineberg (Eds.), *Knowing, teaching, and learning history: National and international perspectives* (pp. 284–305). New York: New York University Press.

Levstik, L.S., & Barton, K.C. (1996). "They still use some of their past": Historical thinking in elementary children's chronological thinking. *Journal of Curriculum Studies, 28,* 531–576.

Levstik, L.S., & Barton, K.C. (1997). *Doing history: Investigating with children in elementary and middle schools.* Mahwah, NJ: Lawrence Erlbaum Associates.

Loewen, J.W. (1995). *Lies my teacher told me: Everything your American history textbook got wrong.* New York: New Press.

Loewen, J. (1998). *Lies across America: What our historic sites get wrong.* New York: New Press.

Lowenthal, D. (1998). *Possessed by the past: The heritage crusade and the spoils of history.* New York: Cambridge University Press.

Malinowski, B. (1948). *Magic, science, and religion and other essays.* Glencoe, IL: Free Press.

McNeill, W.H., Kammen, M., & Craig, G.A. (1989). Why study history? Three historians respond. In P. Gagnon & the National Commission on History in Schools (Eds.), *Historical literacy: The case for history in American schools* (103–118). New York: Macmillan.

Ministry of Education. (1997). *Social studies in the New Zealand curriculum.* Wellington: Ministry of Education (Te Tahuhu o te Matauranga).

Mouffe, C. (1992). Preface: Democratic politics today. In C. Mouffe (Ed.), *Dimensions of radical democracy: Pluralism, citizenship, community* (pp. 1–14). New York: Verso.

Nash, G., Crabtree, C., & Dunn, R. (1997). *History on trial: Culture wars and the teaching of the past.* New York: Knopf.

National Center for History in the Schools. (1992). *Lessons from history: Essential understandings and historical perspectives.* Los Angeles, CA: National Center for History in the Schools.

National Center for History in the Schools. (1994). *National standards for grades K-4: Expanding children's world in time and space.* Los Angeles, CA: Author.

National Council for the Social Studies. (1994). *Expectations of excellence: Curriculum standards for social studies.* Washington, DC: Author.

National Education Association. (1894). *Report of the Committee of Ten on secondary school studies.* New York: American Book Company.

National Education Association. (1916). *The social studies in secondary education: Report of the Committee on Social Studies of the Commission on the Reorganization of Secondary Education of the National Education Association.* Washington, DC: Government Printing Office.

Novick, P. (1988). *That noble dream: The "objectivity question" and the American historical profession.* New York: Cambridge.

Openshaw, R. (1998). Citizen who? The debate over economic and political correctness in the social studies curriculum. In P. Benson & R. Openshaw (Eds.), *New horizons for New Zealand social studies* (pp. 19–42). Palmerston North: Educational research and development press.

Paker, W.C. (1996). Advanced ideas about democracy: Toward a pluralistic conception of citizen education. *Teachers College Record, 98*, 105–128.

Parker, W.C., Cogan, J.J., & Ninomiya, A. (1999). Educating world citizens: Toward multinational curriculum development. *American Educational Research Journal, 36*, 117–145.

Parenti, M. (1999). *History as mystery.* San Francisco, CA: City Lights.

Ravitch, D., & Finn, C.E. (1987). *What do our 17-year-olds know? A report on the first national assessment of history and literature.* New York: Harper and Row.

Rogoff, B. (1990). *Apprenticeship in thinking: Cognitive development in social context.* New York: Oxford University Press.

Rosenzweig, R., & Thelen, D.P. (1998). *The presence of the past: The popular uses of history in American life.* New York: Columbia University Press.

Schwartz, B. (1990). *George Washington: The making of an American symbol.* Cornell, NY: Cornell University Press.

Schwartz, B. (2000). *Abraham Lincoln and the forge of national memory.* Chicago: University of Chicago Press.

Seixas, P. (1993). Historical understanding among adolescents in a multicultural setting. *Curriculum Inquiry, 23,* 301–327.

Segall, A. (1999). Critical history: Implications for history/social studies education. *Theory and Research in Social Education, 27,* 358–374.

Shills, E. (1971). Tradition. *Comparative Studies in Society and History, 13,* 122–159.

Stone, L.E. (1994). *The education feminism reader.* New York: Routledge.

Tryon, R. (1921). *The teaching of history in junior and senior high schools.* Boston: Ginn and Company.

VanSledright, B.A. (1997). And Santayana lives on: Students' views on the purposes for studying American history. *Journal of Curriculum Studies, 29,* 529–557.

VanSledright, B.A. (1999). On the importance of historical positionality to thinking about and teaching history. *The International Journal of Social Education, 12*(2), 1–18.

Wade, R.C. (1997). Community service-learning: A guide to including service in the public school curriculum. Albany: State University of New York Press.

Wertsch, J.V. (1985). *Vygotsky and social formation of mind.* Cambridge, MA: Harvard University Press.

Wertsch, J.V. (1991). *Voices of the mind: A sociocultural approach to mediated action.* Cambridge, MA: Harvard University Press.

Wertsch, J.V. (1998). *Mind as action.* New York: Oxford University Press.

Wertsch, J.V., Del Rio, P., & Alvarez, A. (Eds.). (1995). *Sociocultural studies of mind.* Cambridge: Cambridge University Press.

Woyshner, C.A., & Gelfond, H.S. (Eds.). (1998). *Minding women: Reshaping the educational realm.* Cambridge: Harvard University Press.

CHAPTER 7

INTERROGATING PRIVILEGE, PLURALITY AND POSSIBILITIES IN A MULTICULTURAL SOCIETY

Ellen Durrigan Santora

INTRODUCTION

Successful development and maintenance of a multicultural social studies curriculum is intertwined with the social, cultural, political, and economic forces of the nation, the individual states, and their unique communities. Presently, because of social, political, and demographic changes, the concerns and purposes of multicultural education are being redefined within an epistemic shift (Welch, in McLaren, 1997) that is taking place throughout the United States and Canada. As we move from the limited perspectives afforded by Eurocentric world views, much that was previously accepted without question is giving way to the ambiguity, uncertainty, complexity and fluidity necessitated in the engagement of multiple ways of knowing and their divergent perspectives. Research that once championed the duality that set reason above emotion and elevated the production of rational thinking grounded in empirical evidence is giving quarter to experiential knowledge grounded in spiritual, emotional, relational, as well as rational thought. Those who once sought answers in empirical data, now search for understanding by posing questions, describing webs of fluid relationships, and narrating interconnected stories (see, e.g., Preissle-Goetz & LeCompte, 1991; Grant, 1999).

Multicultural education and the research that supports it are an intrinsic part of this epistemic shift. Earlier efforts to address students of color and new populations of European immigrant students viewed diversity through the normative lens of the dominant culture as a deviation from mainstream ways of knowing and doing. Such views, while encouraging the appropriation and colonization of selected ethnic practices into the "melting pot" we fondly call our "shared culture," fostered educational approaches that sought to "correct" deviant practices and educate and socialize students in the "normalizing" ways of the dominant group. Shifting to more inclusive ways of knowing implies using the confluence of new knowledge and perspectives that flows from the waters of multiple cultural streams to transform one's assumptions, values, beliefs, and ways of experiencing.

Evidence of the stress that resides within this shift can be seen in many dimensions of schooling. Traditionally oriented administrators and boards of education now talk with fear in their voices about school violence and student alienation and often connect these behaviors to students who live on the margins of mainstream culture. Disciplinary policies have a disproportionate impact on minority student suspensions and expulsions. In addition, a school culture dominated by curriculum standards, competency testing and high accountability has caused many social studies teachers, who were only marginally committed to multicultural education, to resort to direct instruction strategies that encourage memorization of standard sets of knowledge. Students who fail to pass standardized and statewide assessment tests are being segregated into special classes. Indeed, the term "at risk" has nearly become synonymous with students of color (Ladson-Billings, 1999). There is growing concern that high stakes testing will drive students who have been considered "at risk" out onto the streets with neither the social nor the academic skills to compete in de-industrialized, high-tech markets.

In addition to the concerns noted above, social studies curricula have been repeatedly contested,[1] and in the process, attempts to fashion culturally relevant learning experiences have been discouraged, diluted, and deleted (Nash, Crabtree & Dunn, 1997; Cornbleth & Waugh, 1995). The media working in tandem with special interest groups such as the religious right and textbook publishers have played a significant role in forging and maintaining public opinion regarding social studies education that constrains the development of students' critical understanding of ways in which diversity has both contributed much to that which our society holds in common and highlighted our need to attend to issues of democracy, equality, and social justice (Johnson & Avery, 1999; Provenzo, 1990; Loewen, 1995). In the current school environment, the evidence suggests there is reason to fear for the future of multiculturalism (Welch, in McLaren, 1997).

For some, this signifies a battle spawned from within the tensions of competing world views. Lather (1991) characterizes these challenges as an "explosion of contradictory and competing knowledges, power arrangements that are both sedimented and constantly shifting, and a lack of an agreed upon foundational knowledge" (p. 71). Differences in race, class, gender, sexual orientation and faith define contemporary classrooms in ways that challenge white middle class educators' and students' traditional assumptions, beliefs, values, knowledge, theories and practices. Critiques emanating from the pluralism of marginalized groups challenge the universality, truth-value, fixity, rationality, objectivity, and neutrality attributed to Western European and androcentric liberal thought. To educate from a more culturally inclusive and relevant position, educators need to reconceptualize how culture is socially and historically constructed and to situate power relations within that construction process (Grant & Sachs, 1995; Kincheloe & Steinberg, 1997). The theory and research I have chosen to review in this chapter address these concerns by arguing that multicultural education should focus on transforming dominant beliefs, values, assumptions, and experiences in ways that will support collective and public action to improve the education and living conditions of all subordinated groups.

In many ways, this review of the research related to multicultural social studies education has become both a "window and mirror" (Style, 1996, cited in Crocco, 1998, p. 128) into my own development as a student, a teacher and a researcher. As I began to interpret and synthesize the disparate array of theories and research, I became acutely aware of the extent to which the selection and sorting process was a reflection of my own identities as an immigrant daughter, a veteran teacher of culturally diverse students and a classroom researcher. I found myself privileging the voices of teachers, students, and classroom researchers[2] and situating those studies within a Deweyan ideology of democratic education (1916) and the various theories that contribute to the discourse of critical multiculturalism including critical multiculturalists' conceptions of cultural democracy (Banks, 1997; Darder, 1991, 1997; Gay, 1994); Pang, Gay, and Stanley's (1995) ideas about an "expanding community"; an eclectic blend of feminist critiques of power and dominance, (e.g., Code, 1991; Gilligan, 1982/1993; Giroux, 1991; Harding, 1991; hooks, 1984) and African American women's thought as it relates to dialogue, agency and the complex and overlapping oppressions of race, class, and gender (e.g., Hill Collins, 1990; Ladson-Billings, 1996). I use these frames to suggest that critical multicultural education research is blazing a distinct and emancipatory path through the frontiers of democratic pluralism for a more epistemologically sensitive social studies education. Chief among the obstacles it faces, however, are assumptions and visions grounded in the racial and cultural identities of white middle class students, educators and policy makers.

THEORETICAL POSSIBILITIES FOR TRANSFORMATION AND EMANCIPATION

Dewey, a modernist who was decidedly anachronistic in his thinking, foreshadowed a new age in education. As one of the earliest thinkers to connect democracy with day-to-day classroom interaction, he recognized the connection between learning at home and learning in school, articulated the significant role of culturally diverse students' experiences in the construction of knowledge, and saw the benefits of students engaging in collaborative problem-solving tasks (Dewey, 1916). He envisioned classrooms as communities of learning wherein students experienced working together in culturally pluralistic and democratic ways. Arguing that democracy was both a way of living and a moral imperative, he was able to weave together the ethical, moral, critical and social goals of education.

Applying Dewey's thinking about students' full participation to the pluralism of today's schools conditions the practice of cultural democracy (see Ramirez & Casteñeda, 1974) within the classroom. Darder (1991, 1997), Gay (1994), Ladson-Billings, (1996) Banks (1997) and others (e.g., Sleeter & Grant, 1994) have appropriated the idea of "cultural democracy" into a critical theory of cultural democracy that recognizes democracy as an ongoing struggle focused on issues of power, culture, and authority. Within a cultural democracy, oppressed groups would use their voices to create conditions for their own emancipation and empowerment. Placing social studies classrooms within a sociocultural context, a culturally democratic pedagogy recognizes that cultural and racial experiences are too often hidden within the silence of students of color, and the role of the teacher is to liberate those voices so that they might contribute to culturally pluralistic constructions of emancipatory knowledge (Darder, 1991, 1997). The creation of expanded or inclusive communities of learners that respond to both unity and diversity in emancipatory ways necessitates bridging the social, cultural, ethical, and epistemological gaps between diverse people. For individuals whose identities are found within their ethnic group, achieving a sense of identity with one's expanded community requires both the "deconstruction and transformation of messages, perceptions, and images about ethnic groups" and learning experiences that prepare one for the privileges and responsibilities of citizenship without hierarchy in a culturally pluralistic democracy (Pang et al., 1995, p. 305).

Feminist theories raise compelling questions for social studies educators who subscribe to Dewey's (1916) model of democratic education as a "conjoint communicated experience" (p. 87). First, schooling needs to address the importance of personal narrativity or the ability to articulate personally meaningful experiences in terms of one's knowledge (Hollingsworth, Gallego, & Standerford, 1995; Middleton, 1993; Noddings, 1992). Second, feminist standpoint theorists tell us that society consists of a variety of groups each of which occupies a position in an unequal, hierarchical order, and knowledge, although dialogical, is intricately connected to one's position within this order (Code, 1991; Harding, 1991). Cross-cultural and cross-racial groups of students and educators therefore must reflect on and communicate their "positions" in order to discover the nature of group oppression and its influence on the classroom experience of all students. Third, voice is a powerful metaphor for the ability of marginalized groups to connect their private and public worlds and to have their stories heard (Gilligan, 1982/1993). Finally, democracy, as it is grounded in diversity, equivalent rights, and risk-taking, is a fluid and dynamic process involving the quest for a common good in both the public and private spheres of people's coexistence (Bloom, 1998).

Feminist pedagogues facing a pluralistic, postmodern reality realize that teaching practices cannot be prescribed from outside the classroom environment and that what is emancipatory in one setting cannot necessarily be generalized to the next. Consequently, feminist pedagogy shifts the focus of teaching from techniques and structures to identity, group consciousness, plurality, interactions, uncertainty, and agency. It engages students' experiences as central to teaching and learning, questions dichotomous and oppositional thinking as being grounded in the existence of hierarchical relationships and supported by a politics of domination and subordination, and creates spaces for students to exercise their voices and their agency by focusing on emancipatory knowledge, skills and attitudes. Especially important to social studies education is its quest for new meanings for citizenship, community, and governance (Arnot & Dillabough, 1999; Bernard-Powers, 1996; Bloom, 1998; Giroux, 1991; hooks, 1994; Stone, 1996; Weiler, 1988).

On the path to improving the relevance of education to African-American youth, African-American women educators (Gordon, 1995; Hill Collins, 1990; King, 1995) have engaged in mapping out the tenets of an African-American epistemology. Marginalized by the discourse of both white feminists and masculinist Afrocentrism,[3] these African-American women believe that race, class and gender are interlocking strands in the fabric of oppression. African-American womanist[4] thought, articulated from "the margins,"[5] distinguishes itself by privileging wisdom gathered from lived experiences, asserting the need for dialogue as a means to assess knowledge claims, and granting primacy to an ethic of caring that assumes one's personal accountability as an agent of knowledge, consciousness and emancipatory action (Hill Collins, 1990).

Perhaps no better example of an African-American womanist epistemology-in-use exists than that found in the collective wisdom of Ladson-Billings (1994) and the teachers she describes in *The Dreamkeepers, Successful Teachers of African American Children.*

> Their common thread of caring was their concern for the implications their
> work had on their students' lives, the welfare of the community, and unjust

social arrangements. Thus, rather than the idiosyncratic caring for individual students (for whom they did seem to care), the teachers spoke of the import of their work for preparing the students for confronting inequitable and undemocratic social structures. (Ladson-Billings, 1995, p. 474)

Not only does Ladson-Billings show us this epistemology in use in the teaching strategies of her participants, but she also describes the epistemological process as it is used to generate the collective knowledge resident in this empowered community of educating professionals. Hooks (1994) argues that extending such dialogue is a simple starting place for teachers, scholars and critical thinkers to cross boundaries created by differences in race, class, gender, sexuality, professional hierarchies, academic disciplines, and so on. Cross-cultural dialogue of this nature would necessarily highlight participants' multiple and competing epistemologies, challenge their deeply imbedded assumptions and biases, and reveal the nature of knowledge as dynamic and incomplete (Hill Collins, 1990).

The dialogic nature of African American women's epistemological theories emanates from a culture grounded in active opposition to oppression and subordination. Baber (1995) elicits the connections between civic competency learned through resistance and the significance of dialogue in her discussion of multivocality. She urges us to consider educators of color as leaders in the articulation of meaningful multicultural curricula. By virtue of their participation in a critical subculture *and* the macroculture, educators of color possess a deeper understanding of issues of race, culture, equity and social justice than do most European Americans. They know that white educators must confront racial and class identities and acknowledge that these are defined within ongoing relationships to "the other" in order to move ahead in negotiating social studies curricula that will support participatory citizenship in a culturally diverse society.

Cornbleth and Waugh (1995) galvanize the need to integrate African-American womanist thought into the curriculum negotiation process by identifying two alternatives, a black studies perspective and reciprocal history (Morrison, 1992, cited in Cornbleth & Waugh, 1995; Wynter, 1992), as the foundations for a history-social studies curriculum that responds to cultural diversity. Such a curriculum would involve students in collectively and reciprocally "analyzing and questioning the prescriptive rules of the prevailing social and political power structures and the cultural landscape" and encourage them "to raise and pursue 'deciphering' questions, in other words to think critically from their own and others' standpoints" (Cornbleth & Waugh, p. 196).

The aims of multicultural curriculum transformation in social studies are complex and are enhanced by the cultural, racial, and gendered differences of researchers within the discipline. Generally, researchers and theorists stress the need for social studies educators to create learning experiences that: enrich and deepen students' understanding of racial, ethnic, religious, and gendered realities; defuse bias, prejudice, and stereo-typical representations; encourage cross-cultural empathy and understand-ing; and enhance students' understanding of the synergy of unity and diversity (Baber, 1995; Ladson-Billings, 1992; Pang et al., 1995). To accomplish this, Crocco (1998) suggests that teachers should begin by articulat-ing a curriculum that is both a "window and mirror" (Style, 1996, cited in Crocco, 1998, p. 128) to students' racial and cultural experiences. We should also expand social studies knowledge with the interpretations and perspectives of scholars of color and women scholars and develop students' understanding of the social construction and reconstruction of knowledge (Banks, 1995, 1996). Through the development of a critical consciousness (see Kincheloe, 1993), teachers and their students should demonstrate an understanding of the moral and political nature of social studies education (Palonsky, 1995) and use this as an avenue to challenging the assumptions and biases of mainstream white, middle class American culture (Kincheloe & Steinberg, 1997). To foster the growth of positive race, class and gender identities, teachers need to create respectful and caring classroom environ-ments (Crocco, 1998; Ladson-Billings, 1994) in which students know and value cultural diversity and work collectively to achieve common goals (Pang et al., 1995). Most important, teachers must foster the development of competence in cultural pluralism as a condition of full democratic citi-zenship in a culturally pluralistic community and encourage students' development and participation as socially responsible citizens who willingly and actively confront subordination, oppression and social injustice (Lad-son-Billings, 1992).

ACKNOWLEDGING WHITE PRIVILEGE AS A FORCE IN MAINTAINING CULTURAL RESISTANCE

The opening of this chapter implied that social, cultural, political, and eco-nomic forces within the nation present obstacles to the development and implementation of more culturally and gender relevant social studies curricula.

Decisions made concerning multicultural social studies content within broader contexts, such as those posed by the defeat of the National History Standards and the debates in New York and California (see Cornbleth & Waugh, 1995; Nash et al., 1997), are accompanied by similar contextual influ-ences within the schools themselves. Interpreting school and classroom research (see, e.g. Brantlinger, 1994; Davidson, 1996; Ehrenberg, Goldhaber, & Brewer, 1995; Feiman-Nemser & Remillard, 1996; Nieto, 1996), we can assume that a racial and cultural mismatch between today's students and their teachers exacerbates the epistemological challenges already present in cultur-ally diverse social studies classrooms. Racial identification and cultural assumptions, their tacit understandings of schools and communities, and their expectations and assumptions of both dominant and marginalized groups shape the way teachers design and implement culturally sensitive curriculum as well as their interactions with culturally and racially different students.

Interrogating the culture of white dominance, McIntosh (1988/1997) foreshadows a research agenda that directs our attention to the assumptions and biases "hidden" within a culture of whiteness. By portraying a series of white experiences of unearned privilege, she suggests the accountability whites must accept for the perpetuation of racial subordination. Weiler (1988) observes that white women teachers working for change do not identify themselves as white because they are trapped by world views constructed within an unequal racial structure shaped by an unconscious culture of white dominance and privilege. Conversely, blacks have always considered whiteness a separate and distinct culture and have connected it to the systemic nature of social injustice (hooks, 1992). King (1991) refers to the failure of whites to acknowledge their cultural position as "dysconscious racism." We must question whether teachers who have *only* white communities of reference, who lack knowledge of life within the African American communities, and who harbor the dysconscious racism that encourages "colorblindness" can succeed in teaching African American students (Ladson-Billings, 1994). The invisibility of race in the lives of many white teachers causes them to minimize the role of racism in the lives of people of color, contributes to their misunderstanding concerning the experiences of students of color, and creates obstacles to interracial collaboration in confronting inequality and social injustice.

The world views of European American teachers are largely different from those of their students of color, and these world views play a fundamental role in teachers' discursive patterns. The research of Wills (Mehan, Lintz, Okamoto, & Wills, 1995; Wills, 2000), Almarza (1997), Santora (1997, 1999), Swartz (1992, 1998), Kornfeld and Goodman (1998), and DiPardo and Fehn (2000) illuminate ways in which this happens in social studies education and with multicultural curriculum reform. Using the metaphor of "cultural baggage," Wills (Mehan et al., 1995; Wills, 2000) advances the idea that teachers and students bring their own racial and cultural biases and assumptions about historical context and significance into the classroom. These biases include where and when in the curriculum it is appropriate to teach about people of color and women. White teachers of predominantly white students rarely provide opportunities for students to develop an understanding of the reality of power and the multifaceted and dialogical nature of conflict in historical interactions between European Americans and African Americans and between European American and Native Americans (Mehan et al., 1995). Without this understanding of the historical relations between whites and peoples of color, white students cannot be expected to make sense of the profound implications of racial inequality in the lives of members of both dominant and subordinate races.[6]

Based on student interviews and classroom observations, Almarza (1997) unveils ways in which teachers convey messages of cultural invisibility to students. These teachers' exclusion of substantive content about the history and contributions of Mexican-Americans, their slighting of culturally relevant learning strategies, and their privileging of white students during teacher-centered class discussions create conditions whereby their Mexican-American students enter into a vicious and self-destructive cycle of "silent resisting" (Foley, 1990; McClure, 1978, cited in Almarza, 1997).

Studying Hispanic,[7] Asian and European American students' cross-cultural interaction in a classroom where their white teacher was determined to ameliorate status conditions among her students, Santora (1997, 1999, 2000) describes the nesting of multiply layered, socioculturally-related contexts. The most significant among these were: a school/community history of middle class parents' challenges to equal educational opportunity initiatives, white middle class dominance of school policy, conflicting staff development initiatives, a school culture that privileged individual over collective achievement, the teacher's culturally embedded beliefs and practices and limited pedagogical content knowledge, and student resistance nurtured by biased assumptions about schooling. These contexts interacted to dilute the teacher's commitment to enact an inclusive history curriculum and provide for students' equal status interaction.[8] This dilution, embedded in a teacher discourse of whiteness that occasionally bordered on overt racism, contributed to students' cross-cultural and cross-gender conflict and caused students, as a means of self-protection, to define social studies content in terms of teacher-provided texts and teacher-controlled participation. While I agree with Almarza that teachers need to reflect on their assumptions related to culturally diverse students and develop more culturally sensitive structural, discursive, and pedagogical practices, my research indicates, as Wills has anticipated, that for multicultural education to succeed, change must be both deep and pervasive.

The interaction of students' culturally embedded preferences with those of their teachers plays a major role in teachers' willingness to either sustain or challenge the status quo. Juxtaposing two studies (Kornfeld & Goodman, 1998; Swartz, 1998) demonstrates the possibility of contrasting preferences of largely white middle class students and students of color for multicultural approaches to social studies education. Kornfeld and Goodman report being met with "the glaze" of resistance when they confronted predominantly European American students with activities that focused on uncertainty and ambiguity. On the other hand, Swartz (1998) describes the wide-eyed, rapid fire responses of urban, predominantly African American students as their teachers posed higher order questions related to the possibility of a pre-Columbian African presence in the Americas. The important and relevant problem posed in their lesson and the teachers' adept questioning techniques confirmed these students' beliefs that Africans had long been invisible from mainstream history. They saw this lesson as an opportunity to engage their personal knowledge in deciphering the puzzles of "lost history" in transformative ways.

Thus while Kornfield and Goodman's attempts to jar students from their reliance on school interpretations of historical events and engage them with multiple perspectives met with resistance, the students in Swartz's study used the ambiguity created by the introduction of alternative perspectives to vindicate their own culturally based historical understanding. Levstik (1997) sheds light on this by suggesting that history taught through the engagement of multiple perspectives may, in fact, contradict some children's "perceived need to know the truth" and may violate the wishes of many parents (p. 50). Taken together, these studies may suggest that middle class students, supported by their parents, are dysconsciously resisting the threats posed by alternative perspectives to the knowledge that has so long supported their dominance within the classroom culture.

The ways in which teachers overtly resist implementation of emancipatory curriculum are highlighted in two recent studies. Di Pardo and Fehn's (2000) study of the implementation of a "Cultural Issues" course in a "white high school" exposes the reality of teacher self-censorship or "neutralizing" when confronted with the social injustices evident within the ecology of their own educational environments. Their negotiated course content was marked by the silencing of "touchy issues" and the "pervasive search for safe ground" (pp. 187–188). When Hollingsworth, Gallego and Standerford (1995) attempted to implement a program that emphasized school, language, personal, community, and critical literacies as part of social studies literacy, the teachers used a discourse of accountability as a tool for resisting the engagement of social issues. In an act that perhaps reflects the complicity of researchers in perpetuating a white bias, Hollingsworth and her associates questioned their own ethics of imposing a program that was not fully accepted by their social studies teacher-participants. With a more critical perspective, DiPardo and Fehn argue that before multicultural reforms can be effective, educators must acknowledge their sociocultural biases and the obstacles these present to frank discussion of oppression and privilege.

Boyle-Baise (1995) and Baber (1995) suggest that the development of racial and cultural consciousness by white teachers would have a positive effect in fostering culturally responsive social studies education reform, and they recognize the need for cross-cultural dialogue in this pursuit. Boyle-Baise argues that white educators who have reflected on their own journeys as multicultural educators can provide windows into ways the invisibility of one's whiteness contributes to the perpetuation of racism. As a social studies educator, Baber (1995) argues that the dual ability of African American educators to engage in a microcultural critique and negotiate their own positions within the macroculture provides them with deeper insights concerning the continued existence of racism and other types of oppression within schools and classrooms. Therefore, she asserts that educators of color should lead in helping white educators to critically examine "the ways one's privileged status creates contradictions between actions and ideologies, and between the realities of our society and its democratic ideals" (p. 352) and how these lead to monovocal constructions of social studies knowledge.

In documenting their own collaborative attempts to engage in a reflective deconstruction of whiteness as racial text, Lalik and Hinchman (2000) tell us it is not an easy task. However, if white teachers construct a reality that does not acknowledge white privilege and the responsibility of white people in perpetuating "dysconscious racism," they will be unable to see multicultural education as a mandate for social change (hooks, 1992). In addition, acknowledging the presence of systemic racism and the role of "whiteness" in its existence is vital to developing a positive racial identity and critical to white engagement in interracial collaboration on issues of political and social change (King, 1991; Ladson-Billings, 1994, 1999; Sleeter, 1996). As white educators begin to understand the construction of their own racial identities, their role in perpetuating the gap between reality and ideology, and the significance of a social epistemology in the development of civic competency, "we can forge solid [interracial] alliances and coalitions to create a community of authentic, emancipatory, liberatory, critical, and transformative voices" (Baber, 1995, p. 352).

TRANSFORMATIVE KNOWING AND EPISTEMOLOGICAL RELEVANCE

From the perspective of transformative feminist theorists, knowledge is positional and reflects both the reality observed and the subjectivity of the knower (Code, 1991; Harding, 1991; Minnich, 1990). Despite its truth claims, knowledge is partial and predominantly a product of human interests, values, and normative assumptions. Consequently, conditions of race, class, gender, culture, and ethnicity influence and limit the construction as well as the use of knowledge (Code, 1991). Like feminist pedagogy, multicultural education involves students in the social construction and reconstruction of knowledge. Identified alternately as part of a transformative (Banks, 1995) or culturally relevant pedagogy (Ladson-Billings, 1995), the social construction of knowledge focuses on making connection between autobiographical experiences and the creation and articulation of new knowledge. Teachers encourage students to identify and question the situational context and "positionality of knowers as they construct their own interpretations of reality" (Banks, 1995, p. 153). Students look for complexity and multiplicity as they explore and make judgments about people, places, and events in light of their own experiences, histories, and perspectives (Ladson-Billings, 1995) and in anticipation of improving the social conditions of the lives of people within subordinated groups.

In reflecting on the teaching of core knowledge, knowledge construction, and the diversity of students' culturally informed perspectives, Banks

(1996) describes five types of knowledge that exist in contemporary class-rooms: personal and cultural, popular, mainstream academic, school, and transformative academic knowledge. Transformative knowledge consists of previously marginalized facts, paradigms, and interpretations that challenge, expand on, and "substantially revise" mainstream academic knowledge (Banks, 1996, p. 9). The work of a number of social studies researchers (Barton, 1995; Dimitriadis, 2000; Epstein, in press, 1997; Seixas, 1993, 1997) furthers our understanding of how these knowledges shape students' social studies experiences. Students come to school primed with knowledge gleaned from family stories, neighborhood wisdom, the media, and prior school experiences. They use these sets of knowledge to filter school history and reach conclusions about its relevance to their own lives and its historical significance.

Evidence suggests, however, that most teachers are not asking students to tap into and/or critically explore their personal and cultural experiential knowledge nor their knowledge of popular culture in the construction of historical and social understanding (Dimitriadis, 2000; Downey & Levstik, 1991; Epstein, in press, 1997). Downey and Levstik (1991) ask social studies educators to address this unnatural bifurcation of student and family autobiographies and school history by exploring ways to braid personal and cultural history together into a more integrated school history. Levstik and Barton (1996) conclude that children across grade levels link history to personal issues and naturally use family stories as well as other personal connections to construct meaningful historical knowledge. And Seixas (1993, 1997) argues that family histories and experiences strongly influence the ways in which culturally diverse high school students frame historical content. Ironically, however, school history offers little to address the concerns, fears, and questions raised by students' family stories, and students fail to reflect critically on or to integrate family oral histories with mainstream school history (Seixas, 1993).

Using race as an analytical category, Epstein (in press, 1997) collected and analyzed qualitative data from fifth, eighth and eleventh grade urban African American and European American students' selection of pictures of historically significant people and events. She argues that as early as the fifth grade, historical perspectives are influenced by students' racial identities. Black youth attribute historical significance primarily to events and people who relate most directly to African American experiences with racism and oppression, are distrustful of traditional historical narratives, and attribute historical authority to family members, black teachers and black media. African American students question the principle of individual rights and characterize black-white relations as marked by black resistance to white supremacy. Concurrently, white students recognize that African Americans have been denied basic rights and freedoms; however, they generally avoid directly implicating white people, and they fail to grant historical significance to instances of racial violence. Like Darder (1991) and

O'Connor (1997), who found that successful and resilient Latino and African American students were culturally competent in both the dominant and their primary cultures, Epstein (1997) concludes that eleventh grade students construct a "double historical consciousness" or two perspectives on United States history—one mirrors traditional historical understandings as portrayed in history textbooks, and the other focuses on effects of and reactions to systemic racism.

From within a community center program, Dimitriadis (2000) reveals that popular culture's portrayals of the black experience can elicit African American youth's criticism of black history as it is managed and taught in public schools and that unlike school-taught black history, popular culture's portrayals of black history provide resources that generate group consciousness and energize reflective political action. Discrediting the discourse of "rights" generated in social studies classes, his student-participants used images of the Black Panthers as portrayed in the fictionalized cinematic representation, *Panther,* to critically explore viable responses to an impending Ku Klux Klan march in their Midwest city.

My own study (Santora, 1998b) of seventh grade social studies students' cross-cultural interaction within collaborative learning groups as they worked with primary source documents related to the contemporary movement of Latino people into the United States discloses a tension between the epistemologies of white middle class students' and their Hispanic peers. White middle class students' attribution of highest significance to teacher-distributed primary source documents can interfere with their ability to acknowledge and critically consider evidence provided from within Hispanic students' stores of personal and cultural knowledge. Echoing Seixas's (1993) call for the explicit teaching of common ground rules, rules of evidence and interpretation, and skills for understanding the relationship of their family and community stories to historical texts and Epstein's (in press) call for teachers to attend to the need for a more honest depiction of history, I stress the need for teachers to provide learning experiences that will assist students in developing the necessary dialogic and discipline-specific skills and attitudes[9] to exercise cross-cultural sensitivity alongside a critical interrogation of personal, cultural, mainstream academic, and transformative knowledge. In short, students themselves must engage the tension as well as the synergy that exists between unity and diversity within a spirit of civility in order to build what Pang, Gay and Stanley (1995) call expanded communities of transformative knowers.

While the primary concern of each of these researchers has been students' limited opportunity to interlace their own experiences and histories with those learned in school, Wineburg (1999), whose study lies outside the ideology of critical multiculturalism, warns us that students' historical thinking requires the bracketing of their own knowledge and experiences in order to understand people and events within the epistemological and cultural frameworks evidenced within their historical contexts. Recognizing that bracketing is but one way to view historical events, social studies educators who juxtapose school and student perspectives become aware of the need to teach students to value their experience and their histories as important sources of knowledge while encouraging them to think and interact with cultural humility in order that they might exercise cultural and historical understanding of multiple perspectives. Such student competencies alongside the need to honestly confront issues of race, class, gender and sexuality in social studies classrooms, are vital if students are to become active participants in cross-cultural communities of learners and empowered citizens in a cultural democracy.

Because education unavoidably privileges selected ways of knowing and forms of knowledge that favor some groups of students over others, incorporating multiple forms of social studies knowledge in critical ways implies that teachers must confront the dilemma that putting personal and cultural knowledge on the same plane with school knowledge can and will conflict with the beliefs of many about the foundations of knowledge. In the absence of more racially, ethnically, and gender-integrated representations of history in school texts, creating spaces for students to engage each other's perspectives is essential. Such an engagement can foster the growth of expanded communities of learning and contribute to the development of more culturally democratic social studies classrooms.[10]

DEVELOPING TRANSFORMATIVE, ACTION-ORIENTED TEACHING/LEARNING COMMUNITIES

Culturally relevant teaching and learning imply high expectations of both teachers and students and an authentic approach to learning that includes the use of students' personal, cultural, and indigenous knowledge[11] alongside transformative and mainstream academic scholarship (Asante, 1994; Banks, 1995, 1996, 1997; Harris, 1992; Keto, 1989; Kincheloe & Steinberg, 1997; Swartz, 1992, 1998). While researchers have done much to identify and label the challenges diversity poses for social studies education and have made a significant effort to translate their findings into practical suggestions, implementation has been extremely limited. Social studies educators have been particularly remiss in fostering students' ability to interact in culturally affirming and socially responsive ways. Broadening our ideas about what constitutes appropriate social studies content while focusing that content on the community, school and classroom appears to offer possibilities for bridging students' different epistemologies, expanding their perspectives of their own and others' realities, and empowering them as active agents in reconstructing the conditions of schooling. Ethnographic action research done within the context of individual classes suggests that shifting some of the focus of social studies programs in more communally introspective ways will help teachers and students develop a critical understanding of the ways in which their own and each others' cultural and racial identities have been historically and socially constructed (Nelson-Barber & Harrison, 1996; Sheets & Hollins, 1999; Steinberg & Kincheloe, 1998). Responding to this need Kincheloe and Steinberg (Kincheloe 1989/1991, 1991, 1993; Villaverde & Kincheloe, 1998; Steinberg & Kincheloe, 1998) advocate engagement in autobiographic, ethnographic and historiographic research as means for both teachers and students to situate themselves culturally and historically within existing power structures and to recognize the interconnection of their lives through the cycles of oppression that constitute their shared histories. Given the development of their collective and critical consciousness, they can work together to forge more culturally responsive and authentic learning experiences and ultimately to assume social responsibility for improving the conditions of their own and others' lives.

Teachers Learning from Students, Communities, and Families

Much of the multicultural education literature abounds with practical suggestions or techniques for addressing cultural diversity in schools and classrooms (see, e.g., Bennett, 1999; Schniedewind & Davidson, 1997; Tiedt & Tiedt, 1995). Little emphasis, however, has been given to the need for teachers to situate themselves culturally and racially as "gatekeepers" (see Thornton, 1994) of social studies knowledge. Recently a group of studies has emerged that more authentically addresses Ladson-Billings (1994) concerns about the importance of such self-reflective understanding. These studies (Baldwin, 1996; Mehan et al., 1995; Moll, Amanti, Neff, & Gonzalez, 1992; Olmedo, 1997a; Patterson, Baldwin, Gonzales, Guadarrama, & Keith, 1999; Torres-Guzman, Mercado, Quintero, & Viera, 1994) use teachers' and students' engagement in autobiographical and ethnographic research and oral history as ways for teachers to learn about their students' indigenous knowledge and use that knowledge to design experiences that will help prepare students to understand and resist oppression based on differences in race, class, gender, perceived ability and sexual orientation.

For teachers to know nothing about their students beyond their classroom performance presents a major roadblock to student learning (Delpit, 1995). According to Mehan and his associates (1995), teachers must modify both their discursive patterns and their curriculum. They need to develop an understanding of their own "dysconscious racism," to bring them into conformity with the demographics of their classroom. Moll and his colleagues (as cited in Mehan et al., 1995) have found that when teachers and researchers work together ethnographically to study the cultural patterns and "funds of knowledge" that exist in the community(ies) served by their school, develop units of study for student inquiry about their community, and modify classroom structures to include community members sharing their knowledge, both teachers and students gain. Through their work, teachers involved in "funds of knowledge" research projects develop an understanding of the community and an appreciation for its rich cultural resources. Students are pleased when the school validates their parents' knowledge and tacit understandings. "Funds of knowledge" projects also help teachers understand the importance of the knowledge exchanged through social and familial networks to the maintenance of households in Mexican American communities (Torres-Guzman et al., 1994). Olmedo (1997a, 1997b) suggests that "funds of knowledge" gained from students' oral histories, in addition to providing varied perspectives from which students can construct historical knowledge, can also be used to address the disjunction between school knowledge and personal and cultural knowledge. Patterson (1999) reports that when classroom teachers study their students' families' "funds of knowledge," they are provided with authentic experiences that challenge the "dysconscious racism" embedded in their professional practices and school cultures and are energized to seek changes in school policy as advocates for their students and their students' families. Baldwin (1996) found that when teachers' develop an understanding of students' language, culture, experience and voices as essential elements within their classes, this knowledge changes the way both teachers and students view power and collaboration in the classroom and ultimately alters their perceptions of what it means to be active participants in a cultural democracy.

The "Conjoint Communicated Experience" and Culturally Democratic Community-building

Many models of transformative education exist within the field of multicultural education. Some have been the subjects and objects of research; others have not. Few have been part of a social studies program; most have emerged from within language and literacy, ESL, and bilingual education. While it can reap huge rewards in terms of developing students' cross-cultural and interracial understanding and their expanded sense of community, engaging students in needed dialogic experiences that involve a plurality of divergent as well as convergent, dissonant as well as consonant voices whose meanings condition each other adds to the complexity of social studies education. Together with student risk-taking, cross-cultural interactions such as these necessarily imply a great deal of teacher risk-taking as well as a rethinking of the epistemological foundations of most white middle class teachers' beliefs about classroom learning. Facilitating such dialogic experiences demands teachers possess the ability to navigate both within and across students' race-, class-, and gender-mediated perspectives. In addition, student engagement in cross-cultural dialogue necessitates teachers' willingness and ability to provide a forum in which students can consider and confront systematic injustice. Stanley (1992) argues that such engagements require a "pragmatic competence" that will allow participants to work on transformative projects both from within their own and through others' world views.

Three research projects distinguish themselves for their descriptions of students and teachers engaging in cross-cultural dialogue as a form of social praxis—a way of changing ideas about what constitutes culturally relevant education. By shifting a literature curriculum to a curriculum of identity politics, Nelson-Barber and Harrison (1996) found that opportunities to explore personally relevant social issues of students' own choosing using a variety of literary and rhetorical genres written from a plurality of perspectives encouraged culturally diverse high school students to engage in action-oriented dialogue. Students readily and competently used issue-laden texts in conjunction with their own life experiences to demythologize notions of identity as singular and static and to engage in identity politics as a form of resistance to oppressive representations and "implicit societal standards" that threaten one's affirmation of cultural difference. The need to untangle and "decipher" their misunderstandings ultimately enhanced students' ability to see each other's perspectives more clearly and incorporate them in the development of more sophisticated understandings. Nelson-Barber and Harrison attribute this curriculum's success to providing a classroom context that positions students as "insiders" in the educational process and encourages them to "forge a connection with one another" (p. 262) that does not require them to hide or relinquish their identity.

When Baldwin[12] (1996) employed a multicultural focus in her American Studies class, her students became ethnographers of their own cultures, the culture of the high school, and "other cultures." Students' questions, problem-posing, suggestions, and dialogue recursively worked to define the specifics of a dynamic curriculum, class activities, presentations, interpretations, action-oriented responses, and assessment. Because the class was socioculturally divided between the "Hoodrats" and "Beverly Hills" the importance of forming "a viable social community before [students] could become a viable learning community" (Ladson-Billings, 1994, cited in Baldwin, 1996, p. 147) became imperative. Discussions of personal experiences and their own stereotypical thinking about race and class differences played a significant role in shaping student dialogue about class activities and in developing a more cohesive learning community. Students became concerned about how they contributed to their own oppression. Toward the end of the semester, students found that four of the key elements evident in videotaped class discussions—individualism, communication, feelings, and involvement—were responsible for forging the unity that developed within their class. According to Baldwin, her teacher-research demonstrated the interconnectedness of human relationships, curricular decisions and pedagogical practices.

Altering the normal relationship between teachers, researchers, and students, students involved in the Bronx Middle School Collaborative[13] conducted ethnographic research in the community in partnership with a teacher and university researcher (Torres-Guzman et al., 1994). Students, teachers, and researchers used their shared reflections on data to generate new understandings of what constitutes a successful educational experience for Puerto Rican Latino(a) youth. Writing and involvement in conference presentations contributed enormously to their literacy competencies. Such empowering forms of inquiry and presentation encourage the development of transformative learning environments, a sense of solidarity that transcends differences in culture and academic ability, and an ethic of care and responsibility for one's own communities.

Social Action: Building Competencies for Citizenship in a Cultural Democracy

Several programs across the country have provided students whose primary language is not English with opportunities to learn through cross-cultural dialogue and social action (e.g., "A Report," 1995; Hollins, King, & Hayman, 1994; Walsh, 1996). For the past eight years, multiethnic bilingual education students at Oxnard High School in California working with Bill Terrazas, Jr. have challenged the educational system's irrelevant curriculum and racist practices through their student activist group (SCaLD, 1996). These students are known throughout the state for their advocacy of cultural and linguistic democracy, a caring, critical, and transformative pedagogy and real-life perspectives. The sources of their empowerment are the collectivity and solidarity of their engagement against social injustice in the school and the community.

Environmentally related social action projects have emerged from the classes of teachers who have emancipatory and transformative visions of science, social studies, and language and literacy education (e.g., Bidlack & Bidlack, 1993; Scharle, 1993; Torres-Guzman et al., 1994). Perhaps the most significant in terms of multicultural education is a project undertaken by alternative school students as part of the Intercambio Research Project. This project is of interest to social studies educators because it empowers Latino(a) science students (the Toxic Avengers) as active, collaborative, and competent citizens by providing first hand experiences with government as students strive to create a healthier community environment (Torres-Guzman et al., 1994). Projects such as these provide opportunities for students to use cross-cultural dialogue, knowledge construction, reflection, and action-oriented responses as means of achieving self-empowerment, solidarity of purpose, collective agency, and an integration of language and citizenship literacies with community action.

While most of the research has been historical in nature, drama has also been advanced as a powerful and authentic tool for encouraging cross-cultural dialogue about real problems, cooperative work, and collective and emancipatory social action (Chilcoat & Ligon, 1998; Gay & Hanley, 1999; Santora, 1998a). Drama pedagogy, as described by Gay and Hanley, is a process that includes theme selection, improvisation, play writing, rehearsals, production, performance, and reflection. When students become involved in a theatrical production related to issues of race, class, and gender, they bring to the production process their unique experiences and abilities, their cultural baggage, and their assumptions, beliefs and values. As a dramatic performance that centers on students' experiences develops, students become aware of and sensitive to the perspectives of their peers, and they use this awareness to engage in collective agency that cuts across boundaries of race, class and gender. Drama, often marginalized by the social studies and other school disciplines, "allows students to release and shape new meanings, empowering them to create new knowledge that may transform their own lives as well as the lives of others" (Chilcoat & Ligon, 1998, p. 540). As demonstrated in the Bryn Mawr Summer School for Women Workers and the Mississippi Freedom Schools, theater productions liberate the soul by developing in their organizers and players a consciousness that takes responsibility for the narration and publication of social injustices experienced in one's own community (Chilcoat & Ligon, 1998; Santora, 1998a).

Each of these successive descriptions of transformative learning and teaching brings us to a deeper understanding of what it means to involve oneself and facilitate the involvement of one's students in collaborative cross-cultural acts of social praxis. Teachers must actively and honestly engage themselves in leaning about the cultures of their students and white teachers need to do this with an understanding of their own complicity in the subordination and oppression of people of color. All teachers need the will to confront the resistance of students, parents, colleagues and administrators who wish to maintain the status quo. Furthermore, they must have the desire and the ability to maintain their classrooms as places where students equitably, respectfully, and responsibly engage in critical cross-cultural dialogue about significant social issues. Finally, teachers must actively commit themselves to the belief that social studies education appropriately engages students in collective research leading to social action that responds to the inequality and social injustice that students see in their own lives.

CONCLUSIONS

Through this review I have sought to complicate some of the dichotomies propagated in educational discourse as they relate to multicultural social studies. Unity and diversity, emotion and reason, the private and public aspects of students' lives, and teaching and learning become complementary conditions for creating classroom communities that engage in dialogic thinking and see social studies education as preparation for and practice in using the beliefs, attitudes, abilities, and knowledge needed to maintain transformative, socially responsive citizenship in a culturally pluralistic society. Dichotomies, springing from a western political discourse and epistemological dualisms, have been successfully challenged by teachers, researchers and students working collectively to find responses to the nagging issues of race, class, culture and gender. By shifting emphases to students' identities, diversity, group consciousness, the uncertainty of knowledge and social agency, educators who weave together the ethical, moral, critical and social goals of education have succeeded in expanding the communities to which students willingly, cooperatively, and actively commit themselves.

Social studies education, however, lacks research describing students' engagement with cross-cultural dialogue in social studies classrooms. Cohen and her colleagues (Cohen, 1986/1994; Cohen & Lotan, 1995), who have studied student status conditions for years, inside and outside classrooms, and have worked with teachers to design intervention strategies that promote full participation in cooperative learning groups (see Cohen, Lotan, Scarloss, & Arellano, 1999), still find these strategies, designed to upset student expectations for (in)competence, fall apart in many classrooms. Bickmore (1993) and Santora (1997) have expressed similar concerns with respect to both whole class instruction and cooperative group learning in social studies classes. More recently, studies have enabled us to attend to the failure of many white teachers to acknowledge their own "dysconscious racism" and its role in alienating and promoting the alienation of students of color. However, such studies are only a part of a more complex puzzle. Until we understand more about how and why students are culturally and racially marginalized by each other and the classroom conditions within which this marginalization occurs, intervention becomes difficult.

Freedman, Simons, Kalnin, Casareno and the M-Class teams across the nation (1999) suggest that research collaboratives composed of teachers and university researchers can penetrate the barriers to teachers and students' engagement in cross-cultural dialogue, and social praxis with teacher research. As a teacher researcher, Baldwin (1996) encourages us to involve students in our research efforts by urging them to share their perceptions and experiences with each other as well as with their teachers both as a means of inquiry and a way in which they can transcend their own differences. This is essential to defining their public lives in relation to each other and engaging in acts of social praxis. From a social studies teaching perspective, this would necessitate a heightened emphasis on student and teacher identities, community building, engagement with multiple perspectives, and the exploration of culturally relevant issues from relational, ethical and moral perspectives. Such a program would require that teachers focus, in holistic and authentic ways, on the attitudes, skills and knowledge needed to engage in sensitive and critical cross-cultural dialogue and navigate in the public sphere to accomplish collective goals. This must become a major focus in social studies education if we are to foster the growth and development of expanded, democratic and transformative communities of culturally diverse adults.

NOTES

1.   Curriculum confrontations are not a new experience for social studies educators. Conflicts and adjustments within society and between nations have repeatedly meant renewed examination of what children learn in history and the social sciences. The responses within the field have been outlined in a number of books and articles (see, e.g., Davis, 1996; Hertzburg, 1981; Jenness, 1990; Nash, Crabtree, & Dunn, 1997; Stanley & Nelson, 1994).

2.   Because of a number of recent reviews of multicultural teacher education, I have included research related to teacher education only as it relates to research focusing on a precollegiate context. (see Grant, 1994; Ladson-Billings, 1995, 1999; Zeichner & Joeft, 1996).

3.   Messner (1994) uses the term "masculinist Afrocentrism" to refer to a militant assertion of black manhood as one of its central tenets. Afrocentrism as an ideology also addresses the needs of black males for strong black male leadership. An example of this would be the way in which large numbers of black men speak of the importance of respect.

4.   "Womanist" was first used by Alice Walker to describe Black feminists who were "critically" concerned about the interests of all people, men and women of all races and classes (Ladson-Billings, 1996). Women within this tradition acknowledge having little or no experience with "femininity" as a social and cultural ideal reserved primarily for middle and upper class women.

5.   "On the margins," a term coined by bell hooks (1984), is a social position that provides black women a unique standpoint from which they can more clearly understand, deconstruct and resist the complexity of power and its role in maintaining racial oppression.

6.   Here, I have amended Wills' interpretation to include the effects of racism on the perpetrators as well as the victims (see Freire, 1970/1981, p. 42).

7.   My use of the term Hispanic is consistent with the way these students, whose parents and sometimes themselves came from a multitude of Latin American nations, referred to themselves. The term Asian is used to refer to a collective of Chinese-American and Japanese-American students, and European American refers to white, non-Hispanic students whose heritages encompass a range of European cultures.

8.   Also see Cohen (1986/1994) and Cohen and her colleagues (Cohen, Lotan, Scarloss, & Arellano, 1999) for a more complete description of how equal status interaction is promoted in the groupwork context.

9.   While they must be taught and learned in integrated, holistic and authentic ways and can in no way be separated from content, these skills and attitudes might include, for example, those considered under the headings of reflective inquiry, equal status participation (see Cohen, 1986/1994), genuine sensitivity and receptivity to narrative, culturally distinct voices, communicative virtues (see Burbules & Rice, 1991), a critical consciousness (see Kincheloe, 1993, 1997), ethical and moral reasoning, social responsibility, civic participation, content-specific understandings, and multicultural competencies. More complex than the sum of critical thinking and communication skills, this set of skills would include the ability to suspend judgment, accept uncertainty and reject absolutes, draw others into a discussion in search of alternative perspectives, articulate varied perspectives, reflect on each other's evidence and arguments, understand how others might reach different conclusions, engage in reflective self-criticism, and re-evaluate one's own arguments in a spirit of openmindedness. These abilities would also encompass an understanding of when and how to seek clarification, query the sources of one's evidence, solicit contextual information, identify positionality, and shift one's own position. Students who are involved in cross-cultural interaction must be able to engage each other dialogically to seek common ground, articulate differences, weigh alternatives in light of democratic values, delineate sources and effects of power, and integrate experiential with textual information. For dialogic thought to be translated into collective empowerment, students need the ability to draw multiple perspectives together in consensus-building and action-oriented ways.

10.   As a pedagogy of hope and possibility, critical multiculturalists recognize that no one type of education will appeal to all teachers, parents, and students. However, they do believe that it is important to provide students with the emancipatory tools through which they can, if they choose, expand their communities and their horizons. As issues surface that highlight particular world views, it is important that students have an opportunity to discuss these issues with each other, gain from a reciprocal exchange of knowledge, and seek common ground and mutual understanding. Solidarity may not be possible, critical thinking may be thwarted, and conflict may become bitter. These are the risks about which Ellsworth (1989/ 1992) and Baber (1995) warn and those to which Stanley (1992) and Pang, Gay, and Stanley (1995) attempt response. Cross-cultural dialogue is an essential part of students' developing understanding of both the richness of diversity and the challenges it poses within a democratic society; it is the way through which students can engage the tension between unity and diversity. It is also the route through which they can learn to respect and protect culturally diverse people's rights and dignities (Pang et al., 1995). It is not necessary for educators to relinquish utopian perspectives because they create dissonance within the classroom and the community; it is necessary that they facilitate students' engagement with dissonance in both respectful and positive ways—ways that include both self-examination and critical reflection—that place "the goals of the pluralistic community above individuality" (Pang et al., p. 326).

11.   Indigenous knowledge is that knowledge that emerges out of the lived experiences of subordinated people and is transmitted over time within a specific cultural or geographic location. It helps people cope with their sociological and agricultural environments. Indigenous knowledge has traditionally been subjugated within the Eurocentric school experience (Kincheloe & Steinberg, 1997).

12.   Baldwin was an ESL teacher teaching an American Studies elective in a Texas high school.

13. The Bronx Middle School Collaborative is part of the Intercambio Research Project. The Intercambio Research Project has five sites in New York and Puerto Rico with the common goal of seeking alternative ways of "seeing and acting on the ... reality of schooling for Puerto Rican Latino children" (Torres-Guzman et al., p. 105).

REFERENCES

Almarza, D.J. (1997). *The construction of whiteness in history classrooms: A case study of seventh and eight-grade [sic] Mexican-American students.* Unpublished doctoral dissertation, University of Iowa.

Arnot, M., & Dillabough, J. (1999). Feminist politics and democratic values in education. *Curriclum Inquiry, 29*(2), 159–189.

Asante, M.K. (1994). *Classica Africa.* Philadelphia: Temple University Press.

Baber, C.R. (1995). Leaders of color as catalysts for community building in a multicultural society. *Theory and Research in Social Education, 23*(4), 342–354.

Baldwin, S.C. (1996). *Developing multicultural awareness among high school students through inquiry.* Unpublished doctoral dissertation, Texas A&M University.

Banks, J.A. (1995). Transformative challenges to the social science disciplines: Implications for social studies teaching and learning. *Theory and Research in Social Education, 23*(1), 2–20.

Banks, J.A. (1996). *Multicultural education, transformative knowledge and action: Historical and contemporary perspectives.* New York: Teachers College Press.

Banks, J.A. (1997). *Educating citizens in a multicultural society.* New York: Teachers College Press.

Barton, K.C. (1995, April). *"My mom taught me": The situated nature of historical understanding.* Paper presented at the American Educational Research Association, San Francisco, CA.

Bennett, C.I. (1999). *Comprehensive multicultural education: Theory and practice.* Boston: Allyn Bacon.

Bernard-Powers, J. (1996). Guest editorial: Engendering social studies: Perspectives, texts, and teaching. *Theory and Research in Social Education, 24*(1), 2–7.

Bickmore, K. (1993). Learning inclusion/inclusion in learning: Citizenship education in a pluralistic society. *Theory and Research in Social Education, 21*(4), 341–384.

Bidlack, C., & Bidlack, R.W. (1993). The magic of Elsah Creek. *Social Education, 57*(7), 372–380.

Bloom, L.R. (1998). The politics of difference and multicultural feminism: Reconceptualizing education for democracy. *Theory and Research in Social Education, 26*(1), 30–49.

Boyle-Baise, M. (1995). The role of the European American scholar. *Theory and Research in Social Education, 23*(4), 332–341.

Brantlinger, E.A. (1994). The social class embeddedness of middle school students' thinking about teachers. *Theory into Practice, 33*(3), 191–198.

Burbules, N.C., & Rice, S. (1991). Dialogue across differences: Continuing the conversation. *Harvard Educational Review, 61*(4), 293–416.

Chilcoat, G.W., & Ligon, J.A. (1998). Theatre as an emancipatory tool: Classroom drama in the Mississippi Freedom Schools. *Journal of Curriculum Studies, 30*(5), 515–543.

Code, L. (1991). *What can she know? Feminist theory and the construction of knowledge.* Ithaca, NY: Cornell University Press.

Cohen, E.G. (1986/1994). *Designing groupwork: Strategies for the heterogeneous classroom* (2nd ed.). New York: Teachers College Press.

Cohen, E.G., & Lotan, R.A. (1995). Producing equal-status interaction in the heterogeneous classroom. *American Educational Research Journal, 32*(1), 99–120.

Cohen, E.G., Lotan, R.A., Scarloss, B.A., & Arellano, A.R. (1999). Complex Instruction: Equity in cooperative learning classrooms. *Theory into Practice, 38*(2), 80–85.

Cornbleth, C., & Waugh, S. (1995). *The great speckled bird: Multicultural politics and education policymaking.* New York: St. Martin's Press.

Crocco, M.S. (1998). Crafting a culturally responsive pedagogy in an age of educational standards. *Theory and Research in Social Education, 26*(1), 123–129.

Darder, A. (1991). *Culture and power in the classroom: Critical foundations for bicultural education.* New York: Bergin and Garvey.

Darder, A. (1997). Creating the conditions for cultural democracy in the classroom. In A. Darder, R.D. Torres, & H. Gutiérrez (Eds.), *Latinos and education: A critical reader.* New York: Routledge.

Davidson, A.L. (1996). Making and molding identity in schools. Albany: State University of New York Press.

Davis, O.L. (1996). *NCSS in retrospect.* Washington, DC: National Council for the Social Studies.

Delpit, L. (1995). *Other people's children: White teachers, students of color, and other cultural conflicts in the classroom.* New York: New Press.

Dewey, J. (1916). *Democracy and education.* New York: Free Press.

Dimitriadis, G. (2000). "Making history go" at a local community center: Popular culture and the construction of historical knowledge among African American youth. *Theory and Research in Social Education, 28*(1), 40–64.

DiPardo, A., & Fehn, B. (2000). Depoliticizing multicultural education: The return to normalcy in a predominantly white high school. *Theory and Research in Social Education, 28*(2), 170–192.

Downey, M.T., & Levstik, L.S. (1991). Teaching and learning history. In J.P. Shaver (Ed.), *Handbook of research on social studies teaching and learning* (pp. 400–410). New York: Macmillan.

Ehrenberg, R.G., Goldhaber, D.D., & Brewer, D.J. (1995). Do teachers' race, gender, and ethnicity matter? Evidence from the National Education Longitudinal Study of 1988. *Industrial and Labor Relations Review, 48*, 547–561.

Ellsworth, (1989/1992). Why doesn't this feel empowering? Working through the impressive myths of critical pedagogy. In C. Luke & J. Gore (Eds.), *Feminisms and critical pedagogy* (pp. 297–324). New York Routledge.

Epstein, T.L. (in press). Race, research and history education. *Theory into Practice.*

Epstein, T.L. (1997). Sociocultural approaches to young people's historical understanding. *Social Education, 61*(1), 28–31.

Feiman-Nemser, S., & Remillard, J. (1996). Perspectives on learning to teach. In F.B. Murray (Ed.), *The teacher educator's handbook: Building a knowledge base for the preparation of teachers* (pp. 63–91). San Francisco: Jossey-Bass.

Foley, D. (1990). *Learning capitalist culture: Deep in the heart of Tejas.* Philadelphia: University of Pennsylvania Press.

Freedman, S.W., Simons, E.R., Kalnin, J.S., Casareno, A. & the M-Class Teams (1999). *Inside city schools: Investigating multicultural classrooms.* New York: Teachers College Press and the National Council of Teachers of English.

Freire, P. (1970/1981). *Pedagogy of the oppressed.* New York: Continuum.

Gay, G. (1994). *At the essence of learning: Multicultural education.* West Lafayette, IN: Kappa Delta Pi.

Gay, G., & Hanley, M. S. (1999). Multicultural empowerment in middle school social studies through drama pedagogy. *The Clearing House, 72*(6), 364–370.

Gilligan, C. (1982/1993). *In a different voice: Psychological theory and women's development.* Cambridge, MA: Harvard University Press.

Giroux, H. (1991). *Postmodernism, feminism, and cultural politics: Redrawing educational boundaries.* Albany: State University of New York Press.

Gordon, B.M. (1995). Knowledge construction, competing critical theories, and education. In J.A. Banks & C.A. McGee Banks (Eds.), *Handbook of research on multicultural education.* New York: Macmillan.

Grant, C.A. (1994). Best practices in teacher preparation for urban schools: Lessons from the multicultural teacher education literature. *Action in Teacher Education, 16*(3), 1–18.

Grant, C.A. (Ed.). (1999). *Multicultural research: A reflective engagement with race, class, gender and sexual orientation.* London: Falmer Press.

Grant, C.A., & Sachs, J.M. (1995). Multicultural education and postmodernism: Movement toward a dialogue. In B. Kanpol & P. McLaren (Eds.), *Critical multiculturalism: Uncommon voices in a common struggle.* Westport, CN: Bergin and Garvey.

Harding, S. (1991). *Whose science? Whose knowledge? Thinking from women's lives.* Ithaca, NY: Cornell University Press.

Harris, M.D. (1992). Africentrism and curriculum: Concepts, issues and prospects. *Journal of Negro Education, 61*(3), 301–316.

Hertzburg, H.W. (1981). *Social studies reform: 1880–1980.* Boulder, CO: Social Science Education Consortium.

Hill Collins, P. (1990). *Black feminist thought: Knowledge, consciousness and the politics of empowerment.* London: Routledge.

Hollingsworth, S., Gallego, M., & Standerford, N.S. (1995). Integrative social studies for urban schools: A case for multiple literacies. *Theory and Research in Social Education, 23*(3), 204–233.

Hollins, E.R., King, J.E., & Hayman, W.C. (Eds.). (1994). *Teaching diverse populations: Formulating a knowledge base.* Albany: State University of New York Press.

hooks, b. (1984). *Feminist theory: From margin to center.* Boston: South End Press.

hooks, b. (1992). Representing whiteness in the black imagination. In L. Grossberg, C. Nelson, & P. Treichler (Eds.), *Cultural studies.* New York: Routledge.

hooks, b. (1994). *Teaching to transgress: Education as the practice of freedom.* New York: Routledge.

Jenness, D. (1990). *Making sense of social studies.* Washington, DC: National Council for the Social Studies.

Johnson, T., & Avery, P.G. (1999). The power of the press: A content and discourse analysis of the United States History Standards as presented in selected newspapers. *Theory and Research in Social Education, 27*(4), 447–471.

Keto, C.T. (1989). *The Africa-centered perspective of history and social sciences in the twenty-first century.* Blackwood, NJ: K. A. Publications.

Kincheloe, J.L. (1989/1991). *Getting beyond the facts: Teaching social studies in the late twentieth century.* New York: Peter Lang.

Kincheloe, J.L. (1991). *Teachers as researchers: Qualitative inquiry as a path to empowerment.* New York: Falmer.

Kincheloe, J.L. (1993). *Toward a critical politics of teacher thinking.* Westport, CT: Bergin and Garvey.

Kincheloe, J.L., & Steinberg, S.R. (1997). *Changing multiculturalism.* Philadelphia: Open University Press.

King, J.E. (1991). Dysconscious racism: Ideology, identity, and the miseducation of teachers. *Journal of Negro Education, 60*(2), 133–145.

King, J.E. (1995). Culture-centered knowledge, black studies, curriculum transformation and social action. In J.A. Banks & C.A. McGee Banks (Eds.), *Handbook of research on multicultural education.* New York: Macmillan.

Kornfeld, J., & Goodman, J. (1998). Melting the glaze: Exploring student responses to liberatory social studies. *Theory into Practice, 37*(4), 306–313.

Ladson-Billings, G. (1992). The multicultural mission: Unity and diversity. *Social Education, 56*(5), 308–311.

Ladson-Billings, G. (1994). *The dreamkeepers: Successful teachers of African American children.* San Francisco: Jossey-Bass.

Ladson-Billings, G. (1995). Multicultural teacher education: Research, practice and policy. In J.A. Banks & C.A. McGee Banks (Eds.), *Handbook of research on multicultural education* (pp. 747–759). New York: Macmillan.

Ladson-Billings, G. (1996). Lifting as we climb: The womanist tradition in multicultural education. In J.A. Banks (Ed.), *Multicultural education, transformative knowledge and action: Historical and contemporary perspectives* (pp. 179–200). New York: Teachers College Press.

Ladson-Billings, G. (1999). Preparing teachers for diverse student populations: A critical race theory perspective. In A. Iran-Nejad & P.D. Pearson (Eds.), *Review of research in education* (pp. 211–248). Washington, DC: American Educational Research Association.

Lalik, R., & Hinchman, K.A. (2000, April). *Examining our constructions of race in teacher education: Beyond empathy and other oppressions of white liberalism.* Paper presented at the American Educational Research Association, New Orleans, LA.

Lather, P. (1991). *Getting smart: Feminist research and pedagogy with/in the postmodern.* New York: Routledge.

Levstik, L. (1997). "Any history is someone's history": Listening to multiple voices from the past. *Social Education, 61*(1), 48–51.

Levstik, L.S., & Barton, K.C. (1996). 'They still use some of their past': Historical salience in elementary children's chronological thinking. *Journal of Curriculum Studies, 28*(5), 531–576.

Loewen, J.W. (1995). *Lies my teacher told me: Everything your American history textbook got wrong.* New York: The New Press.

McIntosh, P. (1988/1997). White privilege: Unpacking the invisible knapsack. In B. Schneider (Ed.), *Race: An anthology in the first person.* New York: Crown Trade Paperbacks.

McLaren, P. (1997). *Revolutionary multiculturalism: Pedagogies of dissent for the new millennium*. Boulder, CO: Westview.

Mehan, H., Lintz, A., Okamoto, D., & Wills, J.D. (1995). Ethnographic studies of multicultural education in classrooms and schools. In J.A. Banks & C.A. McGee Banks (Eds.), *Handbook of research on multicultural education* (pp. 129–144). New York: Macmillan.

Messner, M.A. (1994). White men misbehaving: Feminism, Afrocentrism and the promise of a critical standpoint. *Social Studies Review, 33*(2), 36–41.

Middleton, S. (1993). A postmodern pedagogy for the sociology of women's education. In M. Arnot & K. Weiler (Eds.), *Feminism and social justice in education* (pp. 124–145). London: Falmer.

Minnich, E.K. (1990). *Transforming knowledge*. Philadelphia: Temple University Press.

Moll, L., Amanti, C., Neff, D., & Gonzalez, N. (1992). Funds of knowledge for teaching: Using a qualitative approach to connect homes and classrooms. *Theory into Practice, 31*, 132–141.

Nash, G.B., Crabtree, C., & Dunn, R.E. (1997). *History on trial: Culture wars and the teaching of the past*. New York: Knopf.

Nelson-Barber, S., & Harrison, M. (1996). Bridging the politics of identity in a multicultural classroom. *Theory into Practice, 35*(4), 256–263.

Nieto, S. (1996). *Affirming diversity: The sociopolitical context of multicultural education*. White Plains, NY: Longman.

Noddings, N. (1992). Social studies and feminism. *Theory and Research in Social Education, 20*(3), 230–241.

O'Connor, C. (1997). Dispositions toward (collective) struggle and educational resilience in the inner city: A case analysis of six African American high school students. *American Educational Research Journal, 34*(4), 593–629.

Olmedo, I.M. (1997a). Voices of our past: Using oral history to explore funds of knowledge within a Puerto Rican family. *Anthropology of Education Quarterly, 28*(4), 550–573.

Olmedo, I.M. (1997b). Family oral histories for multicultural education curriculum perspectives. *Urban Education, 32*(1), 42–62.

Palonsky, S.B. (1995). Reaction: Reconsidering the social studies. *Theory and Research in Social Education, 23*(1), 26–30.

Pang, V.O., Gay, G., & Stanley, W.B. (1995). Expanding conceptions of community and civic competence for a multicultural society. *Theory and Research in Social Education, 23*(4), 302–331.

Patterson, L., Baldwin, S., Gonzales, R., Guadarrama, I., & Keith, L. (1999). Claiming our ignorance and making new friends: A different approach to family involvement. *Networks: An On-line Journal for Teacher Research, 2*(2). [On-line Journal] http://www.oise.utoronto.ca/~ctd/networks/journal/Vol%202(2).1999 oct/article1.html.

Preissle-Goetz, J., & LeCompte, M.D. (1991). Qualitative research in social studies education. In J.A. Shaver (Ed.), *Handbook of research on social studies teaching and learning*. New York: Macmillan.

Provenzo, E.F. (1990). *Religious fundamentalism and American education: The battle for the public schools*. Albany: State University of New York Press.

Ramirez, M., & Casteñeda, A. (1974). *Cultural democracy, bicognitive development and education*. New York: Academic Press.

A report on "New places." An international research project: Making schools better places for newcomers. (1995). *Orillero: Newsletter of De Orilla a Orilla, 1*, 1–3. [On-line newsletter] http://orillas-web.upr.clu.edu/Orilleros/places.html.

Santora, E.D. (1997). *An ethnographic case study of the sociocultural contexts of collaborative groupwork in a multicultural, seventh grade social studies/language arts core class.* Unpublished doctoral dissertation, The Pennsylvania State University, State College.

Santora, E.D. (1998a). Bridging differences in culture and class: The Bryn Mawr Summer School for women workers in industry. In L.M. Burlbaw (Ed.), *Curriculum history, 1998.* College Station, TX: Society for the Study of Curriculum History.

Santora, E.D. (1998b, November). *Discourses, dualisms, dialogues, and diversity: Roots of and routes to the empowerment of culturally diverse students within collaborative groups.* Paper presented at the College and University Faculty Association Annual Meeting, Anaheim, CA.

Santora, E.D. (1999, April). *Sociocultural context of collaborative groupwork in a multicultural seventh grade social studies/language arts core class.* Paper presented at the American Educational Research Association, Montreal, Canada.

Santora, E.D. (2000, April). *Weaving the tapestry of classroom culture: The personal, professional and pedagogical.* Paper presented at the American Educational Research Association, New Orleans, LA.

Scharle, C.M. (1993). The lesson that flew: A political-action primer for students. *English Journal, 82*(7), 39–43.

Schniedewind, N. & Davidson, E. (1997). *Open minds to equality: Learning activities to promote race, sex, class, and age equity.* Boston: Allyn Bacon.

Seixas, P. (1993). Historical understanding among adolescents in a multicultural setting. *Curriculum Inquiry, 23*(3), 301–327.

Seixas, P. (1997). Mapping the terrain of historical significance. *Social Education, 61*(1), 22–27.

Sheets, R.H., & Hollins, E.R. (Eds.). (1999). *Racial and ethnic identity in school practices.* Mahwah, NJ: Lawrence Erlbaum.

Sleeter, C.E. (1996). *Multicultural education as social activism.* Albany: State University of New York Press.

Sleeter, C.E., & Grant, C.A. (1994). *Making choices for multicultural education: Five approaches to race, class, and gender* (2nd ed.). New York: Macmillan.

Stanley, W.B. (1992). *Curriculum for utopia: Social reconstructionism and critical pedagogy in the postmodern era.* Albany: State University of New York Press.

Stanley, W.B., & Nelson, J.L. (1994). The foundations of social education in historical contexts. In R.A. Martusewicz & W.M. Reynolds (Eds.), *Inside out: Contemporary critical perspectives in education* (pp. 265–284). New York: St. Martin's Press.

Steinberg, S.R., & Kincheloe, J.L. (Eds.). (1998). *Students as researchers: Creating classrooms that matter.* New York: Falmer.

Stone, L. (1996). Feminist political theory: Contributions to a conception of citizenship. *Theory and Research in Social Education, 24*(1), 36–53.

Students for Cultural and Linguistic Democracy (SCaLD). (1996). Reclaiming our voices. In C. Walsh (Ed.), *Education reform and social change: Multicultural voices, struggles, and visions* (pp. 129–145). Mahwah, NJ: Lawrence Erlbaum Associates.

Swartz, E. (1992). Multicultural education: From a compensatory to a scholarly foundation. In C. Grant (Ed.), *Research and multicultural education: From the margins to the mainstream* (pp. 32–43). London: Falmer Press.

Swartz, E. (1998). Using dramaturgy in educational research. In S.R. Steinberg & J.L. Kincheloe (Eds.), *Students as researchers: Creating classrooms that matter* (pp. 113–135). London: Falmer Press.

Teidt, P.l., & Teidt, I.M. (1995). *Multicultural education: A handbook of activities resources, and information.* Boston: Allyn Bacon.

Thornton, S. (1994). Perspectives on reflective practice in social studies education. In E.W. Ross (Ed.), *Reflective practice in social studies* (pp. 35–42). Washington, DC: National Council for the Social Studies.

Torres-Guzman, M.E., Mercado, C.I., Quintero, A.H., & Viera, D.R. (1994). Teaching and learning in Puerto Rican/Latino collaboratives: Implications for teacher education. In E.R. Hollins, J.E. King, & W.C. Hayman (Eds.), *Teaching diverse populations: Formulating a knowledge base* (105–127). Albany: State University of New York Press.

Villaverde, L., & Kincheloe, J.L. (1998). Engaging students as researchers: Researching and teaching Thanksgiving in the elementary classroom. In S.R. Steinberg & J.L. Kincheloe (Eds.), *Students as researchers: Creating classrooms that matter* (pp. 149–166). Bristol, PA: Falmer Press.

Walsh, C.E. (Ed.). (1996). *Multicultural voices: Struggles and visions.* Mahwah NJ: Lawrence Erlbaum.

Weiler, K. (1988). *Women teaching for change: Gender, class and power.* New York: Bergin and Garvey.

Wills, J.S. (2000, April). *Missing in interaction: Diversity, narrative, and critical multicultural social studies.* Paper presented at the American Educational Research Association, New Orleans.

Wineburg, S. (1999). Historical thinking and other unnatural acts. *Phi Delta Kappan, 80*(7), 488–499.

Wynter, S. (1992, April). *The challenge to our episteme: The case of the California textbook controversy.* Paper presented at the American Educational Research Association, San Francisco.

Zeichner, K., & Joeft, K. (1996). Teacher socialization for cultural diversity. In J. Sikula (Ed.), *Handbook of research on teacher education* (pp. 525–547). New York: Macmillan.

CHAPTER 8

MOVING THE CENTER OF GLOBAL EDUCATION: FROM IMPERIAL WORLD VIEWS THAT DIVIDE THE WORLD TO DOUBLE CONSCIOUSNESS, CONTRAPUNTAL PEDAGOGY, HYBRIDITY, AND CROSS-CULTURAL COMPETENCE

Merry M. Merryfield

INTRODUCTION

It is time for social studies educators to move beyond the global education conceived in the Cold War. In the 1970s the seminal work of Lee Anderson (1979), Chadwick Alger (1974), James Becker (1979), and Robert Hanvey (1975) contributed greatly to the social studies by conceptualizing citizenship education for a global age. Global education developed worldmindedness by expanding the social studies' Eurocentric curriculum with more content on Africa, Asia, Latin America, and the Middle East and infusing voices from people in these world regions to develop skills in perspective consciousness (Becker, 1979; Hanvey, 1975). Globally-oriented social studies curricula added to the traditional U.S. foreign policy view of the world by examining how nonstate actors such as individuals, multinational corporations, and nongovernmental organizations (as diverse as CARE, the International Monetary Fund, the Grameen Bank, Greenpeace, the National Council of Churches, the Palestinian Liberation Organization) were interacting globally and changing the world (Alger, 1974; Alger & Harf, 1986; Anderson, 1979). Teachers began to teach concepts such as globalization, economic interdependence, and global political systems and situated environmental and human rights issues in a world context so that students would learn how they and their communities influence and are influenced by the actions and beliefs of people around the planet (Merryfield, 1998). Adopted by the National Council for the Social Studies in 1982, elements of global education have been integrated into the social studies curriculum in many states and school districts to help young people understand their increasingly interconnected world.

In the 1980s and 1990s while Americans witnessed the fall of the Berlin Wall and the breakup of the Soviet Union and felt the effects of global labor markets, computer technology, and the spread of AIDS, global educators taught young people to understand these and other unprecedented changes through dimensions of global education: local/global connections, perspective consciousness, cross-cultural awareness, global history, and global economic, political, ecological and technological systems and issues. Social studies educators have often used popular metaphors such as the global village or spaceship earth and slogans such as "think globally, act locally" to help their students envision their place and choices in a global age. From the 1970s to the early 1990s there were criticisms and occasional attacks on global education, usually from religious or conservative groups that were concerned about biased instructional materials or points of view they perceived as detrimental to American education (Buehrer, 1990; Lamy, 1991; Nash, Crabtree, & Dunn, 1997; Schukar, 1993). However, few questioned the assumptions implicit in the seminal scholarship in global education that (1) globalization is neither good nor bad, it is simply the result of long-term trends in technological progress, (2) globalization demonstrates the superiority of western capitalism, free markets, and democracy over communism, and (3) if schools educate young Americans in the dynamics of globalization, their generation will be able to sustain the American way of life and the role of the United States within the world system (Alger & Harf, 1986; Anderson, 1979; Becker, 1979; Lamy, 1991; Leetsma, 1979; Pike, 2000; Werner, 1990).

Recently these and other assumptions have been challenged by a tidal wave of popular protest and scholarly literature questioning the meaning, inevitability, and outcomes of globalization. Most common are fears that people and countries are losing political or economic control as seen in *The Global Trap: Globalization and the Assault on Democracy and Prosperity* (Martin & Schumann, 1997) and *Losing Control? Sovereignty in an Age of Globalization* (Sassen, 1996), or dilution of cultural identity as written about in *The Clash of Civilizations and the Remaking of the World Order* (Huntington, 1998) and *Globalization and Identity* (Meyer & Geschiere, 1999). Crossing many disciplines and paradigms, writers are concerned that globalization is increasing political polarization, economic and technological inequities, and cultural conflicts in such works as *Capitalism in the Age of Globalization* (Amin, 1997), *the Lexus and the Olive Tree* (Friedman, 1999), *Jihad vs. McWorld: How Globalism and Tribalism Are Reshaping Our World* (Barber, 1995), and *Articulating the Global and the Local* (Cvetkovich & Kellner, 1997).

Other writers, such as Robert Kaplan (2000) in *The Coming Anarchy*, Cameron McCarthy in *The Uses of Culture* (1998), Saskia Sassen (1998) in *Globalization and Its Discontents*, and Edward Said (1993) in *Culture and Imperialism*, have addressed the paradoxes of divergent, even conflicting local and global forces that are occurring at the same time, even in the same places, and the resulting hybridity of ideas, experiences, and cultures that increasingly characterize the human experience. In the last few years people engaged in new electronic technologies have begun to ask how the Internet and World Wide Web are affecting people's world views and the felt realities of globalization. Scholars raise critical issues about the power of electronic media and communication in globalization and changes in culture, community, work, politics, education and identity in *Communication and Global Society* (Chen and Starosta, 2000), *Electronic Literacies* (Warschauer, 1999), *Culture of the Internet* (Kiesler, 1997), "Telecommunication in the classroom: Rhetoric versus reality" (Fabos & Young, 1999), and *women@internet: Creating New Cultures in Cyberspace* (Harcourt, 1999). The effects of globalization on education may mean moving from national to global curricula for world citizenship as in "Educating world citizens: Multinational curriculum development" (Parker, Ninomiya, & Cogan, 1999) and *Reconnecting from National to Global Curriculum* (Pike & Selby, 1995). Or globalization may necessitate fundamental restructuring and innovation to avoid a worsening of educational inequities and educational irrelevance as noted in *Globalization and Education* (Burbules & Torres, 2000) and *Education and the Rise of the Global Economy* (Spring, 1998).

The thesis of this chapter is that it is time to reconceptualize global education. Although some of the seminal work of global educators from the 1970s is undoubtedly still relevant, we need to globalize global education through literature, theories, and diverse perspectives that reflect the complexity of the planet in the early twenty-first century. The field needs to be informed by interdisciplinary and multidisciplinary scholarship from many cultures and the issues and concerns of people currently invisible in the curriculum in the United States. However, the task does not end with inclusion—the addition of perspectives so that students understand the felt needs and realities of the majority of the world's peoples. More important, students must examine the origins and assumptions that underlie the mainstream, Eurocentric, Cold War framework that divides the world into "us" and "them" and analyze alternative frameworks for understanding people and the planet past and present. The challenge is in moving the center of global education from institutionalized divisions of people and ideas to the complexity of the interaction and syncrety of the global human experience.

I have organized this chapter into three pedagological processes that I believe are particularly relevant for teachers who want to decolonize social studies content and prepare young people to interact in a variety of contexts with people different from themselves. Within each of these I discuss both theoretical work and ideas for application in social studies classrooms. The first process examines the pedagogy of imperialism. Students inquire into relationships between empire-building and knowledge construction and examine how the educational legacy of imperialism shapes mainstream academic knowledge today (Willinsky, 1998). Unlike the global education of the 1970s, this process requires that students identify how imperialist assumptions frame knowledge and information in their lives and analyze how this framework limits their ability to understand many of the world's people, changes, and conflicts. Second is the process of illuminating world views of people on the planet who are usually omitted, marginalized or misrepresented in mainstream academic knowledge. If global education is to be truly global, it is critical that students learn from the experiences, ideas, and knowledge of people who are poor, oppressed, or in opposition to people in power. Unlike the global education of the 1970s, this process brings to the center of the curriculum concerns for equity in representation and pedagogy for social justice (Freire, 1995; Gioseffi, 1993; Harding, 1998; Ladson-Billings, 1994; McCarthy & Crichlow, 1993; Ngugi, 1993; Said, 1993). Students learn from people whose experience and knowledge differ from dominant discourse (Ashcroft, Griffiths, & Tiffin, 1989; Chavez Chavez & O'Donnell, 1998; Gioseffi, 1993). The third process is cross-cultural experiential learning within different contexts of power. Unlike the cross-cultural awareness conceptualized by Hanvey (1975), cross-cultural experiential learning goes beyond the academic study of differences to place people in real-life situations in which they experience the complexities of deep culture, the tangible privileges that come with the power of the mainstream, and the frustrating inequities of marginalization or outsider status. Cross-cultural experiential learning requires students to demonstrate their ability to use cultural knowledge and skills in actual cross-cultural communication and conflict management (Brislin & Yoshida, 1994; Cushner, McClelland, & Safford, 1992; Gochenour, 1993; Johnson & Johnson, 1992; Slavin, 1992; Sleeter, 1995). These three processes can be integrated and developmentally sequenced within K-12 social studies.

PROCESS ONE: ANALYZING HOW THE EDUCATIONAL LEGACY OF IMPERIALISM SHAPES TODAY'S MAINSTREAM ACADEMIC KNOWLEDGE

We need to learn again how five centuries of studying, classifying and order-ing humanity within an imperial context gave rise to peculiar and powerful ideas of race, culture, and nation that were, in effect, conceptual instruments that the West used both to divide up and educate the world. (Willinsky, 1998, pp. 2–3)

In order to recognize the effects of imperialism on today's mainstream academic knowledge and identify how it limits understanding of the world, students must delve into relationships between empire-building and the development of what we call today mainstream academic knowledge, the normative knowledge validated by educational institutions as the objective truth (see Banks, 1995, for a multicultural critique of mainstream aca-demic knowledge in the social studies). In *Learning to Divide the World*, John Willinsky (1998) examines how histories and literature written under impe-rialism "live on, for many of us, as an unconscious aspect of our education" as mainstream academic knowledge (p. 3). Willinsky (1998) builds upon the postcolonial theory of Orientalism (Said, 1978) to demonstrate how the "educational legacy of imperialism" shapes mainstream knowledge through its framework of opposition, its priorities for learning, its divisions and constructions of the world's peoples, and its "scientifically underwrit-ten racism" (p.4). Whether the dichotomous terms are The Orient/The Occident, First World/Third World, free/communist or industrialized/ developing nations, there is an "us"—usually the white middle class descen-dants of Western Europeans who are said to have developed democracy and today make the world safe—and "them," the Others who are divided from real Americans by their culture, skin color, language, politics, or other differences. Others have noted the legacy of imperialism in Anglo-phone countries in the teaching of "European diffusionism," racialized identities, and a reliance upon American and European constructions of other peoples and the world (Blaut, 1993; Freire, 1995; Harding, 1998; McCarthy, 1995, 1998; Omi & Winant, 1993; Pratt, 1992, 1996).

An analysis of the legacy of imperialism could begin with students exam-ining the European struggle from the fifteenth to eighteenth centuries to make sense of the unprecedented sights that they came unto contact within their explorations of Africa, Asia, and what they named "the new world." At first mythical creatures from Pliny's *Historia Naturalis* filled the maps and biblical prophecies were used to explain new lands and phenom-ena. Eventually the contrast between accepted knowledge of the world and their own experiences led the early European explorers and colonizers to recognize that "much of their learning had been shaken, if not undone, and they needed to rebuild that world anew" (Willinsky, 1999, p. 23).

Rabasa's (1993) chapter 'Allegories of Atlas' in *Inventing A-M-E-R-I-C-A: Spanish Historiography and the Formation of Ethnocentrism* offers insights into the construction of Mercator's (1636) *Atlas*, his world maps, and their impact on education. Students can analyze maps, histories, literature, and visuals to trace early changes in European thinking about other places and cultures and juxtapose constructions by the people they were interacting within Africa, Asia and the Americas. Instructional materials that pull together literature, primary sources, and critiques are available from Rethinking Schools, The Network for Educators on the Americas (NECA), and many of the African, Asian and Middle Eastern Title VI area studies centers in the United States. Numerous scholars have produced collections that are especially pertinent to the social studies, such as *On Prejudice: A Global Perspective* (Gioseffi, 1993), *The Africa that Never Was: Four Centuries of British Writing about Africa* (Hammond & Jablow, 1992), *The Post-Colonial Studies Reader* (Ashcroft, Griffiths & Tiffin, 1995) and the CITE series (*Through Japanese Eyes, Through Indian Eyes*, etc.).

As exploration led into empire, the interpretation of these new worlds developed into a vast scholarship that provided new explanations and an reordering of both past and present knowledge. "Like architects after an earthquake, many lettered Europeans saw a chance to rebuild a world" (Willinsky, 1998, p. 24). Over five centuries, knowledge was generated in the name of imperialism's intellectual interests by scientists, naturalists, ethnographers, historians, geographers, journalists, painters and poets. This "research and development arm of imperialism" informed its "educational project" and made "the whole world coherent for the West by bringing all we knew of it within the imperial order of things" (Willinsky, 1998, pp. 10–11). The extensive literature from "the colonies," visual images from sketches, paintings and photos, and the incredible physical acquisitions brought back to Europe provide fertile ground for an examination of how Europeans interacted with and made sense of their new environments.

Willinsky's meticulous details and references are rich resources in themselves for the social studies classroom. In "The Imperial Show and Tell," he provides many examples of how not only animals and artifacts were exhibited for European edification, but also people of color. For example, in 1810 a Xhosa girl of sixteen was brought to London where she was exhibited nude as the "Hottentot Venus." Her body became the subject of cartoons and vaudeville plays and, as she became famous, the show moved to Paris. When she died at 25, her body was dissected by Georges Cuvier, the founder of comparative anatomy, who took this opportunity to compare her organs to those of orangutans and then prepare and present her genitalia to the Academie Royale de Medecine to demonstrate the "African perversity, deformation and pathology" said to be caused by Africans' primitive sexual appetites and lack of moral turpitude (Gilman, 1985, as quoted in Willinsky, 1998, pp. 59–60; see Gilman, 1986 for an in-depth examination of this case of using science to define moral differences as well as others in colonial Europe). To examine hybridity and make connections across time and place, students could analyze examples of Europeans' depictions of both white and African women, African women writers own descriptions of their lives and the whites they knew, white American literature about white and African American women, and African American women's writing, such as Michelle Wallace's (1993) "Negative Images: Towards a Black Feminist Cultural Criticism."

Willlinsky (1998, pp. 23–87) vividly illustrates how the roots of western education are embedded in European dedication to describing, organizing, labeling and interpreting everything they perceived of interest as they "discovered" new worlds. New academic disciplines of anthropology and sociology were developed and old disciplines of history, geography, and anatomy were revised so that these new bodies of knowledge could be pursued and taught. Colonial rule and trade gave rise to many structures for knowledge about the world: experimental agriculture and the import of "exotic" plants and animals for botanical and zoological gardens, lectures before learned societies on theories of race, encyclopedias, ethnographies of "primitive peoples" and museums in which to view their artifacts, and travel literature, plays and fiction that takes the reader into different cultures through European eyes (Willinsky, 1998, pp. 23–87).

In analyzing the effects of museums, exhibitions, zoos, and other collections from the Empire, Willinsky illustrates how enduring these "instruments of public instruction" have been in teaching as scientific truth European constructions of the cultures, geographies, and histories of Africa, Asia, and the Americas. In chapters such as "History and the Rise of the West," "Geographies of Difference," "Science and the Origin of Race," he details the imperial framework of knowledge production and its legacy in today's schools. It was the best anthropological, geographical, and historical knowledge that Europe could offer that defined the differences between civilized and uncivilized, East and West.

Has the imperial framework survived to shape education on the world today? Students can test Willinsky's ideas by examining the mainstream academic knowledge of their school or community. They could also compare scholarly publications or texts from previous generations with those of today. In deciding what should serve as data for analysis of mainstream academic knowledge, teachers and students could choose to focus on academic scholarship (textbooks, journals) in libraries and museums or include popular knowledge through trade, business or government documents, cultural or leisure attractions (theme parks, plays, exhibitions, fairs, circuses), and media (newspapers, TV, films, music, cartoons). How can one judge if an imperial framework lives on in our accepted academic or everyday knowledge? Here are some questions to consider: Is there a portrayal of "the Other" (people of color in the United States or peoples in Africa, Asia, the Middle East) based only upon European or American perceptions and scholarship? Is there a focus on differences between peoples who are like "us" and people who are different from us? Is there attention to differences that make the Other appear as ignorant, amusing, violent, exotic or bizarre? Do whites dominate discourse and set the agenda with people of color given much less attention, voice, or complexity of character than the whites? Do whites interact on exotic backdrops with people of color serving minor roles? Are there omissions of discrimination or justifications of inequities or oppression? Does culture or nationality equal racial differences or ethnic purity? Is there more interest in the "pure" or traditional that the realities of dynamic cultural change? Is there use of colonial language, literature, or points of view, such as a rationalization for imperialism (as in manifest destiny)? Are there assumptions that Americans or Europeans know what is best for people in African, Asian or Latin American countries?

An inquiry into the imperial legacy could also focus on a particular group of people or a world region. Work across thirty years demonstrates that ignorance, stereotypes, and incomplete knowledge continues to characterize what Americans teach and learn about Africa and African peoples (Beyer & Hicks, 1968; Brantlinger, 1986; Crofts, 1986; Merryfield, 1986, 1989; Osunde, Tlou, & Brown, 1996; Ukpokodu, 1996; Wiley, 1982). In a recent action research project (Merryfield, 2001), twenty-one classroom teachers worked with their elementary, middle and high schools students to evaluate educational materials in their school on their African content and interview people in their neighborhoods about their knowledge of Africa. They found that the complexity of the continent's over fifty countries and the diversity of its hundreds of cultures and languages was almost always simplified or reduced to "African." Over ten negative examples of differences (poverty, ethnic conflicts) between Africans and Americans were found for every one positive difference (strong family bonds). An inordinate amount of attention was given to people who are the most different from Americans (the Masai, the San) instead of more representative African ethnic groups. European's pejorative language (such as "bushman" and "witch doctors") and stereotypes ("jungles," "huts," "tribal warfare") are still used (see Crofts, 1986, and Merryfield, 1986, on pejorative language and imperialist assumptions). African animals and artifacts are often given more attention than people (especially at the elementary level), and it is only when white people have explored, settled, traded or sent in troops that people know anything about African history or geography. There were also some findings indicative of changes from an imperial framework, such as the identification of library books, instructional materials and media that teach about Africa through authors, primary sources, and web sites from the Continent (Merryfield, 2001). In the next section we look beyond the educational legacy of imperialism and examine theories and practices that take students into the lives, voices, experiences, knowledge and theories of people who have postcolonial world views.

PROCESS TWO: UNDERSTANDING THE WORLD VIEWS OF PEOPLE UNDERREPRESENTED IN MAINSTREAM ACADEMIC KNOWLEDGE

If global education is to be world-centered, it is critical that students learn from the knowledge and experiences of people who, because of their race, gender, class, culture, national origin, religious or political beliefs, are ignored, stereotyped or marginalized in mainstream academic knowledge. Unlike the global education of the 1970s, this process brings to the center of the curriculum the voices of people past and present who were silenced because they had little or no power to be heard. As students analyze this new knowledge and synthesize its connections with the legacy of imperialism and mainstream academic knowledge, new global understandings begin to emerge that have less to do with divisions among people or nations that they do with the borrowing of ideas, the evolution and hybridity of cultures, the syncrety of shared experience and enduring human conflicts. In this section I have focused on three ideas that can contribute to a postcolonial pedagogy.

Developing a Double Consciousness

Challenging the imperial legacy of racism in American life, the great African American scholar, W.E.B. DuBois, wrote about its effects on identity and world view:

> It is a peculiar sensation, this double-consciousness, this sense of always looking at one's self through the eyes of others, of measuring one's soul by the tape of a world that looks on in amused contempt and pity. One ever feels his twoness—an American, a Negro: two souls, two thoughts, two unreconciled strivings; two warring ideals in one dark body, whose dogged strength alone keeps it from being torn asunder. (DuBois, 1989, p. 3; the first edition was published in 1903)

Unlike the perspective consciousness of global education (Hanvey, 1975) that teaches students to become aware that other people may have views of the world profoundly different from their own, double consciousness is an act of survival in coping with the institutionalized violence and pervasive discrimination of racism. In early twentieth century America, Black children grew up conscious not only of their own culture that they learned from family and community but also the white culture that oppressed them as inferior because of their race. White people did not need to develop a double consciousness as they were never in the position where their survival depended upon their understanding of how Blacks perceived them. The work of DuBois (1965, 1989), which spans many decades and world regions, is an example of seminal literature that illuminates the world view of people struggling with the inheritance of imperialism in dividing people by the color of their skin into superior and inferior categories. In his own famous words, "the problem of the Twentieth Century is the problem of the color-line" (DuBois, 1989, p. 29).

The realities that create a double consciousness are a global phenomenon. Understanding two world views develops when people are separated or discriminated against because of their race, language, religion, national origin, or other differences (Gilroy, 1993; Narayan, 1988). In conceptualizing *The Black Atlantic* as black consciousness that is intercultural and transnational for people of the African diaspora, Paul Gilroy (1993) was drawn to the work of Jewish thinkers as they have also struggled with identity, a double consciousness, slavery, and diaspora. Writers have used other terms to describe the multiple perspectives that people develop to deal with oppression. In writing about the effects of the ultimate oppression, genocide, Anna Newman (1998) describes how her father's "double visions, a double knowing of sorts that infiltrates every corner of his life" paralleled his view before Auschwitz and his experiences afterwards (p. 430).

The ramifications of double consciousness can be examined across many contexts through biography and other nonfiction. Manthia Diawara (1998), a professor of Comparative Literature and Film at New York University, tells of his return to Guinea after 32 years away in the book, *In Search of Africa*. To work on a commentary on Sekou Toure and better understand Negritude, a topic central to his teaching and scholarship, Diawara visits Guinea, looks up old friends, explores old neighborhoods and reflects upon his own and Guinea's psychological changes. He expects to be welcomed back as an insider but finds himself treated as a tourist, an American, a foreigner. At one point he becomes lost in the city only to realize he has walked into Camp Boiro, "Sekou Toure's infamous prison, from which no one had ever come out alive" (Diawara, 1998, p. 37). The flash of fear he experiences triggers reflections on William Sassine, a Guinean writer "whose novels describe the loneliness and ineptitude of people in the face of the crushing force of Afro-Pessimism" through "wordplay that draws on Mandinka idioms to bend the meaning of French expressions" (p. 40). Diawara uses his experiences in returning to Guinea to inform his rethinking of Sassine's work, especially Camara, a character who returns to Guinea to be "berated by an acquaintance who accuses him of loving white people more than his own brothers and of scorning the things that Guineans accomplished" (p. 40). Throughout the book Diawara captures the disconcerting experience of seeing old friends and places through the consciousness of childhood memories at the same time as through the eyes of a New Yorker, an outsider, and recognizing that neither Americans nor Guineans see him as one of them. He uses these insights to reexamine diaspora themes in African and African American literature such as return narratives and Richard Wright, resistance literature and Malcolm X (Diawara, 1998).

The ability to see one's world both from the mainstream and from the margins is one of the shared characteristics of multicultural and global educators (Merryfield, 2000). In analyzing profiles of the lived experiences of 80 American and Canadian teacher educators who were recognized by peers as exemplary in the ways in which they prepare teachers in multicultural and global education, I found that most identified experiences that led to a consciousness of what it is like to be considered inferior, to be placed on the periphery of society, to be looked at as an outsider who does not and will never belong. For people of color in the study, these experiences happened early in life as part of growing up in white America. Many white educators did not develop this consciousness until they left North America and lived overseas. In order to make sense of these experiences, they looked critically at fundamental assumptions about reality, truth, power, and culture that they had before taken for granted. By highlighting disconsonance between identity and contexts of power, the experiences became milestones in the development of a consciousness of multiple realities. For many educators, there were parallels in recognizing that the multiple realities that exist in a community or country also exist globally. This recognition is what has led many people concerned with domestic diversity and social justice to make connections with people supporting global diversity and human rights and become interested in how global perspectives can inform multicultural education. For others in the study, the recognition of the interconnectedness of local and global intersections of power, discrimination, and identity has turned their attention to multicultural education in order to pursue local ramifications of globalization (Merryfield, 2000).

Synthesizing Differences Through Contrapuntal Literature and Histories

The work of Edward Said has much to offer in understanding the hybridity that comes from the conflict, accommodation, borrowing and rethinking across diverse people's experiences, knowledge, and world views. Said (1978, 1993) grew up within the conflicting realities of being a Christian Palestinian in a British and French colonial world. His study of colonialism and imperialism led to the development of Orientalism, a theory to explain the "Western style for dominating, restructuring, and having authority over the Orient" (Said, 1978, p. 3). Said analyzed the characteristics of European literature and history from the Enlightenment onwards to understand how and why Europeans had assigned particular meanings to the part of the world they called "the Orient," when those meanings were in conflict with the ways in which Asian and Arab peoples perceived themselves. Among his many works, I have found *Orientalism, Culture and Imperialism,* and *Covering Islam* particularly relevant because of extensive attention to geographical divisions, language, people, books, and events that we teach about in the social studies. Said's analyses are thought provoking as he reminds us that many of the terms we use to divide the world—The Middle East, The Far East, The Third World—are man-made constructions that Europeans developed to situate the Other. Orientalist divisions (for example, East is East and West is West), perspectives (Europeans are civilized, and Orientals are barbaric), phrases ("the mysterious East"), and images (a scantily clad oriental woman as courtesan in an Egyptian harem) define the "Orientals." It is a colonialist presumption that Europeans were the experts and the peoples they colonized were not able to define themselves (1978, pp. 26–28, 216).

Through Orientalism Europeans have projected their perspectives (and myths and misinformation) upon not only upon the Western world but also upon the peoples of Asia, Africa and elsewhere whom they have oppressed. As in double consciousness, those colonized by the Europeans had to contend with the colonizer's reality. Said saw Europe's orientalist perspectives dynamically interacting with the cultural identities of peoples who were colonized and that interaction continuing to influence identity and thought after independence. "Indeed all culture as hybrid (in Homi Bhabha's complex sense of that word) and encumbered, or entangled and overlapping ... strikes me as *the* essential idea"(Said, 1993, p. 317).[1] Teaching about hybridity of cultures counters the imperial legacy of dividing the world and provides complex and dynamic knowledge about two major characteristics of globalization: increasing cultural hybridity and the fusion or syncrety of political, military, health, economic or religious ideas that once were isolated or opposed to each other (see Bhabha, 1986, and Parry, 1987, for other postcolonial constructions of hybridity).

In *Culture and Imperialism*, Said articulates a pedagogy for countering Orientalist history and literature that applies to the social studies. Students can "look back at the cultural archive" and "reread it not univocally but *contrapuntally,* with a simultaneous awareness both of the metropolitian history that is narrated and of those other histories against which (and together with which) the dominating discourse acts"(1993, p.51). By adding new perspectives and knowledge to American or European constructions of history, culture, political or economic systems, contrapuntal writing and reading can illuminate other world views and provide insights into how identity, power, and history interact. Contrapuntal pedagogy in the social studies is not simply the provision of different perspectives. Instead the focus is on the interaction and integration of cultures, the dynamic process in which the colonizer and the colonized were changed as they experienced each other's lifestyles, technologies, goods, and ideas about the natural world, community, spirituality, and governance.

An example of the new knowledge would be the study of Orientalism or Africanism and, to take a related set, the study of Englishness and Frenchness.

These identities are today analyzed not as God-given essences, but as results of collaboration between African history and the study of Africa in England, for instance, or between the study of French history and the reorganization of knowledge during the First Empire. In an important sense we are dealing with the formation of cultural identities understood not as essentializations ... but as contrapuntal ensembles, for it is the case that no identity can ever exist by itself and without an array of opposites, negatives, oppositions: Greeks always require barbarians, and Europeans Africans, Orientals. (Said, 1993, p. 52)

By organizing contrapuntal history or cultural studies by events or ideas valued by the Other, students can identify the power that comes with who frames the questions and recognize the limitations of knowledge that focuses on differences. In *Uses of Culture*, Cameron McCarthy (1998) criticizes multiculturalists, who in their efforts to view the world through the "gaze of the subaltern," "stack African Americans, Latinos, and Native Americans against Polish-Americans, Italian Americans, Jewish Americans, etc. (p. 156)." Instead of continuing the colonial division of the Other, he encourages educators to "study the historical and contemporary heterogeneity of human interactions and lives"(McCarthy, 1998, p. 160). Thus, a postcolonial curriculum does not focus on or try to reconstruct "pure" or authentic" cultures that may have existed before imperial contact. The myth of the noble savage comes to mind as a part of some people's efforts to romanticize so-called untouched "primitive" cultures. Post-imperial global educators might even question whether such cultural isolation or ethnic purity has ever existed as global history documents the continual movement, diffusion, and metamorphoses of cultures (Wiley, 1986).

Decolonizing the Mind

A third scholar whose work can inform global education within the social studies is Ngugi wa Thiong'o, a Kenyan writer who experienced the Gikuyu liberation movement (the Mau Mau rebellion in colonialist language) against British colonialism. As a young teacher and writer, Ngugi was jailed when his plays and books were perceived as subversive by the postindependence government. He examines the effects of racism and oppression on identity and language and looks closely at the role of schools in perpetuating what he calls a colonized mind. In *Decolonising the Mind*, Ngugi (1986) explores how the identity developed during the dehumanization of colonization has lived on in many Kenyans' minds a generation after independence. He illustrates how a colonial mentality deeply permeates many people's thinking today because it is not only embedded but unexamined. Thirty years after independence, many Kenyans do not question the colonialist assumptions that Kenyan languages and literature are appropriate for lower levels of learning such as primary education or basic literacy while English and British literature are prerequisites for higher education (Ngugi, 1986).

Decolonizing the mind, as in transformative multicultural education (Banks, 1995), helps people become conscious of how oppressors force their world views into oppressed peoples' lives in such ways that in later generations people may never realize that their ideas and choice are affected by colonialist or neo-colonist perspectives. It is not only subjugated peoples who have a colonized mind. When white students assume they are superior to others because of their race, they are exhibiting similar colonialist assumptions. The pedagogy of decolonizing the mind is congruent with Willinsky's examination of the educational legacy of imperialism described above as it focuses on examining where norms, assumptions and underlying beliefs came from and what effect they have on people's lives.

In *Moving the Centre*, Ngugi (1993) offers a solution to the postcolonial inheritance of cultural imperialism, especially, the imperialism of the English language, by "moving the center." Not unlike the use of "margins and mainstream" written of by Grant (1992), center and periphery denote geo-power relationships. Ngugi's goal is to "shift the base from which to view the world from its narrow base in Europe to a multiplicity of centres … from Asia, Africa and South America" (Ngugi, 1993, p. 6). He is concerned with moving the center within countries and globally to include all cultures so that none is excluded or, as he describes Third World literature in American universities, "treated as something outside the mainstream" (Ngugi, 1993, p.10).

DuBois, Said and Ngugi are some of a growing number of writers whose ideas can open minds and help young people better understand the diversity and conflicts of the human experience past and present. If we move the center of the social studies curriculum to include the experiences, knowledge, and world views of people who are now ignored or underrepresented, young Americans will have a broader, more complex understanding of global realities.

PROCESS THREE: SUSTAINED AND REFLECTIVE CROSS-CULTURAL EXPERIENTIAL LEARNING

Although cross-cultural interaction and immersion are mentioned within the social studies by some multicultural and global educators, there is little evidence that most K–12 social studies teachers or teacher educators have had sufficient training in theories of cross-cultural psychology or methods of intercultural education to put these ideas into practice (Merryfield, 1995; Powell, Zehm, & Garcia, 1996; Wilson, 1982, 1983, 1993b; Zeichner & Hoeft, 1996; Zeichner & Melnick, 1995). On one hand there is a plethora of rhetoric about the need to prepare students to work with diverse people, and on the other a paucity of scholarship on the ability of teachers or teacher educators to do so. In this section I identify work that can inform the social studies on cross-cultural and intercultural learning. Due to space constraints and the complexity of these theories, my overview serves as an introduction with recommendations for further reading and resources. I begin with literature on understanding lived experiences.

Reflecting Upon Lived Experiences in Culture Learning

Cross-cultural experiential education builds upon the lived experiences that students and teachers bring with them into the classroom. What is lived experience? Max Van Manen (1990) describes the temporal nature of lived experience:

> Various thinkers have noted that lived experience first of all has a temporal structure: it can never be grasped in its immediate manifestation but only reflectively as past presence ... Lived experience is the breathing of meaning ... Thus a lived experience has a certain essence, a 'quality' that we gain in retrospect (1990, p.36).

Van Manen also points out how reflective writing interacts with experience and "teaches us what we know, and in what way we know what we know" (1990, p. 127). Through a poststructuralist perspective, Deborah Britzman (1994) suggests that a person's experiences and identity interact in a complicated construction of self and experience. One's identity shapes how experiences are seen and how they are interpreted over time. This perspective challenges conventional assumptions that experiences have some essentialist effect or meaning (Britzman, 1994; Brodkey, 1987; McCarthy, 1990, 1998; Scott, 1991). They argue that power undergirds the construction of identities and interpretation of experiences. This area of research is informed by Foucault's (1980) discourse of experience. It is in creating narratives of one's experience that who a person is and what the person experienced become one.

This interaction across identity, power, and experience is central to understanding how cross-cultural experiences create meaning in people's lives. It is especially critical to keep in mind when cross-cultural experiential learning places people in different positions of power than they normally experience. Think of the change in the context of power when an African American male student leaves his Africentric school near his home to work in a service learning project with the city's mostly white businessmen. Another type of change in power would be from the periphery to the center when a white female teacher returns to her middle class suburban school after a year of teaching English within the Muslim culture of Northern Nigeria. The dynamic nature of reflection and discourse over time is very complex as people and their narratives of experience may change.

When adults or even high school students look back upon their lives and identify those experiences they now see as significant in shaping their world views they may see meaning that differs from how they made sense of those events at the time when they were actually experiencing them. The retrospective meaning making quality of reflection upon one's lived experiences means that the significance of cross-cultural experiences may change over time and contexts. Teachers need to reflect upon their own lived experiences with people who are different from themselves and analyze how they have developed their perspectives and knowledge of others before they begin such processes with their students (Dilliard, 1996; Ford & Dilliard, 1996; Hoffman, 1996; Merryfield, 1993, Sleeter, 1993, 1995).

Writing about Lived Experiences in Culture Learning

One of the fundamental steps in becoming an effective educator is understanding the cultural background and experiences of one's students so that content and pedagogy are connected to their lives (Ladson-Billings, 1994). Many teachers use writing assignments to identify what students already know or assume about culture or history or to explore their family heritage, their interaction with other people, experiences in other places or with immigration or migration. The act of writing about cross-cultural experiences may complicate reflection and meaning. In a collection of essays entitled *"Race," Writing and Difference*, Henry Louis Gates (1986) raises issues about writing by the Other (whom "the European defined as African, Arabic, Chinese, Latin American, Yiddish or female") as he examines the history of written texts and their portrayal of people of color around the world, a portrayal that is challenged when the Other also writes (p. 2). Historically, writing has served as a powerful tool in creating European "truths" about Africans and Asians, and the ability to write has been considered to be skill that separated Europeans from the Other (Gates, 1986; Said, 1978, 1993). For more than two hundred years white Americans tried to prevent Africans and African Americans from writing at all as they recognized its power:

> By 1750, the chain had been minutely calibrated; the human scale rose from 'the lowliest Hottentot' (black South Africans) to 'glorious Milton and Newton.' If blacks could write and publish imaginative literature, then they could, in effect, take a few giant steps up the chain of being in an evil game of 'Mother, May I?' (Gates, 1986, p. 8)

For people of color, the act of writing about cross-cultural experiences may draw on different goals or epistemologies in the tradition of the Other writing as social or political action against oppression. Because of the interconnectedness of identity, power, lived experience, writing, and reflection, the learning from cross-cultural experiences may differ considerably across a group of students who differ in race, class, gender, language, or national origin. Today postcolonial literature can supply a rich diversity of ideas, experiences, and perspectives on what it means for people of color as "the empire writes back" to the European canon (Ashcroft, Griffiths, & Tiffin, 1989).

Cross-cultural Experiences in Culture Learning

Within the seminal work in cross-cultural psychology and sociology (Allport, 1954; Cole & Scribner, 1974; Dasen, 1992; Hall, 1959, 1976; Kelly, 1955; Secrest & Flores, 1969; Triandis & Berry, 1980) and intercultural experiential education (Bennett, 1993; Brislin, 1986, 1993; Brislin & Yoshida, 1994; Gochenour, 1993; Paige, 1993) scholars have developed theories of cultural interaction, communication, and learning and applied them to educating people to live and work with people of diverse cultures either within their own country or in countries different from their own. Kenneth Cushner (1999) has written extensively on intercultural education for social studies classrooms. His work provides insights into conceptualizing, planning, sequencing, and evaluating cross-cultural learning. *Human Diversity in Education* (Cushner, McClelland, & Safford, 1992) is an especially significant resource for social studies educators in developing an understanding how cross-cultural experiential education integrates the goals of global education and multicultural education to address prejudice, ethnocentrism, and discrimination while teaching skills in cross-cultural communication and interaction and knowledge of diverse cultures. Besides practical suggestions on intercultural activities, Cushner et al. (1992) explore the phenomenon of culture shock within as well as across national boundaries and its implications for American classrooms. Experienced by nearly everyone who adjusts to a new culture, culture shock is the "disorientation that occurs whenever someone moves from their known, comfortable surroundings to an environment which is significantly different and in which their needs are not easily met" (Cushner et al., 1992, p. 44). They conclude that culture shock is a stress which happens every day in American schools when children leave their homes and enter a different culture from the one in which they have been socialized (Cushner et al., 1992). Insights from this literature are relevant to teachers and students who enter new cultures within their school or community and experience disorientation, confusion, or discomfort in dealing with people different from themselves or unfamiliar situations. The emotions and stress that result from encounters with human differences are cumulative. Considering the magnitude of these emotions—the stresses of dealing with the ambiguity of wanting to belong yet being an outsider, the discomfort and insecurity of being treated as different—one can understand how experiences with people different from oneself would be magnified when a person's experiences with diversity are always characterized by being positioned on the margins of society or dismissed as inferior (Collins, 1990; Cushner et al., 1992).

There are two frameworks in the intercultural education literature that are especially relevant for the social studies. First is Milton Bennett's (1993) developmental model of intercultural sensitivity which provides insights into how people move from stages of ethnocentrism toward intercultural competence and how teachers can enhance this process. The ethnocentric stages include (1) denial (either from accidental isolation or deliberate separation), (2) defense as evidenced by denigration (derogatory attitudes, stereotyping, overt hostility) superiority (seeing those who are different as inferior) or reversal (denigration of one's own culture and assumptions of the superiority of another culture) and (3) minimization from either physical (all people have the same physical needs) or transcendent (we are all God's children) universalism. The ethnorelative stages include (4) acceptance of behavioral and value differences (cultural differences are seen as neither good nor bad; they are acknowledged and respected), (5) adaptation of skills for interacting and communicating are enhanced (development of empathy and understanding of pluralism through multiple cultural frames of reference), (6) integration, which include both contextual evaluation and constructive marginality in which a person is "always in the process of becoming a part of and apart from a given cultural context" (Alder, 1977 as quoted in M. Bennett, 1993, p. 59).

In discussing each of the six stages, Bennett describes the psychology of peoples' thought processes and identifies educational strategies and activities that meet the needs of people in that stage. For example, if students are at the denial stage ("there are no cultural differences I need to know about"), activities such as holding an international festival or visiting an exhibit of Chinese art would help people develop recognition of some differences without overwhelming them with profound cultural contrasts. However, if they are at the stage of minimization where cultural differences are recognized but trivialized (the 'one world' view of "we are really more alike than different, so I don't have to worry about all those differences"), activities are needed to help students recognize the significance of cultural contexts. To give a practical significance to cultural differences, Bennett recommends using simulations and shared experiences with people from other cultures that reward people's recognition of both profound cultural differences and the need to learn how to interact differently because of them. It is important that people learn that there are times when "just being themselves" with people of other cultures may mean their behaviors are inappropriate, even insulting (M. Bennett, 1993).

In the same book, Janet Bennett (1993) expands upon cultural marginality, the experience of many students today who are on the margins of two or more cultures. Her work on encapsulated marginals (people who are troubled or alienated by the ambiguity of their identity) and constructive marginals (people are never not "at home" and find advantages in "dynamic in-betweenness") is very useful for understanding the connections between teaching cultural content and teaching diverse student populations.

The second framework, called "The Culture-General Framework," can inform both teaching about different cultures as well as communication and interaction across cultures. Developed through the research of Brislin et al. (1986), its eighteen themes are grouped into three categories—emotions, knowledge and cultural differences. Emotions that often develop with cross-cultural experiences include: (1) anxiety over unfamiliar demands, (2) disconfirmed expectations when situations differ from what was expected, (3) the need to belong but being unable to do so as an outsider, (4) the ambiguity of not understanding messages being sent in the new culture, yet having to respond, and (5) confrontation with one's own prejudices. The five emotions can be examined by teachers and students as they are immersed in different levels of cross-cultural learning from a service learning project with a local mosque to a study abroad project in rural Mexico, or especially when five Kosovar refugees join the fifth period's global history class. These emotions are also very relevant for professional development programs as most educators these days find themselves (and their students) coming into contact with people from cultures that they may know little about. For example, when more than 15,000 Somali immigrants were resettled in Columbus, Ohio in the 1990s, not only did the Somalis experience such emotions in dealing with the schools, but many American teachers and students also developed the same feelings as the Somalis were different in many ways from other immigrants they had known. Recognizing the power of these emotions is the first step in improving teaching and learning.

Knowledge areas that incorporate many cross-cultural differences but are difficult to understand include work, time and space, language, roles (based on gender, age, religious beliefs, inherited position, etc.), the importance of the group versus importance of the individual, rituals versus superstition, social hierarchies/class/status, and values (Brislin et al., 1986). These areas can provide teachers with a structure to move beyond the superficiality of dress, holidays and food or a focus on the exotic and bizarre. (I once observed a fourth grade teacher's *one and only* lesson on Botswana entitled "Why Africans eat bugs.") A Columbus middle school teacher I work with applied this part of the Culture-General Framework to her teaching of India. In the previous year, the students had read a section in their cultural geography book, watched a video on Hinduism, mapped different ethnic groups and religions and visited a local Indian grocery store and restaurant. Now the class became involved in researching patterns of belief and behavior. Groups of two or three students selected a concept from the list above and collected data from the library, the Internet, and Indians living in the community to learn how beliefs affect behavior. By the end of the project the students not only understood some the diversity of contemporary Indian cultures better than ever before, they also recognized how their own cultural patterns are transmitted and changed over generations, yet rarely examined. Interest and motivation were sparked by the focus on beliefs and Indians became more than "school work." They were real people, key-pals, friends they wanted to visit some-day. When fighting broke out in Kashmir later in the school year, the students were eager to find out what was happening because one of their key pals in New Delhi had grown up in Kashmir and had shared with them some photos of his village when explaining his family's place in the social hierarchy. Using the events as a teachable moment, the teacher invited five Indian students from a local university to work with her students and prepare some instructional materials for some other middle school students to learn about cultural conflicts in India. But first she had her students develop cross-cultural handouts on "making our Indian visitors comfortable" based upon their research on beliefs and behaviors.

Third, the Culture-General Framework describes bases of cultural differences, those ways that people in different cultures think about and evaluate information: the differences in how people (1) categorize, (2) differentiate, (3) make ingroup/outgroup distinctions, (4) differences in learning styles, and (5) differences in how people attribute or judge the causes of behavior. This work can be used to develop culturally relevant pedagogy as well as cross-cultural understanding (Brislin et al., 1986). Several publications of Intercultural Press focus on instructional activities and cross-cultural assignments that clarify these differences or demonstrate their significance in everyday interactions. I recommend *Experiential Activities for Intercultural Living* (Seelye, 1996) and *Cross-Cultural Dialogues* (Stori, 1994) for preparing preservice teachers to recognize the power of cultural differences in the way people make judgments, choose to ask questions, make sense of body language, develop expectations, etc.

Finally there is some research on how cross-cultural experiences contribute to the development of multicultural and global educators. Teachers' narratives, stories, and theories take us into the process of educators' thinking about events, how experiences lead to insights, and the dynamic processes of constructing or deconstructing meaning (Day, 1993; Deering & Stanutz, 1995; Finney & Orr, 1995; Gomez, 1996; Schubert & Ayers, 1992; Wilson, 1998; Wolk & Rodman, 1994). Angene Wilson (1982, 1983, 1986, 1993a, 1993b, 1997; 1998) has written extensively about how their cross-cultural experiences positively affect how social studies educators think and teach about the world and its people. Her article, "Oburoni Outside the Whale: Reflections on an Experience in Ghana," provides powerful insights into the contexts of power and how identity can be transformed through immersion in another culture (Wilson, 1998). Within narratives of classrooms and schools are compelling stories of experiences in social studies and global education. Martha Germaine's (1998) *Worldly Teachers* takes us into the lives of six American teachers as they leave their teaching positions in the Midwest or East Coast, move to either China or Japan to teach, and then return back home and resume their teaching here. Other research describes the intersections of lived experience, cultural diversity, equity, and education through the perspectives of teachers and students in urban schools (Fine, 1991; Kozol, 1991, Meier, 1995), African American and African Canadian teachers (Foster, 1997, Henry, 1998), and immigrant students (Olsen, 1997).

Teachers and students come to schools with lived experience that inform their understanding of identity, human differences, power, hybridity, cultural change, and other constructs of social studies. These lived experiences provide the foundation for specialized cross-cultural experiential learning in social studies classrooms, in the community, in service learning projects and experiences within and across different cultures. Few people forget the lessons learned when they experience first hand what it feels like when one's human differences are the basis for being welcomed into the center or pushed toward the periphery of a society.

CONCLUSIONS

Last week I returned to Ohio from a conference in Seoul in which several Korean historians, representatives from the Ministry of Education, and five American social studies professors pondered the teaching of world history, content on Korea in American classrooms, and global education for both American and Korean students. We met in the wake of the historic July 2000 meeting of the leaders of North Korea and South Korea and in the anticipation of a hundred North and South Koreans crossing the border to visit family members they had not seen or heard from in almost fifty years. There is no more profound example of Cold War divisions than the two Koreas today. Since curriculum guides, standards, textbooks and other social studies materials were on the agenda, the Korean professors puzzled over evidence that Americans are teaching that the Cold War is over, that it ended with the fall of the Berlin Wall and the break up of the Soviet Union. Americans are teaching that they have won the war with communism—yet what about North Korea? Do Americans know troops are facing off on the border? They queried American use of "Third World" and wondered why their highly industrialized, well-educated, democratic country is categorized as though it has more in common with Burma or Nigeria that it does with the United States.

As we drove past the U.S. Army base in Seoul, my Korean colleagues described the anger of some Koreans who see the soldiers as American imperialists and the differences in how the older generation remembers the war. At the King's palace, a colleague shared with me how Korean social studies teachers teach about the Japanese occupation from 1910 to 1945, about being forced to give up their Korean names and take Japanese ones, about the King's home being turned into a zoo, and about Japanese "use" of Korean women. With evidence everywhere of American multinationals, food, fashion, services, websites, and media (films, rock videos, CNN, and Armed Forces Network-Korea, to name a few), one Korean colleague shared her concerns that economic development and globalization mean westernization of Korean culture and values.

As I rode the subway, talked with Korean teachers at a social studies conference, experienced teenage hangouts with a former student, I faced a very unpleasant reality that is at the heart of this chapter. The issues, ideas and lifestyles on the minds of Koreans today (and most other people in Asia, Africa, Latin America) are not being taught in American classrooms. Yes, American students will study the Korean War, and they may even learn about reunification talks if they happen to have a social studies teacher who values current events. But unless things change, young Americans will continue to be taught to place Korea in certain categories defined by imperial and Cold War frameworks: Asia, World War II, The Cold War/containment, the Korean Conflict, anticommunist allies, and perhaps trading partners or "emerging" democracies. None of these categories will lead to understanding what is important to Koreans today, their changing culture and values, their concerns and issues, their complex connections to China and Japan, their Koreanization of American and Japanese pop culture.

Here is where a reconceptualized global education can make a difference. Social studies students examine the construction, assumptions and legacy of imperial knowledge that leads Americans to place Koreans and others in such categories, analyze the perspectives and ideas of Koreans and other underrepresented people and the hybridity of their ideas and experiences. They learn from face to face, online and simulated cross-cultural experiences with Koreans and Korean immigrants in their neighborhood. They place the vast changes over the last fifty years within a global perspective of issues facing other people and the planet. They understand globalization, *the* defining issue of our time.

NOTE

1.   The italics or references in quotations are the authors' own throughout this chapter.

REFERENCES

Alger, C.F. (1974). *Your city and the world/The world and your city.* Columbus, OH: Mershon Center.

Alger, C.F., & Harf, J.E. (1986). "Global education: Why? For whom? About what?" In R.E. Freeman (Ed.), *Promising practices in global education: A handbook with case studies* (pp. 1–13). New York: The National Council on Foreign Language and International Studies.

Allport, G.W. (1954). *The nature of prejudice.* New York: Addison-Wesley.

Amin, S. (1997). *Capitalism in the age of globalization.* London: Zed Books.

Anderson, L. (1979). *Schooling for citizenship in a global age: An exploration of the meaning and significance of global education.* Bloomington, IN: Social Studies Development Center.

Ashcroft, B., Griffiths, G., & Tiffin, H. (Eds.). (1989). *The empire writes back: Theory and practice in post-colonial literature.* London: Routledge.

Ashcroft, B., Griffiths, G., & Tiffin, H. (Eds.). (1995). *The post-colonial studies reader.* New York: Routledge.

Banks, J.A. (1995). Transformative challenges to the social science disciplines: Implications for social studies teaching and learning. *Theory and Research in Social Education 23*(1), 2–20.

Barber, B.R. (1995). *Jihad vs. McWorld: How globalism and tribalism are reshaping the world.* New York: Random House.

Becker, J. (1979). *Schooling for a global age.* New York: McGraw Hill.

Bennett, J.M. (1993). Cultural marginality: Identity issues in intercultural training. In R.M. Paige, (Ed.), *Education for the intercultural experience* (pp. 109–135). Yarmouth, ME: Intercultural Press, Inc.

Bennett, M.J. (1993). Towards ethnorelativism: A developmental model of intercultural sensitivity. In R.M. Paige, (Ed.), *Education for the intercultural experience* (pp. 21–71). Yarmouth, ME: Intercultural Press, Inc.

Beyer, B.K., & Hicks, E.P. (1968). *Image of Africa: A report on what American secondary school students know and believe about Africa south of the Sahara.* Pittsburgh: Project Africa, Carnegie Mellon University.

Bhabha, H.K. (1986). Signs taken for wonders: Questions of ambivalence and authority under a tree outside Delhi, May 1817." In In H.L. Gates (Ed.), *Race writing and difference* (pp. 163–184). Chicago: University of Chicago Press.

Blaut, J.M. (1993). *The colonizer's model of the world: Geographical determinism and Eurocentric history.* New York: The Guilford Press.

Brantlinger, P. (1986). Victorians and Africans: The geneology of the myth of the dark continent. In H.L. Gates (Ed.), *Race writing and difference* (pp. 185–222). Chicago: University of Chicago Press.

Brislin, R. (1993). *Understanding culture's influence on behavior.* Fort Worth, TX: Harcourt Brace & Company.

Brislin, R.W. (Ed.). (1986). *Applied cross-cultural psychology.* Beverly Hills, CA: Sage Publications.

Brislin, R., Cushner, K., Cherrie, C. & Yong, M. (1986). *Intercultural interactions.* Newbury Park, CA: Sage Publications.

Brislin, R., & Yoshida, T. (Eds). (1994). *Improving intercultural interactions.* Thousand Oaks, CA: Sage Publications.

Britzman, D.P. (1994). Is there a problem with knowing thyself? Towards a post-structuralist view of teacher identity. In T. Shanahan (Ed.), *Teachers thinking, teachers knowing: Reflections on literacy and language education* (pp. 53–75). Urbana, IL: NCRE.

Brodkey, L. (1987). Postmodern pedagogy for progressive educators. *Journal of Education 169*(3) 138–143.

Buehrer, (1990). *New age masquerade.* Brentwood, TN: Wolgemuth & Hyatt.

Burbules, N.C., & Torres, C.A.(2000). *Globalization and education.* New York: Routledge.

Chavez Chavez, R. & O'Donnell, J. (Eds). (1998). *Speaking the unpleasant.* Albany: State University of New York Press.

Chen, G., & Starosta, W.J. (2000). *Communication and global society.* New York: Peter Lang.

Cole, M., & Scribner, S. (1974). *Culture and thought.* New York: John Wiley.

Collins, P.H. (1990). *Black feminist thought.* New York: Routledge.

Crofts, M. (1986). Africa. *Social Education 50*(5), 345–350.

Cvetkovich, A., & Kellner, D. (1997). *Articulating the global and the local.* Boulder, CO: Westview Press.

Cushner, K. (1989). Assessing the impact of a culture-general assimilator. *International Journal of Intercultural Relations, 13*, 125–146.

Cushner, K. (1999). *Human diversity in action.* New York: McGraw-Hill.

Cushner, K., McClelland, A., & Safford, P. (1992). *Human diversity on education: An integrative approach.* New York: McGraw-Hill.

Dasen, P.R. (1992). Cross-cultural psychology and teacher training. In J. Lynch, C. Modgil, & S. Modgil (Eds.). *Cultural diversity and the schools: prejudice, polemic or progress?* (pp. 191–204). London: Falmer Press.

Day, C. (1993). The importance of learning biography in supporting teacher development: An empirical study. In C. Day, J. Calderhead, & P. Denicolo (Eds.), *Research on teacher thinking: Understanding professional development* (pp. 221–232). PA: The Falmer Press.

Deering, T.E., & Stanutz, A. (1995) Preservice field experience as a multicultural component of a teacher education program. *Journal of Teacher Education, 46*, 390–394.

Diawara, M. (1998). *In search of Africa.* Cambridge, MA: Harvard University Press.

Dillard, C.B. (Spring/summer 1996) Engaging pedagogy: Writing and reflecting in multicultural teacher education. *Teaching Education 8*(1), 13–21.

DuBois, W.E.B. (1965). *The world and Africa: An inquiry into the part that Africa played in world history.* New York: International Publishers.

DuBois, W.E.B. (1989). *The souls of Black folks.* New York: Bantam Books.

Fabos, B., & Young, M.D. (1999). Telecommunication in the classroom: Rhetoric versus reality. *Review of Educational Research 69*(3), 217–259.

Fine, M. (1991). *Framing dropouts: Notes on the politics of an urban public high school.* Albany: State University of New York Press.

Finney, S., & Orr, J. (1995). "I've really learned a lot, but...": Cross-cultural understanding and teacher education in a racist society. *Journal of Teacher Education, 46*, 327–333.

Ford, T.L., & Dillard, C.B. (1996) Becoming multicultural: A recursive process of self-and social construction. *Theory Into Practice, 34*, 232–238.

Foster, M. (1990). *Black teachers on teaching.* New York: The New Press.

Foucault, M. (1980). *Power/knowledge: Selected interviews and other writings.* New York: Pantheon.

Freire, P. (1995). *Pedagogy of hope.* New York: Continuum.

Friedman, T.L. (1999). *The Lexus and the olive tree: Understanding globalization.* New York: Farrar, Straus, Giroux.

Garibaldi, A.M. (1992). Preparing teachers for culturally diverse classrooms. In M. E. Dilworth (Ed.), *Diversity in teacher education: New expectations* (pp. 23–39). San Francisco: Jossey-Bass, Inc.

Gates, H.L. (Ed). (1986). *Race, writing and difference.* Chicago: University of Chicago Press.

Germaine, M.H. (1998). *Worldly teachers: Cultural learning and pedagogy.* Westport, CT: Bergin & Garvey.

Gilman, S.L. (1986). Black bodies, white bodies: Towards an iconography of female sexuality an late nineteeeth-century art, medicine, and literature. In H.L. Gates (Ed.), *Race writing and difference* (pp. 223–261). Chicago: University of Chicago Press.

Gilroy, P. (1993). *The black Atlantic: Modernity and double consciousness.* Cambridge, MA: Harvard University Press.

Gioseffi, D. (Ed.). (1993). *On prejudice: A global perspective.* New York: Doubleday.

Gochenour, T. (Ed.). (1993). *Beyond experience: The experiential approach to cross-cultural education.* Yarmouth, ME: Intercultural Press.

Gomez, M.L. (1996). Telling stories of our teaching, reflecting on our practices. *Action in Teacher Education 18*(3) 1–12.

Grant, C.A. (Ed.). (1992). *Research and multicultural education: From the margins to the mainstream.* London: Falmer Press.

Hall, E. (1959). *The silent language.* Garden City, NY: Doubleday.

Hall, E. (1976). *Beyond culture.* Garden City, NY: Anchor.

Hammond, D., & Jablow, A. (1992). *The Africa that never was: Four centuries of British writing about Africa* Prospect Heights, IL: Waveland Press.

Hanvey, R.G. (1975). *An attainable global perspective.* New York: Center for War/Peace Studies.

Harcourt, W. (1999). *women@internet: Creating new cultures in cyberspace.* London: Zed Books, Ltd.

Harding, S. (1998). *Is science multicultural? Postcolonialisms, feminisms and epistemologies.* Bloomington: Indiana University Press.

Henry, A. (1998). *Taking back control: African Canadian women teachers' lives and practice.* Albany: State University of New York Press.

Hoffman, D.M. (1996). Culture and self in multicultural education: Reflections on discourse, text, and practice. *American Educational Research Journal 33*(4), 545–569.

Huntington, S.P. (1998). *The clash of civilizations and remaking of the world order.* New York: Touchstone Books.

Johnson, D.W., & Johnson, R.T. (1992). Social interdependence and cross-ethnic relations. In J. Lynch, C. Modgil, & S. Modgil, (Eds.), *Cultural diversity and the schools: prejudice, polemic or progress?* (pp. 179–189). London: Falmer Press.

Kaplan, R. (2000). *The coming anarchy.* New York: Random House.

Kelly, G.A. (1955). *The psychology of personal constructs.* New York: W.W. Norton.

Kiesler, S. (1997). *Culture of the Internet.* Mahwah, NJ: Lawrence Erlbaum Associates.

Kozol, J. (1991). *Savage inequalities.* New York: Crown.

Ladson-Billings, G. (1994). *The dreamkeepers: Successful teaching of African-American students.* San Francisco: Jossey-Bass.

Lamy, S.L. (1991). A conflict of images: The controversy over global education in U.S. schools. In K. Tye (Ed.), *Global education: From thought to action* (pp. 49–63). Alexandria, VA: Association of Supervision and Curriculum Development.

Leetsma, R. (1979). Looking ahead: An agenda for action. In J.M. Becker (Ed.), *Schooling for a global age* (pp. 233–243). New York: McGraw-Hill.

Martin, H., & Schumann, H. (1997). *The global trap: Globalization and the assault on democracy and prosperity.* London: Zed Books, Ltd.

McCarthy, C. (1990). Rethinking liberal and radical perspectives on racial inequality in schooling: Making the case for nonsynchrony. In N.M. Hidalgo, C.L. McDowell, & E.V. Siddle (Eds.), *Facing racism in education* (pp. 35–49). Cambridge, MA: Harvard Educational Review.

McCarthy, C. (1995). The problems with origins: Race and the contrapuntal nature of the educational experience. In C.E. Sleeter & P.L. McClaren (Eds.), *Multicultural education, critical pedagogy and the politics of difference* (pp. 245–268). Albany: State University of New York Press.

McCarthy, C. (1998). *The uses of culture: Education and the limits of ethnic affiliation.* New York: Routledge.

McCarthy, C., & Crichlow, W. (Eds.). (1993). *Race, identity and representation in education.* New York: Routledge.

Meier, D. (1995). *The power of their ideas: Lessons for America from a small school in Harlem.* Boston: Beacon Press.

Mercator, H.J. (1636/1986). *Atlas or a geographicke description of the world.* Facsimile edition in two volumes. Amsterdam: Theatrum Orbis Terrarum.

Merryfield, M. (1986). *Teaching about Africa.* ERIC Digest. Bloomington, IN: The Social Studies Development Center.

Merryfield, M.M. (Ed.). (1989). *Lessons from Africa.* Bloomington, IN: ERIC and the Social Studies Development Center, Indiana University.

Merryfield, M.M. (1993). Reflective practice in teacher education in global perspectives: Strategies for teacher educators. *Theory Into Practice, 32,* 27–32.

Merryfield, M.M. (1995). Institutionalizing cross-cultural experiences and international expertise in teacher education: The development and potential of a global education PDS network. *Journal of Teacher Education, 46,* 1–9.

Merryfield, M.M. (1998). Pedagogy for global perspectives in education: Studies of teachers' thinking and practice. *Theory and Research in Social Education, 26* (3), 342–379.

Merryfield, M.M.. (2000). Why aren't American teachers being prepared to teach for diversity, equity, and interconnectedness? A study of lived experiences in the making of multicultural and global educators. *Teaching and Teacher Education* 16(4), pp. 429–443.

Merryfield, M.M. (2001, April). *Learning about Africa through African eyes: When teachers and students challenge European and American constructions of Africa and Africans.* Paper presented at the annual meeting of the American Educational Research Association, Seattle.

Meyer, B., & Geschiere, P. (Eds.). 1999. *Globalization and identity.* Oxford: Blackwell Publishers.

Narayan, U. (1988). Working together across difference: Some considerations on emotions and political practice. *Hypatia 3*(2), 31–47.

Nash, G.B., Crabtree, C., & Dunn, R. E. (1997). *History on trial: Culture wars and the teaching of the past.* New York: Knopf.

Neumann, A. (1998). On experience, memory, and knowing: A post-holocaust (auto) biography. *Curriculum Inquiry 28,* 425–442.

Ngugi wa Thiong'o. (1986). *Decolonizing the mind.* London: Heinemann.

Ngugi wa Thiong'o. (1993). *Moving the centre: The struggle for cultural freedom.* London: James Curry.

Olsen, L. (1997). *Made in America: Immigrant students in our public schools.* New York: New Press.

Omi, M., & Winant, H. (1993). On the theoretical status of the concept of race. In C. McCarthy & W. Crichlow (Eds.), *Race, identity and representation in education* (pp. 3–10). New York: Routledge.

Osunde, E.O., Tlou, J., & Brown, N.L. (1996). Persisting and common stereotypes in U.S. students' knowledge of Africa: A study of preservice social studies teachers. *The Social Studies 87*(3), 119–124.

Paige, R.M. (Ed.). (1993). *Education for the intercultural experience.* Yarmouth, ME: Intercultural Press, Inc.

Parker, W.C., Ninomiya, A., & Cogan, J. (1999). Educating world citizens: Multinational curriculum development. *American Educational Research Journal 36*(2), 117–145.

Parry, B. (1987). Problems in current theories of colonial discourse. *Oxford Literary Review 9*(1&2), 27–58.

Pike, G. (2000). Global education and national identity: In pursuit of meaning. *Theory Into Practice 39*(2), 64–73.

Pike, G., & Selby, D. (1995). *Reconnecting from national to global curriculum.* Toronto: International Institute for Global Education, University of Toronto.

Powell, R.R., Zehm, S., & Garcia J. (1996). *Field experience: Strategies for exploring diversity in schools.* Engelwood Cliffs, NJ: Prentice-Hall.

Pratt, M.L. (1992). *Imperial eyes: Travel writing and transculturation.* London: Routledge.

Pratt, M.L. (1996). Me llamo Riboberta Menchu: Autoethnography and the recoding of citizenship. In A. Carey-Webb & S. Benz (Eds.), *Teaching and testimony: Rigoberta Menchu and the North American Classroom* (pp. 57–72). Albany: State University of New York Press.

Rabasa, J. (1993). *Inventing A-M-E-R-I-C-A: Spanish historiography and the formation of ethnocentrism.* Norman: University of Oklahoma Press.

Said, E.W. (1978). *Orientalism.* New York: Random House.

Said, E.W. (1993). *Culture and imperialism.* New York: Alfred A. Knopf.

Said. E.W. (1997). *Covering Islam.* New York: Vintage Press.

Sassen, S. (1996). *Losing control? Sovereignty in an age of globalization.* New York: Columbia University Press.

Sassen, S. (1998). *Globalization and its discontents: Essays on the new mobility of people and money.* New York: The Free Press.

Schubert, W.H., & Ayers, W.C. (Eds.). (1992). *Teacher lore: Learning from our own experience.* New York: Longman Publishing.

Schukar, R. (1993). Controversy in global education: Lessons for teacher educators. *Theory Into Practice 32*(1), pp. 52–57.

Scott, J. (1991). The evidence of experience. *Curriculum Inquiry 17*, 773–797.

Secrest, L., & Flores, L. (1969). Homosexuality in the Philippines and the United States: the handwriting on the wall. *Journal of Social Psychology 79*, 3–12.

Seelye, H.N. (Ed.). (1996) *Experiential activities for intercultural living.* Yarmouth, ME: Intercultural Press.

Slavin, R.E. (1992). Cooperative learning: Applying contact theory in desegregated schools. In J. Lynch, C. Modgil, & S. Modgil (Eds.), *Cultural diversity and the schools: prejudice, polemic or progress?* (pp. 333–348). London: Falmer Press.

Sleeter, C.E. (1993). How white teachers construct race. In C. McCarthy & W. Crichlow (Eds.), *Race, identity and representation in education* (pp. 157–171). New York: Routledge.

Sleeter, C.E. (1995). Reflections on my use of multicultural and critical pedagogy when students are white. In C.E. Sleeter & P.L. McClaren, (Eds.), *Multicultural education, critical pedagogy and the politics of difference* (pp. 415–438). Albany: State University of New York Press.

Spring, J. (1998). *Education and the rise of the global economy.* Mahwah, NJ: Lawrence Erlbaum Associates.

Stori, C. (1994). *Cross-cultural dialogues.* Yarmouth, ME: Intercultural Press.

Triandis, H.C., & Berry, J.W. (Eds.). (1980). *The handbook of cross-cultural psychology.* Boston: Allyn & Bacon.

Ukpokodu, N. (1996). Africa in today's social studies curriculum. *The Social Studies* 87(3), 125–132.

Van Manen, M. (1990). *Researching lived experience.* London, ON: The Althouse Press.

Wallace, M. (1993). Negative images: Towards a black feminist cultural criticism. In S. During (Ed.), *The cultural studies reader* (pp. 118–131). New York: Routledge.

Warschauer, M. (1999). *Electronic literacies: Language, culture and power in online education.* Mahwah, NJ: Lawrence Erlbaum Associates.

Werner, W. (1990). Contradictions in global education. In D. Henley & J. Young (Eds.), *Canadian perspectives on critical pedagogy* (pp. 77–93). Occasional Monograph #1. Winnipeg: The Critical Pedagogy Network and Social Education Researchers in Canada.

Wiley, M. (1982). Africa in social studies textbooks. *Social Education 46*(7), 492–497, 548–552.

Willinsky, J. (1998). *Learning to divide the world: Education at empire's end.* Minneapolis: University of Minnesota Press.

Wilson, A. (1982). Cross-cultural experiential learning for teachers. *Theory Into Practice 21*, 184–192.

Wilson, A. (1983). A case study of two teachers with cross-cultural experience: They know more. *Educational Research Quarterly*, 8(1), 78–85.

Wilson, A.H. (1986). Returned Peace Corps volunteers who teach social studies. *The Social Studies 77*(3), 100–107.

Wilson, A.H. (1993a). Conversation partners: Helping students gain a global perspective through cross-cultural experiences. *Theory into Practice, 32*, 21–26.

Wilson, A.H. (1993b). *The meaning of international experience for schools.* Westport, CT: Praeger.

Wilson, A.H. (1997). Infusing global perspectives throughout a secondary social studies program. In M.M. Merryfield, E. Jarchow, & S. Pickert (Eds.), *Preparing teachers to teach global perspectives* (pp. 143–167). Thousand Oaks, CA: Corwin Press.

Wilson, A.H. (1998). Oburoni outside the whale: Reflections on an experience in Ghana. *Theory and Research in Social Education 26* (3) pp.410–429.

Wolk, R.A., & Rodman, B.H., (Eds.). (1994). *Classroom crusaders.* San Francisco: Jossey-Bass.

Zeichner, K.M., & Hoeff, K. (1996). Teacher socialization for cultural diversity. In J. Sikula (Ed.), *Handbook of research on teacher education* (pp. 525–547). New York, Macmillan Library Reference.

Zeichner, K.M., & Melnick, S.L. (1995, February). *The role of community field experiences in preparing teachers for cultural diversity.* A paper presented at the annual meeting of the American Association of Colleges for Teacher Education, Washington, DC.

CHAPTER 9

PROMISE AND PRACTICE OF COMPUTER TECHNOLOGIES IN THE SOCIAL STUDIES: A CRITICAL ANALYSIS

Michael J. Berson, John K. Lee, and Daniel W. Stuckart

INTRODUCTION

Significant expectations have evolved from the development of the personal computer in the 1970s and the appearance of the World Wide Web in the early 1990s. The hyperbole connected to educational applications emerging from the personal computer and World Wide Web has been consistent. Advocates have promoted technological applications as beneficial for a host of educational circumstances. Despite assurances of substantial progress from supporters of technology, some critics claim that social studies instruction has not appreciably changed in the last twenty years (Martorella, 1997; White, 1997). With social studies educators continuing to promote technology, a critical review of technology's effect on social studies is in order. This assessment critically addresses the development of educational technology related to social studies.

SOCIAL STUDIES AND TECHNOLOGY IN THE RESEARCH LITERATURE

Conceptualizations of Social Studies and Technology

The most common conceptualization of technology has been as a collection of tools. Berson (1996) suggested six areas of social studies computer use including drill and practice, tutorials and study guides, games and simulations, inquiry and problem solving, graphics, and word processing and writing. Ehman and Glenn (1987) proposed a heuristics for conceptualizing social studies and technology as it relates to instruction to include the computer's ability to aid in the presentation of content, assist students in learning, help students apply what they have learned, and assess student learning. Instructional uses of specific technology tools have included simulations, word processing, drill and practice, databases, tutorials, games, problem solving, and the Internet (Becker, 1999; Northup & Rooze, 1990; Ross, 1991).

Other authors have considered the role of technological tools in the context of larger societal structures. Martorella (1997) conceptualized technology in such broad terms. He viewed the computer's role as being an alter ego, citizenship educator, workplace, school, and/or data gatherer. Knapp and Glenn (1996) called for the restructuring of curriculum in schools to take into account the broad influence of technology. Restructured classrooms would make use of technology in three ways, to provide information, to develop knowledge and skills, and to link different locations.

Social Studies Related Technological Agency

Previous reviews of computer use account for the effect of technology by focusing on technology as it influences social studies practice. The Internet and World Wide Web, hypermedia applications, and data instruments such as spreadsheets and databases are forms of technology that influence social studies. An alternative consideration of technology in the form of technological agency would shift the focus from technology to social studies practice. Technological agency refers to the human generated capacity of specific hardware and/or software applications. The extent to which technology facilitates social studies practices is a measure of technological agency. This review will address technological agency through a focus on social studies practices such as civic responsibility, global understanding, and historical awareness. A review of recent research related to specific technologies in social studies will proceed a consideration of technological agency.

Internet and Web-based Resources

Use of the Internet in social studies has increased significantly since 1990 (Becker, 1999). In terms of pedagogy, the use of Internet and web-based resources facilitates direct instruction, research, problem solving, and inquiry (Braun & Risinger, 1999). Online resources also encourage integrative learning in the social studies disciplines (Johnson & Rector, 1997). This effect is particularly salient in history where Ayers (1999) argued that the Internet related advancements in hypertext and hypermedia[1] combined with a renewed social science history could converge to invigorate the professional study of history. Social studies teachers can also make use of multiple perspectives by using and emphasizing authentic history through primary sources available on the Internet (Tally, 1996).

Observers have suggested that learning in social studies becomes more meaningful and realistic when students are able to correspond with other students through e-mail (Barr, 1994; Boldt, Gustafson, & Johnson, 1995). While Postman (1992) criticized the disconnectedness that results from online communication, Berenfeld (1996) suggested that tele-collaboration between students from different schools advances inquiry and distributive problem solving. In one social studies class, students in New York spent a semester working with students in Oizumi, Japan (Maskin, 1996). The experience resulted in new perspectives about each other's cultures, but did not translate into a deeper appreciation of the respective cultures.

Teachers should always attempt to broaden educational experiences for their students. Social studies educators have suggested that the Internet can promote social studies specific needs such as active learning (Gaines, Johnson, & King, 1996). One such type of activity, the Internet virtual field trip, may encourage interest in social studies (Mason & Beal, 1999). Bellen and Scheurman (1998) suggested students' control over navigation on the web, a lack of preparation in advance of a virtual trip, and viewing the trip as an end unto itself could be problematic. Overall, the Internet can stimulate student interest and enhance student's roles as constructivists' learners (Wilson & Marsh, 1995; White, 1996). When students' assume this constructivist stance, they take an active role in analyzing information. The abundance of information on the Internet also gives students a research advantage and generally motivates students (Maskin, 1996). Much of the literature relating to social studies and the Internet takes on a promising tone. In contrast, Braun (1997) proposed that although the Internet could be a positive addition to the social studies, three problematic issues remained un-addressed including the lack of assessment concerning web pages, the effect the Internet would have on moral education, and the absences of critical thinking associated with the use of web resources.

Hypermedia Applications

Computer technologies related to hypermedia, such as multimedia educational software, have relevance in social studies. Higgins and Boone

(1992) found that using hypermedia texts results in a higher retention of social studies material. Hypermedia study guides were also found to be an effective supplement to social studies instruction (Higgins & Boone, 1992). Horton, Boone, and Lovett (1990) showed students made significant gains from pretest to posttest when using hypertext study guides. One particular hypermedia application, HyperCard, allows students to construct knowledge by involving students in decisions concerning the design and content of their HyperCard projects (Jennings, 1994). For example, when students create hypermedia projects they must not only analyze and integrate factual elements of an event, but they must also create the sequential order for specific pages or cards in their presentation. Additionally, students working with HyperCard have the opportunity to design individual cards according to their understanding of the content and their stylistic preference. Decisions related to the construction of hypermedia projects also require critical thinking skills (Fitch, 1997). Multimedia design tools promote students' construction of knowledge and their problem solving ability in social studies (Ferretti & Okolo, 1996). Social studies students can construct their understanding of various ideas using multimedia through explicit instruction, modeling, tutoring, cooperative learning, and databases (Fontana, Dede, White, & Cates, 1993).

Descriptions of teachers' uses of hypermedia are illustrative in terms of their instructional value. Dillner (1993) described a teacher who constructed a hypermedia project to assist students in reading comprehension. This teacher knew her students' individual needs and consequently was able to design a lesson individualized to the developmental level of her students. Other descriptive uses of hypermedia include a report on travel within students' home state (Coady, 1994), a simulation of the election of 1912 (Newmark, 1989), research on history related topics such as the Renaissance (Milton & Spradley, 1996), direct instruction on the geography and weather of western Europe (Adams, 1995), and incorporation with a college level world history course (Fitch, 1997).

Data Instruments

Teachers and students use numerous data instruments in the social studies classroom including word processing, spreadsheets, and data processing. Although the literature on word processing in social studies instruction is scanty, it has consistently been the most popular technology used in social studies classrooms (Becker, 1999). The use of spreadsheets in social studies gives students an opportunity to manipulate various forms of information. The data related skills developed using spreadsheets are portable enough to allow students to use them in other school and work settings. For example, students may compare local characteristics relating to Congressional apportionment and representative government (Roland, 1997).

Many social studies applications of spreadsheets relate to math and thus promote an integrative approach. Hollister (1995) suggested using spreadsheets to advance natural connections between math and social studies. Topical areas such as population demographics and elections are classic examples of the areas where relationships can be highlighted. Spreadsheet related activities might also highlight relationships between science and social studies. The use of scientific data from global information systems (GIS) in spreadsheets reinforces both scientific and social/community related objectives (Raubal, Gaupmann, & Kuhn, 1997).

Databases support critical thinking, promote interpretation of information, and facilitate drawing of conclusions (Rooze, 1986). They can be used, created, or designed by students to promote different types of cognitive behavior (Hunter, 1987). The use of databases can turn students into active processors of information (Hunt & Allen, 1988). Databases also promote civic participation (Braun, Fernlund, & White, 1997), allow students to actively participate in the inquiry process (Hunter, 1987), enhance critical thinking skills (Parisi, 1985), and create research opportunities (Hunt & Allen, 1988).

Technological Agency and the Purposes of Social Studies

Technological agency influences the specific instructional goals of social studies. These influences emerge in the form of social studies practice as evidenced by student and teacher action. Technological agency also reflects the broader purposes of social studies. The broader purposes of social studies as influenced by technology include economic production, human interaction, democracy, and critical thinking.

Technology and Economic Production

Social studies classrooms must be able to meet the demands of the new electronic or knowledge society (Jennings, 1994). Students will need to develop communication, critical thinking, problem solving, and interpersonal skills (McBeath, 1994). These skills translate into the human capital that individuals carry with them as they move through economic society. Possession of these skills allows individuals to confidently pursue knowledge-related jobs and opportunities. Using technology in social studies and other curriculum areas is important because the workplace will demand skills that relate to computer use (Wilson & Marsh, 1995).

There are several examples of learning environments that incorporate elements of learning in the knowledge society. Students' use of information from a variety of sources (both written and oral) will improve their ability to negotiate the landscapes of information commonplace in the knowledge society workplace. Ask the expert and cross-school research projects are examples of learning models that facilitate learning in the knowledge society (Scardamalia & Bereiter, 1996). The "ask the expert" learning model allows students to interact through asynchronous communication with a qualified authority in a specific content field. Cross-school projects bring together students from varied backgrounds to work on a common Internet-based project. These school-based projects models use technology to improve learning involving communication between individuals and groups.

Technology and Human Interaction

Social studies educators must deal with the impact of technology on the development of human communities (Gooler, 1995). When computers made their appearance in schools, there was concern related to the impact of technology on the development of classroom communities. Some argued that the development of social and citizenship communication skills needed to process information was an important consideration (Diem, 1983). Others fear the social consequences of technology and have called for the deceleration of the information revolution (Stoll, 1999). One fear was that human interaction would dissipate in schools as computers took the place of teachers and students interacted only with the computer screen (Langeveld, 1983).

Technology and Democracy

The democratic citizen needs new types of knowledge in this technological age (Glenn, 1990; Sembor, 1997). Smith-Gratto (1989) argued that technology has the potential to threaten democracy by extenuating inequalities in our society. Others have held that technology is necessary in social studies classrooms to teach students how to use the information related to their responsibilities as citizens (Berson & Berson, 2000; Glenn, 1990). Today, effective citizenship includes a range of computer technology skills (Glenn, 1990; Martorella, 1997). In particular, students with disabilities are better able to achieve the citizenship goals of social studies using multimedia technology (Ferretti & Okolo, 1996).

Technology and Critical Thinking

Citizenship in a democracy implies critical thought, and critical thought requires information (Parker, 1991). Technology can make more information available to students than ever before. The Internet, in particular, has the ability to dramatically increase the amount of information available to students. When used within an appropriate instructional strategy, the Internet supports National Council for the Social Studies curriculum standards related to citizenship (Johnson & Rector, 1997).

Technology and Authenticity

Technology offers a new way to capture the actuality of American society in students' lived experiences (Tally, 1996). Students who engage in active learning have personal or authentic experiences that strengthen their understanding of the given topic. Active learning is advanced when teachers and students use technologies such as telecommunications (Barr, 1994; Boldt, Gustafson, & Johnson, 1995). When students communicate with other students or experts as part of a problem solving or critical thinking activity, they are in control of their learning experience. Instead of reacting to teacher directions, students are designing their own learning environment through communication technology (Berenfeld, 1996). This constructivist approach to learning encourages student activity, motivation, and authenticity in learning experiences (Maskin, 1996; White, 1996; Wilson & Marsh, 1995).

Summary

Technology and particularly technological agency can play an effective role in the social studies classroom. While the quantitative evidence that technology positively impacts student learning is weak, the descriptive evidence that it impacts the student experience is strong.

Despite the practice and promise computer technologies bring to the social studies, an examination beyond the discipline reveals a growing critical undercurrent. Both academic writings and the popular media report a movement to question the ideals, assumptions, and manifestations of computer technologies in schools (Rukeyser, 1998a). Furthermore, as federal, state, and local governments continue the trend to appropriate massive expenditures for computer integration and maintenance, the tension between the computer integration advocates and the skeptics promises to intensify. The skeptics offer critical perspectives encompassing several categories: (1) broad social changes; (2) attributes of technology; (3) classroom pedagogy, practice, and achievement; and (4) the amplification of inequality. The common denominator in all perspectives is the challenge to a blind acceptance of computer integration and an ignorance of the social, economic, psychological, and physical costs of such a policy.

TECHNOLOGY AND SOCIETY

Technology Integration Affects Broad Social Change

Education has yet to realize the complete effects of computer integration. However, information technologies influence broad social changes in a variety of ways. Critics lament the loss of master narratives, the debasement of language, the loss of privacy, and a disaffection from geographic place and community.

The Decline of the Master Narratives

Throughout history master narratives have provided the theoretical force for human development. Roszak (1986) calls these "the *master ideas*—the great moral, religious, and metaphysical teachings" (p. 91). An example is, "All men are created equal," a notion grounded in ideas which are driven by values and belief systems. The power of the idea is evident from the countless wars and revolutions fought for its preservation and, in some cases, destruction. The author contends that the cult of information subverts these ideas by elevating data above them. Postman (1992) defines tradition as the power of symbols and the strength of the narratives that created the symbols. He further asserts that technopoly, the deification of technology, usurps symbols and causes a loss of narrative. Birkerts (1994) views the combination of secularization, the proliferation of data, and the loss of narratives as the extinction of human understanding. Humans no longer search for truth; rather, they manage information. The diminishing importance of the master narratives signals another technology casualty, a debasement of the written word.

The Debasement of the Written Word

In the sixteenth century, the printing press eroded the importance of the spoken word. In modern times, information technologies supplant the written word in favor of image domination (Birkerts, 1994; Oppenheimer, 1997; Postman, 1992; Stoll, 1995; Warschauer, 1999). Oppenheimer (1997) and Warschauer (1999) report that computer technologies promote design elements over writing exercises. Students spend more time editing, affixing images, and focusing on overall page design than creating meaningful text.

Information technologies also change the nature and use of language. The printing press, telegraphy, photography, broadcasting, and computer technologies imbue new meanings and subtleties into the language, "It [technology] redefines 'freedom,' 'truth,' 'intelligence,' 'fact,' 'wisdom,' 'memory,' 'history'—all the words we live by" (Postman, 1992, pp. 8–9). Moreover, Birkerts (1994) decries the loss of language finesse and aggrandizement. Information technologies promote "plainspeak" and the dumbing-down of language (p.128). For example, e-mail practice embraces grammatical and syntactical errors. Sloppy discourse suggests a looser association between humans and language; in the technological world, irreverence is not a sin (Talbott, 1995). Computer technologies are not wholly responsible for the erosion of language, but as Birkerts (1994) alleges, information technologies exacerbate the rate of change beyond evolutionary accommodation. Likewise, he views the change as a threat to individuals.

THE EXTINCTION OF INDIVIDUAL SELF AND PRIVACY

Information technology lessens the psychological distances between individuals. A technological world of dense networks and instantaneous information negates the subjective nature of individuals. Technology penetrates individual spheres and displaces privacy with public streams of consciousness. In the process, individual self dissolves into a collective whole regulated by electronic pulses (Birkerts, 1994).

The threat to individual privacy may well become the most prevalent social issue involving computer technologies. Technology alters the power balance between individuals and institutions (Garson, 1995). Modern governments function like giant surveillance entities gobbling up, integrating, and storing data entries. In turn, the government sells and gives away information to enforcement agencies and private interests (Roszak, 1986). Private corporations use the data and surveillance tools to select and monitor employees (Stoll, 1995). The end result is an intrusion into citizens' private lives. The changing dynamics of privacy issues and computer technologies invite urgent exploration in society's political and judicial forums as well as the social studies classroom. In addition to potentially violating individual privacy, information technologies also mitigate the physical distances between individuals.

The Disaffection from Community and Place

The mediated world bridges the gaps between individuals and threatens community organization. "Networks" often misrepresent themselves as "communities" (Talbott, 1995, p. 64). People connected via information technologies rarely constitute a community of human institutions. Instead, electronic connections prevail over personal sources of community.

Putnam (2000) laments the loss of "social capital," community networks that bring value to individuals and society (pp. 19–20). He chronicles the general decline in civic engagement during the second half of the Twentieth Century and conjectures that the Internet may or may not enhance "virtual social capital," questioning whether it truly exists (p. 170). One phenomenon is certain though: The decline in civic involvement predates the rapid infusion and adoption of the information superhighway. In contrast, other elements of electronic technologies appear to bolster individualism at the expense of community, especially the dissemination of news and entertainment. Over the last one hundred years, drama and music have shifted from the theaters and concert halls to the private domains of living rooms and automobiles which "allows us to consume this hand-tailored entertainment in private, even utterly alone" (p. 217).

In the school setting, some observers challenge the notion that computers promote collaboration (Oppenheimer, 1997). Computer-facilitated synchronous and asynchronous exchanges lack the depth and meaning of face-to-face conversations. Moreover, in the schools computer collaboration often involves one student controlling the computer at a time, leading to competition as well as potentially noisy disputes. These observations support child development specialists' concerns that computer technology promotes an unintended outcome, social isolation. Technology potentially advances other dangers as well.

TECHNOLOGY ATTRIBUTES FOSTER PITFALLS AND MYTHS

Technology antagonists argue that computers create a reality fraught with myths and danger (Banks & Renwick, 1997; Oppenheimer, 1997; Roszak, 1986; Rukeyser, 1998b; Stoll, 1995). The precarious state results from the attributes of information technology, which include the dynamics of rapid change and an unhindered proliferation and integration into all aspects of society.

The Consequences of Computer Evolution

Computers have evolved at a rapid rate causing certain skeptics to question the value of public expenditures. After schools acquire the technology, a continuous stream of money is necessary for maintaining the equipment and networks (Banks & Renwick, 1997). Politicians and schools divert money away from other programs in a zero-sum game (Bloom, 1996; Norris, 1999, Rukeyser, 1998a, 1998b; Schmitt & Slonaker, 1996; Watson, 1999). In addition, critics cite the schools' lackluster history in dealing with nonenduring technologies (Cuban, 1986; Oppenheimer, 1997).

Cuban (1986) articulates a pattern beginning in 1920 where schools attempt to integrate new technologies into the classrooms with little success. The process begins with education reformists, backed by researchers and developers, offering bold promises. When teachers fail to implement the new technology, blame is placed on money, the school bureaucracy, and teacher resistance. Eventually the technology is faulted. The notorious process repeats itself with the introduction of the next "latest" technology. By blindly accepting reformist arguments, society acquiesces to technologies' demands.

Society's Submission to Information Technology's Demands

According to Postman (1992) the unquestioned acceptance and embracement of computers is a submission to technology's demands.

> The fact is, there are very few political, social, and especially personal problems that arise because of insufficient information. Nonetheless, as incomprehensible problems mount, as the concept of progress fades, as meaning itself becomes suspect, the Technopolist stands firm in believing that what the world needs is yet more information. (pp. 60–61)

The power of information technology convolutes logic, creates and perpetuates myths, and potentially causes physical and emotional harm.

An unbalanced emphasis on information twists logic and distorts meaning. Information is not knowledge nor is knowledge wisdom (Roszak, 1986; Stoll, 1995). Likewise, when society places great emphasis on an information technology, it sends the message that a mediated environment is more meaningful than the real one. Recent evidence suggests that students increasingly perceive the World Wide Web as the premier authoritative source for information, when in fact, much of it is ill informed and superficial. The popular press also reports a surge in digital plagiarism, students copying and pasting information from the web and offering it as an original work (Oppenheimer, 1997; Rukeyser, 1998b). All this leads to one of the most prevalent myths: The Internet will eventually feature the great libraries of the world online.

The vast bulk of scholarship and other intellectual works are unlikely to appear online because of copyright laws. People want to be paid for their work, and they do not want to offer it for free (Rukeyser, 1998b; Stoll, 1995). Rukeyser (1998b) blames politicians for immortalizing the library myth with empty rhetoric. A harmful policy conclusion is a shift in attention and resources. School administrators divert purchases from substantive printed material to less significant electronic resources. In other words, the emphasis on computer technologies affects the availability of learning resources and threatens physical and emotional well being.

Information technology demands complete conformity and total infusion into society often without regard for the individual physical and emotional costs (Mendels, 1999b, 1999c; Oppenheimer, 1997; Schmitt & Slonaker, 1996; White & Walker, 1998). Mendels (1999b) reports on the emergence of child advocacy groups and their efforts to prevent the computer from becoming as entrenched as television in the psyches of American children. The members blame information technologies for provoking stress in children and the subsequent medical maladies such as depression and hyperactivity. One group, the *Alliance for Childhood,* is composed of educators, psychologists, doctors, and others who advocate the banning of intensive computer use in the elementary grades. Child specialists indicate two major reasons for limiting technology in the early grades. First, children require a broad foundation drawing on all five senses. And second, the tangible world offers greater learning opportunities. Computers, on the other hand, offer a one-dimensional, technical outlook detrimental to early stages of development. One symptom is that children may be isolated from direct interactions with caring individuals, thereby hampering development of strong interpersonal relationships (Oppenheimer, 1997). Additionally, some researchers believe that blatant commercial exploitation increases with the continued infusion of technology (Mendels, 1999c; White & Walker, 1998).

A CRITICAL LOOK AT COMPUTER TECHNOLOGY IN THE SOCIAL STUDIES CLASSROOM

Information technology is not an educational panacea (Mendels, 1999c; Rukeyser, 1998a). As the schools continue to accelerate the growth of computer capital investment, lingering questions remain regarding pedagogy, practice, and student achievement.

Pedagogy

Perhaps the greatest barrier to classroom computer integration is teacher resistance (Cuban, 1986; Cummings 1995, 1996). Cummings (1995, 1996) offers six arguments explaining why teachers resist educational technology: (1) disincentives and lack of incentives; (2) scarcity of knowledge; (3) an established teaching pattern; (4) paucity of resources; (5) potential technical problems; and (6) antiquated institutionalized patterns. Teachers maintain the status quo because teaching is central to their lives and pedagogical change forces uncomfortable value changes (Olson, 2000). Prescriptive measures call for more and better resources, access, training, and vesting teachers with control over policy (Cuban, 1996). Fatemi (1999) cites training as the most important obstacle preventing effective classroom computer integration. He advocates skills and selection training to recognize diverse learning styles. Pedagogical concerns reflect effective practice issues as well.

Practice

Research about computer practice in the social studies classroom is scant and fragmented. However, some critics offer insights into the possible hazards of student practice. Computer integration in the schools focuses on efficiency rather than on how it alters the conception of learning. Therefore, technology ignores why students learn (Postman, 1992). Additionally, computer integration forces the choice between molding children into caring, democratic citizens or dispassionate, efficient learners (Cuban, 1996). A technology focus places emphasis on vocational skills at the peril of critical thinking development (Mendels, 1999b). Furthermore, "edutainment" software is a superficial and ineffective substitute for real experiences (Rukeyser, 1998a). Another hazard is visual learning may not be the best way to develop nonverbal reasoning skills (Oppenheimer 1997). Olson (2000) contends that computer labs are a symbol of a movement to stress generic thinking skills. Computer assisted learning systems usurp the traditional curriculum-based objectives which are time proven and resource rich. He advocates an examination of conventional classroom roles in an effort to establish more effective computer practice. The uncertainty enveloping effective practice emanates largely from controversial achievement studies.

Student Achievement

The paucity of relevant studies addressing social studies classroom computer integration and achievement outcomes aids a raging debate concerning general effectiveness. Skeptics point out that in cases where various studies conclude positive results, they are often based on flawed assumptions and experimentation (Berson, 1996; Oppenheimer, 1997). In addition, results are uneven across disciplines (Schacter, 1999), do not indicate an increase in standardized test scores (Mendels, 1999a; Norris, 1999; Rukeyser, 1998b; Schmitt & Slonaker, 1996), and in some instances, signal less achievement over traditional teaching and learning (Schacter, 1999; Schmitt & Slonaker, 1996). Saye and Brush (1999) conducted a social studies experiment to examine the effects of how students respond to a specially designed multimedia unit on the civil rights movement. Although the researchers caution about generalizing the results, they report evidence of student success in developing historical understanding as a result of the "authentic context" generated by multimedia. Effective pedagogy and practice may lead to increases in achievement, but many citizens do not have access to computer technologies.

The Amplification of Inequality

The Digital Divide

The digital divide separates those who are information rich through their access to telecommunications, computers, and the Internet from the information poor. It does not recognize national boundaries. Rather, it cuts a wide swath between social classes around the world (Human Development Report, 1999). The gap continues to widen in what some scholars view as a glaring contradiction: Never before has a medium existed potentially offering all individuals entrée to information and a conduit to publish diverse views. Yet, prohibitive costs for computer equipment and services, a highly specialized language, and other exclusive barriers limit access to a wealthy, elite few (Warschauer, 1999).

In the United States, the Commerce Department's National Telecommunication and Information Agency (NTIA) compiles statistics about the digital divide. The NTIA reports substantial increases in household purchases and usage of computers, the Internet, and e-mail for the period 1994–1998, but at the same time the agency notes an expanding digital divide largely along geographic, income, and racial lines. Rural and central city areas lag far behind in computers and online services. But, when the agency controls for income, the disparity disappears. Although computer use increases for all income groups, larger incomes continue to outpace the lesser, widening the divide. Likewise, among racial groups, Whites are over three times as likely to own a computer than Blacks and four times than Latinos, even when controlling for income. In terms of age, the young and senior citizens are less likely to own and use a computer. Higher education levels also signal increase use and access. A two-parent family structure is twice as likely to purchase a computer than a single-parent arrangement (NTIA, 1999). In the global community, the digital divide takes on an added dimension.

The Human Development Report (1999) describes a gaping digital divide between affluent, modern nations and poor, traditional countries. The report suggests that corporate entities exercise information hegemony through (1) private research agendas that ignore the needs of poor people; (2) tightened intellectual property rights that shut out developing countries; (3) patent laws that do not recognize traditional forms of knowledge; and (4) the pursuit of profit at the expense of everything else. The report acknowledges that the gap between "haves" and "have-nots" as well as "knows" and "know-nots" is expanding significantly. Future recommendations include the call for strong policy action to recognize the needs of diverse cultures.

THE FUTURE OF TECHNOLOGY IN THE SOCIAL STUDIES

We are confronted with rapid technological change and, as yet, unfilled expectations (Diem, 1999). As the incorporation of technology has grown at a massive rate, accompanying expenditures have paralleled the acquisition of hardware and software in the schools. Despite financial investment in the technological infrastructure of many educational institutions, results have been less than compelling on the subsequent impact on teaching and learning. Whether blame rests with the lack of teacher preparedness, failure to seamlessly integrate technology into instruction, insufficient access to computers, or only partial realization of the potential of the hardware and software to enhance the content, the efficacy of technology for transformation of schools remains unrealized.

Computers have been accompanied by hype and hope, and the resulting view of the future is filled with cautious possibilities. We are adventuring into uncharted territory where our current knowledge and experience are insufficient to predict computer technology that has yet to come. Shaver (1999) has suggested that this innovation may be irrelevant to inducing changes in the experience of schooling our children. Enthusiasm for the potential of technology has further confounded conclusions which fail to separate structural processes from the medium implemented. Due to the lack of resources, ambiguity of educators and contradictory research conclusions, the broad effects of technology on schools has become minimal. Within these seemingly paradoxical themes—that is, rapid and unforeseeable technological change and impact, on the one hand, and caution based on unfulfilled expectations in the past, on the other—what is the future of social studies education in the electronic age of knowledge and distributed intelligence?

If we hope to have a strong basis for reform, the focus of educational development and design needs to be informed by a conceptual framework which explicitly identifies assumptions about teaching, youth, and social exchange. The social studies in the United States has been based on a tradition of developing children's democratic ideals and promoting their civic involvement. A process which contributes to the democratization of youth is a fostering of their personal identity within the context of a strong sense of community. This development can best be enabled by fostering an ability to relate within family and community units. Online exchanges offer the promise of transforming youth development through a global network of individuals who are active in meaningful online participation, but these exchanges may perpetuate biased views of the world that are informed by interactions with predominantly elite segments of society, especially in international contexts, and are devoid of perspectives which promote pluralism through critical self-reflection as well as historical and cultural contexts of power and intolerance. In essence, the caveat to technology and innovation is the presumption that the innovation can influence identity, inform values, foster critical reasoning skills, and instill compassion for others.

The specific features of technology with its rapid developments and ever-advancing innovation are less critical to discussions of future applications than the evolution of increased controls and choices for harnessing the power to access and process information. Technological innovation is both an artifact of society and an influencer of social change (Williams, 1997). Discussions of the promise and practice of computer technologies in the social studies often have failed to address the uncertainty and complexity of implementing innovation. The circular process of evolving new technologies, incorporating and adapting these enhancements into instruction, identifying the utility and outcomes of the innovation, and anticipating future applications emphasizes the intricate interplay of the various stakeholders in the stages of implementation and use. We must concede that we will always have unknowns regarding "the responses of the user and the evolution of social needs" (Williams, 1997, p. 302). As Senn (1999) notes, technology has introduced more questions into the dynamics of social studies instruction, and neither the promises of the techno-optimists nor the warnings of the techno-skeptics have resolved the issues for either the short-term impact or, more critically, the long-term repercussions.

As schools propagate access to technology in education, new challenges to students arise. Even fundamental questions lack answers. With the growing awareness about children and brain functioning, how will computers and virtual experiences alter the human brain? When William Gibson coined the term cyberspace in 1984, he referred to it as a consensual hallucination. How will this digital hallucination entice youth away from real experiences, and what will be the concomitant effect on their socioemotional functioning? What is the effect of computers on learning and motivation? How will technology facilitate expansion beyond our human limitations? If the technology can provide the data, information and knowledge, then parents and teachers have the task of instructing students to manage ideas effectively and wisely. This collection of tools in a mediated environment offers potential efficiency; however, citizenship is dependent on compassionate activism in real contexts as opposed to virtual settings. We need to continually reevaluate the role of information technology in schools as well as the role of schools in the age of information technologies.

Educational innovation has always been a slow process with a reliance on old educational paradigms that direct the use of technology implementation. However, we are at a crossroads with tremendous potential.

> New technology is a voracious infant. Its demands for attention, care, and feeding increase as it grows. Yet we still retain the upper hand. While computers are far more than "just tools," they don't independently make decisions (not yet, at any rate). Our wise decisions now can equip our young to master their machines in the service of rich and productive lives. Thoughtful adult models can teach them how to question the vacuous values of those who try to sell them products or promises. If, on the other hand, we turn youngsters into stimulus-seeking droids able only to follow others' programs, yearn for their products, or click buttons for immediate and trivial rewards, we should not be surprised if real minds ultimately become the servants of virtual ones. (Heally, 1998, pp. 318–319)

Social studies educators need to reflect upon technology to determine what skills it can foster while concomitantly critiquing the social and economic influences it has on children, youth and society (Berson, 2000). The danger of evolving "electronic tourists" (Fabos & Young, 1999) who continue to view the cyberworld through ethnocentric lenses is countered by the prospect of reinventing communications, culture and community as youth learn to evolve new solutions to the problems fostered by the information revolution. Successful solutions will be based on the complexity of a knowledge base that is neither fixed nor unbiased, and flexibility and adaptation will be the skills necessary to assist students and teachers in auspiciously negotiating technology and fostering a meaningful reform which does not trivialize human interaction, community consciousness, or collaboration in the context of global connectivity.

NOTE

1.   Hypertext is a form of web-based electronic text with selective words and phrases linked to additional text. Hypermedia refers to the use of images and audio in addition to text.

REFERENCES

Adams, R.C. (1995). Cool moves: Teaching geography and history with hypercard. *The Computing Teacher, 22*(7), 31–33.

Ayers, E.L. (1999). *History in hypertext.* Retrieved August 24, 1999 [Online] Available: http://jefferson.village.virginia.edu/vcdh/Ayers.OAH.html

Banks, S., & Renwick, L. (1997, June). Technology is still a promise, not a panacea. *Los Angeles Times,* p. A-1. Retrieved January 25, 2000, [Online]. Available: http://www.realworld.org/archives/timesarticle1.html

Barr, H. (1994). Social studies by electronic mail. *The Social Studies 85*(4), 170–173.

Becker, H.J. (1999). Internet use by teachers. Retrieved February 05, 2000, [Online]. Available: http://www.crito.uci.edu/TLC/findings/Internet-Use/startpage.htm

Bellan, J.M., & Scheurman, G. (1998). Actual and virtual reality: Making the most of field trips. *Social Education 62*(1), 35–40.

Berenfeld, B. (1996). Linking students to the infosphere. *T.H.E. Journal, 23*(9), 76–83.

Berson, M.J. (1996). Effectiveness of computer technology in the social studies: A review of the literature. *Journal of Research on Computing in Education, 28*(4), 487–499.

Berson, M.J. (2000). Rethinking research and pedagogy in the social studies: The creation of caring connections through technology and advocacy. *Theory & Research in Social Education, 28*(1), 121–131.

Berson, M.J., & Berson, I.R. (2000). An introduction to global child advocacy: Historical action, contemporary perspectives, and future directions. *International Journal of Educational Policy, Research and Practice, 1*(1), 1–12.

Birkerts, S. (1994). *The Gutenberg Elegies: The Fate of Reading in the Electronic Age.* Boston: Faber and Faber.

Bloom, G.S. (1996). Caveat emptor buyer beware (Technohype). *Thrust for educational leadership.* Retrieved January 25, 2000, [Online]. Available: http://www.realworld.org/articles/Caveat_Empt.html

Boldt, D.J., Gustafson, L.V., & Johnson, J.E. (1995). The Internet: A curriculum warehouse for social studies teachers. *The Social Studies, 86*(3), 105–112.

Braun, J. (1997). Past, possibilities, and potholes on the information superhighway. *Social Education 61*(3), pp. 149–153.

Braun J.A., Fernlund, P.F., & White, C.S. (1998). *Technology tools and the social studies curriculum.* Wilsonville, OR: Franklin, Beedle, and Associates.

Braun, J.A., & Risinger, C.F. (1999). *Surfing social studies: The Internet book.* Washington, DC: National Council for the Social Studies.

Coady, B. (1994). Hypertravel. *The Computing Teacher, 22*(3), 27–29.

Cuban, L. (1986). *Teachers and machines: The classroom use of technology since 1920.* New York: Teachers College Press.

Cuban, L. (1996, October). Techno-reformers and classroom teachers. *Education Week.* Retrieved January 25, 2000, [Online]. Available: http://www.edweek.org/ew/vol-16/06cuban.h16

Cummings, L.E. (1995). Educational technology—A faculty resistance view, Part I: Incentives and understanding. *Educational Technology Review, 4,* 13–18.

Cummings, L.E. (1996, Winter). Educational technology—A faculty resistance view, Part II: Challenges of resources, technology, and tradition. *Educational Technology Review,* 7, 18–20, 30.

Diem, R. (1983). *Social Implications of technology innovations: A study of ethics and attitudes.* (ERIC Document Reproduction Service No. ED 255 403)

Diem, R. (1999). Technology and reform: A retrospective view. In M.R. Nelson, L. Monsen, & Y. Nordkvelle (Eds.), *Reform and change in social studies: 1998 SSEC annual conference* (Research Report No. 47, pp. 19–23). Lillehammer: Lillehammer College.

Dillner, M. (1993). Using hypermedia to enhance content area instruction. *Journal of Reading, 37*(4), 260–270.

Ehman, L.H., & Glenn, A.D. (1987). *Computer-based education in the social studies.* ERIC Clearinghouse for Social Studies/Social Science Education. (ERIC Document Reproduction Service No. ED 284 825)

Fabos, B., & Young, M.D. (1999). Telecommunication in the classroom: Rhetoric versus reality. *Review of Educational Research, 69*(3), 217–259.

Fatemi, E. (1999, September). Building the digital curriculum: Summary. *Education Week.* Retrieved January 15, 2000, [Online]. Available: http://www.edweek.org/sreports/tc99/articles/summary.htm

Ferretti, R.P., & Okolo, C.M. (1996). Authenticity in learning: Multimedia design projects in the social studies for students with disabilities. *Journal of Learning Disabilities, 29*(5), 45–60.

Fitch, N. (1997). History after the web: Teaching with hypermedia. *The History Teacher, 30*(4), 427–441.

Fontana, L.A., Dede, C., White, C.A., & Cates, W.M. (1993). *Multimedia: A gateway to higher order thinking skills.* Washington, DC: Association for Educational Communications and Technology. (ERIC Document Reproduction Service No. ED 362 165)

Gaines C.L., Johnson, W., & King, D.T. (1996). Achieving technological equity and equal access to the learning tools of the 21st century. *T.H.E. Journal, 23*(6), 76–78.

Garson, G.D. (1995). Computer technology and social issues. (ERIC Document Reproduction Service No. ED 381 156).

Glenn, A.D. (1990). Democracy and technology. *The Social Studies, 81*(5), 215–217.

Gooler, D.D. (1995). Perspectives: Technology as content in social studies curricula for young learners. *Social Studies and the Young Learner, 7*(3), 27–30.

Healy, J.M. (1998). *Failure to connect: How computers affect our children's minds—for better and worse.* New York: Simon & Schuster.

Higgins, K., & Boone, R. (1992). Hypermedia computer study guides and the social studies achievement of students with learning disabilities, remedial students, and regular education students. *Journal of Learning Disabilities, 29*(9), 402–411.

Hollister, B.C. (1995). Social math in the history classroom. *Social Education, 59*(1), 14–16.

Horton, S.V., Boone, R.A., & Lovitt, T.C. (1990). Teaching social studies to learning disabled high school students: Effects of a hypertext study guide. *British Journal of Educational Technology, 21*(2), 118–131.

Human Development Report. (1999). *New technologies and the global race for knowledge* (pp. 57–76). Retrieved February 7, 2000, [Online]. Available: http://www.undp.org/hdro/report.html

Hunt, N.P., & Allen, E.G. (1988). Fifth graders do "real work" on the computer. *Social Studies, 79*(2), 78–80.

Hunter, B. (1987). Knowledge-creative learning with data bases. *Social Education, 51*(1), 31–43.

Jennings, J.M. (1994). *Comparative analysis, hypercard, and the future of social studies education.* Paper presented at the Annual Conference of the National Council for the Social Studies, Phoenix, Arizona. (ERIC Document Reproduction Service No. ED 381 439)

Johnson, C., & Rector, J. (1997) The Internet ten: Using the Internet to meet social studies curriculum standards. *Social Education, 61*(3), 167–169.

Knapp, L.R., & Glenn, A.D. (1996). *Restructuring schools with technology.* New York: Allyn & Bacon.

Langeveld, W. (1983). Alternative teaching aids: Or why we can do without new technology in political education. (ERIC Document Reproduction Service No. ED 231 737)

Martorella, P.H. (1997). Technology and social studies: Which way to the sleeping giant? *Theory and Research in Social Education, 25*(4), 511–514.

Maskin, M.R. (1996). "Infotectives" on the "Infobahn": Designing Internet-aided projects for the social studies classroom. *NASSP Bulletin, 80*(582), 59–70.

Mason, C.L., & Beal, C. (1999) Virtual fieldtripping: No permission notes needed; Creating a Middle School Classroom Without Walls. *Meridian: A Middle School Computer Technologies Journal, 2*(1). Available: http://www.ncsu.edu/meridian/jan99/vfieldtrip/index.html

McBeath, R.J. (1994). The impact of paradigm shifts on education. *Educational-Media-International, 31*(3), 165–70.

Mendels, P. (1999a). Focus shifts to effectiveness of education technology. *New York Times.* Retrieved January 25, 2000, [Online]. Available: http://www.nytimes.com/library/tech/99/07/cyber/education/14education.ht ml

Mendels, P. (1999b, December 15). Push for computers in classrooms gathers new foes. *New York Times.* Retrieved January 25, 2000, [Online]. Available: http://www.nytimes.com/library/tech/99/12/cyber/education/15education.ht ml

Mendels, P. (1999c, December 29). The leading issues of '99? Wired schools and accreditation. *New York Times.* Retrieved January 25, 2000, [Online]. Available: http://www.nytimes.com/library/tech/99/12/cyber/education29education.html

Milton, K., & Spradley, P. (1996). A Renaissance of the Renaissance: Using Hyperstudio for research projects. *Learning and Leading with Technology, 23*(6), 20–2.

National Telecommunications and Information Administration (1999, November). *Falling through the net: Defining the digital divide.* [On-line]. Available: http://www.ntia.doc.gov/ntiahome/fttn99/contents.html

Newmark, A. (1989). The election of 1912: A hypertext simulation. *Electronic Learning, 8*(2), 54–56.

Norris, M. (1999). Money well spent? *ABC News.* Retrieved January 25, 2000, [Online]. Available: http://abcnews.go.com/onair/CloserLook/wnt990929_computers.html

Northup, T., & Rooze, G.E. (1990). Are social studies teachers using computers?: A national survey. *Social Education, 54*(4), 212–214.

Olson, J. (2000). Trojan horse or teacher's pet? Computers and the culture of the school. *Journal of Curriculum Studies.* Retrieved January 25, 2000, [Online]. Available: http://www.ed.uiuc.edu/jcs/Vol%2032/OLSON.html

Oppenheimer, T. (1997, July). The computer delusion. *The Atlantic Monthly.* Retrieved January 25, 2000, [Online]. Available: http://www.theatlantic.com/issues/97jul/computer.htm

Parisi, L. (1985). *Computer database: Applications for the social studies.* ERIC Digest No. 25. (ERIC Document Reproduction Service No. ED 264 167)

Parker, W. C. (1991). *Handbook of research on social studies teaching and learning.* New York: Macmillian Publishing Company.

Postman, N. (1992). *Technopoly: The surrender of culture to technology.* New York: Alfred A. Knopf.

Putman, R.D. (2000). *Bowling alone: the collapse and revival of American community.* New York: Simon & Schuster.

Raubal, M., Gaupmann, B., & Kuhn, W. (1997). Teaching raster GIS operations with spreadsheets. *Journal of Geography, 96*(5), 258–263.

Roland, L. (1997). Distributing representatives: Using spreadsheets to study apportionment. *Learning and Leading with Technology, 24*(8), 26–29.

Rooze, G.E. (1986). A strategy for helping students draw conclusions. *Social Studies, 77*(2), 74–76.

Ross, E.W. (1991). Microcomputer use in secondary social studies classrooms. *Journal of Educational Research, 85*(1), 39–46.

Roszak, T. (1986). *The cult of information: The folklore of computers and the true art of thinking.* New York: Pantheon Books.

Rukeyser, W.L. (1998a). Broken promises: Decisions about computer based instruction must be based on data and analysis, not faith, fear and hype. *Thrust for Educational Leadership.* Retrieved January 25, 2000, [Online]. Available: http://www.realworld.org/articles/brokenpromises.html

Rukeyser, W.L. (1998b). Technology in our schools. *Our Children.* Retrieved January, 25, 2000, [Online]. Available: http://www.pta.org/pubs/techsch.htm

Saye, J.W., & Brush, T. (1999). Student engagement with social issues in a multimedia-supported learning environment. *Theory and Research in Social Education, 27* (4), 472–504.

Scardamalia, M., & Bereiter, C. (1996). Engaging students in a knowledge society. *Educational Leadership, 54*(3), 6–10.

Schacter, J. (1999). The impact of education technology on student achievement: What the most current research has to say. *The Milken Family Foundation Publications.* Retrieved January 25, 2000, [Online]. Available: http://www.mff.org/edtech/publication.taf?_function=detail&Content_uid1=1 61

Schmitt, C.H., & Slonaker, L. (1996). Computers in school: Do students improve? High technology doesn't always equal high achievement. *Mercury News.* Retrieved January 25, 2000, [Online]. Available: http://www.mercury-center.com/archives/reprints/edcom011496.htm

Sembor, E.C. (1997). Citizenship, diversity, and distance learning: Video conferencing in Connecticut. *Social Education, 61*(3), 154–159.

Senn, P.R. (1999). If the Internet is the answer, what is the question? In M.R. Nelson, L. Monsen, & Y. Nordkvelle (Eds.), *Reform and change in social studies: 1998 SSEC annual conference* (Research Report No. 47, pp. 19–23). Lillehammer, Norway: Lillehammer College.

Shaver, J.P. (1999). Electronic technology and the future of social studies in elementary and secondary schools. In M.R. Nelson, L. Monsen, & Y. Nordkvelle

(Eds.), *Reform and change in social studies: 1998 SSEC annual conference* (Research Report No. 47, pp. 24–37). Lillehammer: Lillehammer College.

Smith-Gratto, K. (1989). Computer literacy and citizenship n a democracy. *Louisiana Social Studies Journal, 16*(1), 30–33.

Stoll, C. (1995). *Silicon snake oil: Second thoughts on the information highway.* New York: Doubleday.

Stoll, C (1999). *High-tech heretic.* New York: Doubleday.

Talbott, S.L. (1995). *The future does not compute: Transcending the machines in our midst.* Sebastopol, CA: O'Reilly & Associates, Inc.

Tally, W. (1996). Up against authentic history: Helping teachers make the most of primary source materials on-line. *Electronic Learning 16*(2), 40–41.

Warschauer, M. (1999). *Electronic literacies: Language, culture, and power in online education.* Mahwah, NJ: Lawrence Erlbaum Associates.

Watson, K.L. (1999). The cybershift: The Web spawns a new social studies classroom, but what exactly is it? *CSS Journal: Computers in the Social Studies.* Retrieved November 3, 1999, [Online]. Available: http://www.cssjournal.com/klwatson.html

White, C. (1996). Relevant social studies education: Integrating technology and constructivism. *Journal of Technology and Teacher Education, 4*(1), 69–76.

White, C.S. (1997). Technology and social studies: An introduction. *Social Education, 61*(3), 147–148.

White, C., & Walker, T. (1998, May/June). Technology integration in social studies and teacher education: A postmodern critique. *CSS Journal: Computers in the Social Studies, 6*(3). Retrieved December 21, 1999, [Online]. Available: http://www.cssjournal.com/tech.html

Williams, R. (1997). The social shaping of information and communications technologies. In H. Kubicek, W.H. Dutton, & R. Williams (Eds.), *The social shaping of information superhighways: European and American roads to the information society* (pp. 299–338). Frankfurt: Campus Verlag.

Wilson, E.K., & Marsh II, G.E. (1995). Social studies and the Internet revolution. *Social Education, 50*(4), 198–202.

CHAPTER 10

THE FUTURE OF RESEARCH ON SOCIAL STUDIES—FOR WHAT PURPOSE?

James P. Shaver

INTRODUCTION

The quality of the research on social studies education has been criticized frequently and thoroughly over the past 40 years, beginning with Metcalf's (1963) chapter in the *Handbook of Research on Teaching*. A series of later critics has included Shaver and Larkins (1973), Shaver (1979, 1982a, b), Nelson and Shaver (1985), Fraenkel (1987), and Fraenkel and Wallen (1991). Few elements of the research endeavor have been spared in the various analyses. Among the shortcomings identified have been the pursuit of problems irrelevant to the interests and concerns of school practitioners, weak experimental designs, the lack of adequate reliability and validity evidence for dependent variables and the absence of verification of independent variables, studies of too short duration for the results to be generalized to ongoing schooling, the dearth of replication studies, the inappropriate use of tests of statistical significance, and the failure to attend to educational significance.

More recently, authors of brief commentaries to be aimed at "taking stock of our past endeavors and charting new courses" (Ross, 1997, p. 6) during the 25th year of *Theory and Research in Education (TRSE)* lamented anew the continuing poor quality of research on social studies education and the lack of impact on curriculum and instruction (Leming, 1997; Kornfield & Marker, 1997; Shaver, 1997). A year later, in a brief Viewpoint piece, Fraenkel (1998) grumbled that the "host of weaknesses [he had cat-alogued] that characterized much of the social studies research

...."extant" some 10 years earlier, as well as when he and Wallen (1991) pre-pared their chapter for the *Handbook of Research on Social Studies Learning and Teaching*, were "still characteristic of the great majority of social studies research today.... We don't seem to improve on what we do" (p. 272).

Fraenkel (1998) did, however, note "some encouraging signs, the most obvious being the considerable increase in qualitative and historical research studies and use of effect sizes as indicators of practical signifi-cance (instead of relying, as is still so often done, on statistical significance) in quantitative research" (p. 273). A perusal of the last five years of *TRSE* (1995–1999, vols. 23–27) yielded some evidence bearing on Fraenkel's guarded optimism.

FROM P VALUES TO ESs?

First, what can be said at this point in time about effect sizes use? An effect size is a metric for the magnitude of a result that is independent of sample size and scale of measurement (Glass, 1976). Standardized mean differ-ences (*SMDs*) are a widely used type of effect size. Percentages are an example of other statistics that can serve as "difference" effect sizes. Corre-lational effect sizes—e.g., the point biserial correlation and etta^2 for inter-val and ratio scale data, the phi coefficient and Cramer's *V* for frequencies and percentages—are available for researchers who want to interpret their data in terms of association and variance explained (Cohen, 1988; Shaver, 1991, pp. 87–88).

My review of 1995–1999 *TRSE* articles did not yield encouraging results in regard to the use of effect sizes (*ESs*). Eleven articles contained reports of quantitative data collected on students, teachers, and/or parents. In only one article (Hahn, 1996) were *ESs* reported explicitly. (Although not defined, computations using the tabled means and standard deviations indicated that the *ESs* were standardized mean differences.) In a conceptu-ally sound analytic move in light of her convenience samples of students in cooperating teachers' classes (Shaver, 1993), Hahn included no *p* values from tests of statistical significance.

Other authors abstained from the use of tests of statistical significance with data from nonrandom samples, but, unfortunately, did not report effect sizes. If Houser (1995) had reported standard deviations with his means, an interested reader could have computed *ESs*. Singer (1995), Mitchell, Evans, Daly, and Roach (1997), and Prior (1999) overlooked that their percentages could be interpreted as effect sizes or used to compute other *ESs* (i.e., correlation coefficients).

Some authors reported the results of tests of statistical significance despite the lack of random sampling or assignment. Byrnes and Torney-Purta (1995) analyzed data from their nonrandom samples (adolescents selected to participate in an international politics workshop, adolescents from an elite private high school, and adults recruited from graduate programs at a university) using repeated measures, 3 x 2 analysis of variance (ANOVA), with Newman-Kuels post hoc tests, and chi-square. No ESs were reported for their means, and standard deviations or ANOVA tables (with sums of squares) were not included so that readers could compute ESs themselves. They also did not interpret their percentages as ESs and referred incorrectly to chi-square—a test of statistical significance—as a method "similar to Pearson correlations [that] measures the degree of association among [sic] two variables" (p. 269). In addition, the term "significant" was used without a modifier (e.g., "statistical significance") in discussing their results.

tenDam and Rijkschroeff (1996), Hughes (1997), and Saye and Brush (1999) also used tests of statistical significance with nonrandom, convenience samples (11 intact women's history classes and 11 intact comparison classes, 30 students in a college course, and 2 intact classes of 11th graders, respectively), did not report ESs, and relied on p values in discussing their results. Hughes did report means and standard deviations, so ESs could be computed by knowledgeable readers. tenDam and Rijkschroeff and Saye and Brush reported percentages without recognition that they could be interpreted as ESs or converted to correlational ESs.

Although Mitchell et al. (1997) refrained from analyzing their nonrandom percentage data with inferential statistics, they were not similarly circumspect with their correlational analyses. Stepwise multiple-regression analysis might yield an interpretable effect size—in this study, for the association of demographic variables with attitudes toward academic freedom issues (for criticisms of this type of analysis, see Thompson, 1998). However, R^2 was not reported, although an inappropriate test of statistical significance was (p. 63).

Vinson (1998) had a random sample as a basis for his use of chi-square, but overlooked the potential ES interpretations of his percentages. (He also inappropriately reported p values for his reliability and validity coefficients.) Griffith (1999) drew a random sample of elementary teachers. He indicated (p. 381) that he used the t-test to analyze subgroup differences, but then reported no t or p values, or ESs.

The 1995–1999 *TRSE* articles included one review of literature (Wade & Saxe, 1996). Despite the recent emphasis on research review methodology and, in particular, the utility of effect sizes in summarizing research (e.g., Shaver, 1991), Wade and Saxon did not discuss literature-review methodological issues or report ESs (except, incidentally, percentages, p. 344). References were made to statistical significance (e.g., "statistically significant gains" [p. 342]) and to "significance," but with no modifier (e.g., "no significant impacts" [p. 341] and "significant gains" [p. 343]). Results were also referred to in imprecise terms—e.g., "found increases" (p. 341), "displayed better ... abilities," "show only small increases" (p. 342), "showed larger gains ... than" (p. 343), and "is a strong predictor" (p. 345). Effect sizes would have added valuable information for those interested in the outcomes of community service learning.

In short, the last five years of *TRSE* provided little evidence to support Fraenkel's (1998) optimism about the increased use of effect sizes and diminished reliance on tests of statistical significance in research on social education. It is encouraging to note that a few authors are refraining from the use of inferential statistics when they lack random samples, but discouraging to continue to see results reported in terms of *p* values from inferential analyses on nonrandom samples. Moreover, *ESs* are not being reported, or recognized when available.

It is also important to note that the reporting of effect sizes is a necessary but not sufficient step for the educationally meaningful interpretation of quantitative research results. Hahn (1996), for example, reported that she had obtained "no *educationally* significant gender differences ... as indicated by the effect sizes (.00–.22)" (p. 17, emphasis added), but provided no rationale for that conclusion. The magnitude of an *ES* is not per se an indicator of educational significance; large findings may be trivial and small findings important (Shaver, 1985, 1991, pp. 89–91). For example, should an *SMD* = 3.0 on a test of information recall from a textbook be considered an educationally valuable outcome? Put differently, why is Hahn's *SMD* of .22 for a measure of political interest (or .23 for media use, p. 18) not educationally significant? What magnitude of *ES* would have been necessary for educational significance?

Obviously, the establishment of educational significance is no easy task. Not only must the benefit of the result be weighed against the financial and human costs of producing it, but the adequacy of the research itself must be evaluated—for example, did the study, if experimental in design, have internal validity and is the result replicable, generalizable, and consistent across relevant subgroups of students and teachers. The fundamental issue of benefit—i.e., the value of the outcome—is particularly difficult to address, because the assessment-validity evidence necessary to make a case for educational value in the context of justified goals for social studies education is typically not available.

The assessment-validity situation is especially difficult for those who believe that the purpose of social studies education is to have an impact on adult citizenship behavior. Validity coefficients for the strength of association between social studies outcome assessments and later adult behavior are not available, much less evidence to calibrate test scores with later behavior (Sechrest, McKnight, & McKnight, 1996). For example, how many points of change on a political efficacy scale, such as used by Hahn (1996), are necessary to produce a 10% increase in the likelihood that a student will, as an adult, become actively involved in advocacy on a public issue? Even intermediate validity data on what has come to be called the "authenticity" of assessment—i.e., whether the test is based on a conceptually sound construct, such as an adequate model of public-issues analysis; whether the assessment situation represents adequately the real-life situation in which the conceptual frame is to be applied; and whether there is evidence that the assessment scores correspond with the judgments of persons with relevant expertise (Oliver & Shaver, 1974, pp. 183–185, 221–222)—are commonly lacking.

To sum up, there is little evidence of a trend toward the routine reporting of effect sizes in social studies research reports. Hopefully, any movement in that direction will be accompanied by increased awareness that *ES* magnitude is not alone a sufficient basis for judgments about the educational significance of results. Assessment validity is an especially crucial consideration, and major research efforts are needed in that area.

QUALITATIVE AND HISTORICAL STUDIES?

How about Fraenkel's (1998) other "encouraging sign," a "considerable increase in qualitative and historical research studies?" There is no question but that the reporting of qualitative studies of social education has increased. Fraenkel and Wallen noted in 1991 (p. 69) that only 29% of the "empirical" articles published in *TRSE* from 1979 to 1988 were qualitative, with even smaller percentages of reports of qualitative social studies research in other journals. Based on data that Ehman (1998, pp. 241, 243) reported from his analysis of articles in *TRSE* from 1988 to 1997, the percentage of qualitative articles increased to 79% for that period; from 1991 to 1997, 85% of the empirical articles published in the journal were qualitative research reports. I counted 11 qualitative research articles, 58% of the empirical articles in *TRSE*, during 1998 to 1999. No *TRSE* publication trend for historical articles is discernible from Ehman's or my data.

But is the trend toward increased qualitative research "encouraging?" That is, has the research been any more productive than quantitative research in building educational theory or improving social studies education? Not that I have been able to discern. The relative impacts of quantitative and qualitative research on social studies education is an area of inquiry that, to the best of my knowledge, has not yet been adequately pursued. My reading of the literature indicates that engagement in qualitative research has primarily provided a source of intellectual satisfaction for those uncomfortable with or pessimistic about quantitative research, not any increase in understanding of the educational process or knowledge of assistance to educational practitioners.

As Jackson (1993) observed in his friendly commentary on qualitative research, such studies could serve as heuristics for teachers who wish to reflect on their instructional decisions and might sometimes increase teachers' confidence in what they are doing. However, Jackson noted that teachers rarely read qualitative research reports. Why? At least in part because "most [qualitative researchers write] for their like-minded colleagues" hoping that "minimally ... a handful of our peers, which means our fellow qualitative researchers, will read and approve of what we have done." In particular, qualitative studies tend not to be of interest to school people because they "do not directly address the immediate interests of practitioners. They do not tell them how to do their jobs better" (p. 228). Along the same lines, Fraenkel (1998, p. 274) referred to "overlong qualitative reports that describe every detail of what goes on in a single classroom without ever explaining why this particular classroom was worth looking at in the first place."

The emerging analyses of qualitative research sound very much like the critiques of quantitative research over the years. Tanner (1998) made that connection directly. He noted that the tendency to use "technical and esoteric jargon ... to mask the poverty of ideas underlying the research, and to isolate the communication within the cocoons of narrow academic specialties ... is no less the case with much so-called qualitative research" than with quantitative research (p. 346). In short, qualitative research does not appear to have been more successful than quantitative research in generating knowledge germane to social studies education.

WHY SO UNPRODUCTIVE?

What, aside from the usual litany of shortcomings noted at the beginning of this chapter, might account for the lack of productivity of research on social studies education? As a result of experiences as dean of the School of Graduate Studies at Utah State University (USU), I have begun to shape a different type of answer to that question.

One of the responsibilities of USU's graduate dean is to sign the title page of each master's thesis and doctoral dissertation, signifying acceptance in fulfillment of that degree requirement. I am not inclined to put my signature to anything unless I am familiar with its contents. As a result, the sign-off process presented an excellent opportunity to review research and research orientations across several disciplines.

For the most part, the studies that graduate students reported in their theses and dissertations fit my preconceived notions of research in science and the social sciences (including education). In the humanities, I found little difficulty in agreeing to the request that master's students in English be allowed to submit a committee-approved novel or collection of poems for a thesis, rather than having to do empirical research, as had previously been required. What I found somewhat perplexing were the theses and dissertations from engineering.

Utah State University has strong programs in mechanical and aeronautical, electrical and computer, biological and irrigation, and civil engineering. Graduate students work with faculty in producing practical, functional artifacts or methods for producing such artifacts—e.g., computerized irrigation systems to aid agriculture in Thailand; slope-movement-resistant concrete piers for highway bridges; control systems for satellites; real-time transmission of simultaneous, two-way audio and video over telephone lines. However, the theses and dissertations seemed to be almost totally focused on specific projects, with little concern for building a cumulative knowledge base in the literature or for reviewing such a literature as a basis for the research.

I sent one thesis back to electrical and computer engineering with the comment that it lacked any literature review tying the study to past research in the field and so looked like it was just a project report, rather than a scholarly research report. The faculty advisor (who was also the department head) scratched his head, reckoned that I was right, and had the student add a four-page review that laid no foundation for the study. In the meantime, the device the student had developed was in use, facilitating the control of satellites in space.

I never saw another engineering thesis without a literature review, but I sensed that I was dealing with a different type of research domain, although I could not quite piece together the dynamics for that difference. Then I read a working paper by Andy Gibbons (n.d.), a professor in USU's Department of Instructional Technology, in which he built a case for instructional technology as a nonscience activity, relying heavily on a book by an aeronautical engineer, Walter Vincenti (1990), *What Engineers Know and How They Know It.* Vincenti's thesis, synopsized below, is that engineering is technology, not science, not even applied science, and so is a different type of research enterprise with a different epistemology. That is, purpose drives epistemology.

The purpose of science, Vincenti submits, is to understand nature; such knowledge is the focus of scientific research, an end in itself. The basic use of knowledge in science is to create more knowledge. The purpose of engineering, in contrast, is practical and set in a social context: It is to create artifacts that serve humans in a direct, immediate way. Knowledge is not generated for its own sake, but to be used in the design, production, and operation of artifacts that meet recognized social needs. Increased understanding of nature defines progress in science; in engineering, progress is defined by the existence of useful artifacts and increased effectiveness in producing particular kinds of artifacts.

Given the differences in purpose, Vincenti notes, scientists and engineers pursue different types of problems from differing epistemological stances. The role of theory differs as a result. Scientific theory is intended to describe nature, to explain phenomena, and to be used to make predictions as the basis for generating new knowledge. Generality and precision are valued attributes of scientific theory. On the other hand, when engineers do pursue theory, it is for the purpose of contributing to the design, production, and operation of useful artifacts. Engineering theory is typically mathematical, to be used in practical calculations to predict artifact performance. Lack of explanation is tolerated as long as there is sufficient generality and precision for the design and development task at hand; pursuing either elaboration or detail further simply wastes time and money, in light of the purpose of engineering. As a consequence, for example, the textbook treatments of thermodynamics are different in physics and engineering. Physicists are interested in understanding as completely as possible the thermodynamic properties of matter; engineers are interested in those aspects of thermodynamics that will help them to design better artifacts, such as bridges and aircraft.

In the absence of theory, the scientist pursues it. In the same situation, Vincenti observes, the engineer decides whether to try develop a theory or to take the experimentation route to solve the problem at hand. Engineering experimentation differs from scientific experimentation because it is aimed at artifact design, not at knowledge building, although it may result, as the development of engineering theory often does, in outcomes applicable to other problems. The scientist formulates theory-based hypotheses to be tested, then conducts studies, in the ideal, to determine if the hypotheses can be refuted. Rejection is as important as acceptance in theory construction, with either outcome serving as the basis for theoretical reformulation or elaboration and further hypothesis testing. In contrast, Vincenti points out, engineering is a practical problem-solving activity. The challenge is not to conceptualize and test hypotheses to contribute to theory confirmation or disconfirmation, but to construct an artifact that works within practical constraints, as defined by design criteria and specifications. Economy—i.e., limited resources of time, money, and person-power—and zero tolerance for error—because of the potential costs in time, money, and human life, as well as professional reputation—are requirements that distinguish engineering research from scientific research.

The engineer works within design paradigms that begin with project definition and include overall design and then major-component design, with tentative layouts that are based on or checked by mathematical analysis or experimental test. Modifications are usually necessary through several iterations. As well as to check component performance, the engineer does research when the knowledge available is not adequate to the design task. Experimental parameter variation, in which the characteristics of some material, process, or device and/or the conditions under which it will perform are systematically varied and the effects on desired performance assessed, is an important type of engineering research. The purpose is not, as in science, to develop theory, but to produce design data.

The use of scale models is also a characteristic engineering methodology, following from the design purpose. Vincenti notes, for example, that the testing of models in wind tunnels has been essential in the development of airplanes. In one case, wing shape was addressed in that way as a purely technical problem when theory was not available to handle design issues such as how to reduce profile drag without negative impacts on other performance characteristics. In my experience, at USU's Utah Water Research Laboratory small-scale dams with varying parameters are tested in water flumes under differing conditions to explore design decisions for full-scale dams. During USU's Engineering Week, rather than displaying the results of science fair-type research projects, prospective engineering students from regional high schools compete to see whose Popsicle-stick bridge can sustain the most pressure.

Vincenti concedes that science and engineering—or, more broadly speaking, technology, of which engineering is a part—are not categorically different. Both are empirical. Engineers do draw on scientific knowledge when it is relevant and helpful. Both operate within the same laws of nature. Both disseminate knowledge through the same publication mechanisms and both are cumulative in the sense of building on prior knowledge, even though the type of knowledge sought and accumulated is different, and knowledge per se is not the desired end product of engineering as it is of science.

Historians of technology, Vincenti notes, do not consider technology to be a derivative of science, but an autonomous body of knowledge that shares important attributes with science: Technical thought, and therefore the thinking of engineers, "though different in its specifics, resembles scientific thought in being creative and constructive" (p. 4). In that sense, both science and engineering show progress. In fact, Kuhn (1970, p. 161), in his analysis of scientific knowledge-building, commented that because "progress is an obvious attribute of both fields," it is often difficult to perceive the "profound differences between science and technology."

IMPLICATIONS FOR RESEARCH ON SOCIAL STUDIES?

Vincenti's (1990) analysis of the purpose-epistemology connections in science and engineering shed light on the nature of engineering research that had perplexed me as graduate dean. More important, that analysis provided me with a new perspective, focused on the interactive relationship between purpose and epistemology, from which to view the lack of productivity of research on social studies education, as well as of educational research in general.

In contrast with science and its primary goal of expanding human understanding of the natural world, and engineering with its clear focus on artifact design, production, and operation, social studies/educational research is remarkable for its lack of consensus on a research mission. There is, though, ongoing anguish about the paucity of knowledge accumulation, along with a continuing, often somewhat muddled, preoccupation with theory (Thomas, 1997) and a seemingly paradoxical consternation about the absence of impact on classroom practice.

Not surprisingly, disparate epistemological frames and epistemological dissension are the most obvious features of our research area—research on social studies education in particular and educational research in general. In hindsight, it is instructive that I and the editorial advisory board began the *Handbook of Research on Social Studies Teaching and Learning* with a section on "Issues of Epistemology and Methodology." Included are chapters on social epistemology (Popkewitz & St. Maurice, 1991); critical research (including interpretive research [phenomenology, hermeneutics, and reader response theory] and poststructural criticism [Foucault's interpretive analytics and Derrida's deconstruction], Cherryholmes, 1991); qualitative research (e.g., ethnography, field studies, case studies, community studies, life history and biographical studies, and document-content analysis, Preissle-Goetz & LeCompte, 1991); and quantitative research (experimental, quasi-experimental, correlational, causal-comparative, and content analysis research, Fraenkel & Wallen, 1991). That listing is indicative of the lack of a community of social studies researchers imbued with a common research culture.

In light of the increased reporting of qualitative research on social studies education, the lack of a consensual research orientation suggested by the titles of chapters in the forthcoming second edition of the *Handbook of Qualitative Research* (Denzin & Lincoln, in press) is similarly informative. They reflect disagreement over the purpose of such research—the audiences for which the research is to be conducted and the appropriate influence of ethical and political contexts—as well as controversies over the epistemologies that might underlie qualitative research, such as interpretivism, hermeneutics, and social constructivism.

The dimensions of the epistemological controversy in educational research are etched vividly in Guba's (1990) discussion of the ontological, epistemological, and methodological assumptions of four research paradigms—positivism, postpositivism, critical theory ("'ideologically oriented inquiry,' [such as] neo-Marxism, materialism, feminism, Freireism, participatory inquiry, and other similar movements" [p. 23]), and constructivism.

Positivism, with its assumption of an existent reality to be discovered through research, with bias to be excluded through experimental control, is Guba's foil. He notes that postpositivists, in contrast to positivists, recognize that researchers' knowledge of an existent reality is screened through their frames of reference; objectivity is believed to be substantially achievable through cross-criticism and use of a multiplicity of methods, including qualitative inquiry. While still accepting the existence of an external reality, critical theorists go one step further epistemologically, positing the inevitability of the influence of researchers' values on their efforts to discover the existent reality. Dialogue is considered essential to raise and counter false consciousness and come to a true, in the political sense, view of reality. Constructivism has, as Phillips (1998) pointed out, "great 'within group' variation" (p. 139).[1] Some constructivists are akin to critical theorists, acknowledging that knowledge can be a representation of reality, even though constructed within a social, cultural, and political framework. However, Guba's idealist definition, which rejects the possibility of objectivity, falls within what has been termed "radical constructivism" (Nola, 1998; Phillips, 1998). The premise is that positivistic ontological and epistemological assumptions are "badly flawed and must be entirely replaced." In particular, there can be no meaningful distinction between ontology and epistemology, because "'reality' exists only in the context of a mental framework (construct) for thinking about it" (Guba, 1990, p. 25). The purpose of inquiry is "neither to predict and control the 'real' world nor to transform it but to *reconstruct* the 'world' at the only point at which it exists: in the minds of constructors" (p. 27, italics in the original).

The conflicting conceptions of epistemology that frame discussions of educational research in general (see not only Guba, 1990, but the continuing debates in the journal, *Educational Researcher*) are present among social studies educators. Leming (1997) emphasized that point, alluding to "the passion that has surrounded the [social studies] profession's consideration of political and epistemological ideals," which has been "so intense and focused" that sight of the purpose of social studies research, "the interests of children," has been lost (p. 503).

The potpourri, even cacophony, of epistemologies in social studies research, as well as educational research in general, reflects a field without a clear image of itself. Little wonder that it is difficult to discern a central, unifying purpose for that research; intellectual uncertainty and conflict over epistemology are hardly the foundation for a productive research endeavor. It is not surprising that evidence of the disruptive effects of conflicting epistemologies on the research productivity of graduate students and beginning faculty researchers emerged clearly from the narratives collected from qualitative researchers by Miller, Nelson, and Moore (1998).

The epistemological discord not only reflects the lack of a focused research purpose but contributes to it, in a chicken and egg scenario, as budding researchers are introduced to a field distinguished primarily by lack of a research character. Not so in science or engineering where agreed-upon sense of purpose precludes belabored arguments about epistemological issues. Vincenti (1990) noted that although engineers "rarely think about it consciously," their epistemological assumptions show up "in their daily work ... and in the content of their textbooks" (p. 135); engineers "know from experience" about "the character of engineering knowledge as [a technological] epistemological species" (p. 3).

Note, too, that it was Kuhn's (1970) perplexity arising from experiences with social scientists at the Center for Advanced Studies in the Behavioral Sciences that led to his recognition of the role of paradigms in scientific research. Kuhn "was struck by the number and extent of the overt disagreements between social scientists about the nature of legitimate scientific problems and methods." That contentiousness was contrary to "the practice of astronomy, physics, chemistry, or biology [that] normally fails to evoke the controversies over fundamentals that today often seem endemic among, say, psychologists or sociologists" (p. viii) and, I would add, educational, including social studies, researchers.

Kuhn (1970) considered the social sciences to be an immature field of research, in a preparadigmatic state (e.g., pp. 11, 13, 18–20, 163). Masterson (1970) disagreed, arguing that the social sciences are better labeled as "multiple paradigmatic," a "state of affairs in which, far from there being no paradigm, there are on the contrary too many" (p. 74). Her observation is consistent with that of Berger (1994), a sociologist, that "the warranting communities of the [social sciences] are plural and diverse," unlike "those of science, which ... tend to be single-minded, except, perhaps, at the 'frontiers' ... of knowledge" (p. 986). A plurality and overabundance of epistemological stances sums up social studies education as a research field.

CONSTRUCTIVISM IN SOCIAL SCIENCE AND SCIENCE

Along with the degree of epistemological controversy, a major distinction between science and the social sciences (including educational research and research on social studies) is the serious consideration within the latter of radical constructivism as a research paradigm. The denial of an external reality and the possibility of objectivity, basic tenets of the radical constructivist position, amount to a form of intellectual nihilism (Stanley, 1992, pp. 190, 206) that can only exacerbate the poverty of reflections on purpose-epistemology connections in social science and educational research. With the contention that any belief about reality is relative to each individual's construction, the validity of epistemological concerns is denied. The corresponding denial of any purpose for inquiry other than "to reconstruct the world ... in the minds of constructors" (Guba, 1990 p. 27) is self-defeating for researchers who believe that schools and classrooms do exist other than in their own minds. Certainly, that epistemology-purpose derivation stands in stark contrast to the realist purpose-epistemology stance that underlies science.

Conversations with science faculty led me years ago to the at first surprising conclusion that, in contrast to sociologists, philosophers, and historians of science, practicing biological and physical scientists have little interest in or patience with epistemological arguments, especially radical constructivist ones. That perception is confirmed in the literature. The notion that "science is a collective activity in which scientists construct a knowledge of nature rather than uncover it directly from nature" (Shapiro, 1998, p. B5) is given short shrift. As a molecular biologist (Coulson, 1994) put it in a letter to the editor of *Science* in reaction to a constructivist book review (Berger, 1994), "there isn't a practicing scientist in the world who is not a naïve realist, philosophically speaking" (pp. 854–855). In another letter, a chemist (Hagan, 1994) commented that the prevailing relationship [between scientists and sociological studies of science] is benign neglect. Natural scientists, barely aware of the existence or content of science studies, do not bother to question the legitimacy of such scholarship: it is considered irrelevant to the practice of science. (p. 853)

A biologist (Lewis Wolpert, as quoted in Melange, 1997, p. B6) summed up scientists' attitudes as follows:

> This century ... philosophers [of science] have contributed nothing ... of slightest relevance to practising [*sic*] scientists such as myself. I would like help with such problems as the nature and limits of reductionism ... and how to distinguish science from non-science. But philosophers of science seem to be much more interested in problems related to realism: is there a real world out there that we scientists study? How boring. I am a crass and naïve, even militant, realist, which I know I could not defend philosophically, but for my science it is totally irrelevant. Practising scientists have no interest in the philosophy of science and ... view philosophy as a "debilitating befuddlement."

Science is a social activity; decisions as to what problems to pursue and how to interpret results are affected by social contexts, as Begley (1997, 1999) has illustrated well in her pop-science articles. It is, however, "a mistake to move from the sense in which science is nothing but the activities of human beings to think that all the realms of science can be reduced to the social" (Shapiro, 1998, p. B5). That research is done by humans subject to social influences does not mean that the reality under study is socially constructed. Social-influence caveats, such as those of critical theorists (e.g., Cherryholmes, 1991; Popkewitz, 1990; Popkewitz & St. Maurice, 1991), are well-taken, especially for those doing research on human behavior. However, the radical constructivist paradigm has significance only for those who aim to abandon systematic research as a productive enterprise.[2]

SO?

What is my purpose in this discussion of epistemology in engineering and science and the contrasting epistemological cauldron in educational research and social studies research in particular? Certainly, it is not to suggest that social studies researchers should revert to prior efforts to take on the mantle of science. Despite the contrary arguments of some (e.g., Gage, 1996), the research record in educational research, including social studies research, indicates that human behavior is too historically and culturally conditioned and takes place in a context that is too interactionally complex to allow the development of scientific theory (Shaver, 1982b; Thomas,

1997, 1999). A science of social studies education is not a realistic goal. Nor is it my intent to propose that social studies researchers adopt wholeheartedly and unreflectively the epistemology of engineering.

My hope is that consideration of the purpose-to-epistemology relationships in science and engineering will illustrate and even dramatize the major problem in social studies research—the contentious lack of agreement among social studies educators, which Brophy (1997, p. 81) found disconcerting as a newcomer to the field. The discord encompasses not only the nature of social studies education, but the purpose of research on social studies and, therefore, the epistemological assumptions to guide that research. To paraphrase Silberman's (1970, p. 379) admonition about dysfunctional schooling, the problem with social studies research is "mindlessness," lack of consensual thought about purpose and about how epistemological assumptions and research methodologies fulfill or alter purpose. Clarification of purpose must precede fruitful consideration of epistemological and methodological issues, and, therefore, warranted judgments about the quality of research.

Although I have eschewed an intent to advocate for engineering epistemology, I must note that technology, the broader category within which Vincenti locates engineering, is a better fit than science to what social studies educators at universities mostly intend to do. Technology provides a potentially fruitful perspective from which to think about the purposes of social studies research.

Of course, I am not using technology, as is common now (see, e.g., Berson, 2000, p. 127), to refer to electronic and mechanical devices, such as computers. Instead, with Simon (1981), I am thinking of technology as a process in which designers of artifacts are "concerned with how things *ought* to be—how they ought to be in order to *attain goals*, and to *function*" (p. 7, italics in the original). From that frame of reference, technological design "is a social activity directed at a practical set of goals intended to serve human beings in some direct way" (Vincenti, 1990, p. 11). And, as Simon noted, the developmental domain of technology includes nonmaterial outcomes, such as "courses of action aimed at changing existing situations into preferred ones." The focus on design in the above sense is, and should be, "the principal mark that distinguishes the professions [including education, as well as engineering] from science" (p. 129).

Fred Newmann's (e.g., 1990, 1991) research on thoughtful classrooms seems to me to come close to the technological research model, and probably would have come closer had funding been available to continue a programmatic effort. In a letter to Fred (J. P. Shaver, personal communication, November 20, 1990) transmitting my review of four reports of the thoughtfulness classroom research, I commented that, after three years of funded research:

I find your series of studies to be very sensible.... You now have a classroom thoughtfulness instrument in place, have gathered some "normative data" on typical, select, and reorganized social studies departments, and have begun to make a thrust in the area of assessing student thinking outcomes. The really interesting work would lie ahead if you had funding for *at least* another three years: that is, the effort to determine the extent to which classroom thoughtfulness, as you assess it, is related to student gains on measures of thinking based specifically on the goals or objectives of specific teachers and courses, as well as the continuing pursuit of the relations with more general tests of reasoning....

And, of course, the experimental studies still lie ahead. The cross-sectional research is provocative; it would be excellent if you could now turn to experimental studies to determine the extent to which teachers can be helped to manipulate the thoughtfulness of their classrooms and the effects of such manipulation both on higher-order thinking in general and higher-order thinking assessed in terms of teacher-course objectives. In addition, you have not yet had a chance to do any replications of your initial studies, and it is not likely that others will obtain the funding or be able otherwise to do so on anything but a very limited scale.

My point is ... to suggest a major problem in educational research: the lack of adequate resources for the kinds of programs of research that might lead to strong, adequately complex, and replicated results. (Emphasis in the original.)

In his reply to my letter (F. M. Newmann, personal communication, December 5, 1990), Fred commented:

You're absolutely right about the tremendous effort and resources required, *over the long term*, to develop solid knowledge on questions like these.... [O]ver the years, because of shifting funding priorities, I haven't been able to pursue a number of issues I thought I might have just begun to understand..., [with] short-term projects that barely got off the ground before they had to be abandoned. I've tried to maintain some consistency in thematic emphasis, and while this allows me a sense of intellectual continuity, it's a poor substitute for systematically developed empirical work. (Emphasis in the original.)

I have included the rather long quotations to make two points. First, 10 years later, I am now struck by the technological, nonscience tone of my comments on Fred's research. His research goal was not knowledge for its own sake, but to figure out how to propagate thoughtful social studies classrooms, a human service goal. The tasks were, for example, to gather classroom-thoughtfulness parametric (in the engineering sense) data, develop an instrument to assess outcomes, examine classroom-thinking relationships, and determine if and how thoughtful classrooms could be produced. An excellent design/research agenda, if it could have been implemented fully!

That brings me to my second point from the quotations: the need for programmatic research in technology, as well as in science. Vincenti (1990) emphasized that engineering/technology involves a long-term, complicated, and fascinating process. The design and research are multifaceted, with several categories of knowledge (pp. 208ff.) and levels of design, from tentative layout to production and tryout (pp. 7–11). The master's thesis in electrical engineering to which I referred earlier in this chapter was but one small part of a research and development program on satellite control systems at USU's Space Dynamics Lab.

Private and public funding is available for engineering projects and, for the most part, only funded design is done. A difficulty for social studies researchers is that funding is scarce and, as Newmann lamented, usually short term when available. The result is little programmatic research in the field. At the same time, research for a number of unrelated theses and dissertations in social studies education is carried out each year in universities across the nation, as well as around the world.

In 1985, Nelson and I proposed that the energy of faculty and graduate student social-studies researchers be focused via a research consortium that would identify major research problems and coordinate heretofore scattered research efforts (p. 411). None such has been developed and Fraenkel (1998, p. 273) recently made a similar proposal. Now it seems clear that lack of broad consensus on research purpose, along with the attendant squabbles about research paradigms, are major obstacles to any organization of social studies researchers for concerted programmatic research.

WHAT NOW?

The first task before the social studies research community, rather than discussions of research paradigms, epistemological issues, and even research quality and the productivity of research, is to develop a sense of a shared research mission. Only with a clear, even if implicit, consensus on purpose can issues of epistemology be addressed productively—or, even better, largely ignored because the enterprise is proceeding well, as is the case for the most part in science and engineering.

Can, or will, the necessary formulation of common purpose take place among social studies educators? It is important to note that accord on purpose in science and in engineering are not the result of conscious efforts at philosophical construction: An implicit consensus has grown out of years of productive research and technological development and the accompanying education of new generations of scientists and engineers. An understanding of what science and engineering are about, both purpose and epistemology, is passed along (as Kuhn [1970, pp. 5, 10–11, 47] noted for science) as part of undergraduate and graduate education, as a taken-for-granted element in textbooks, faculty lectures, and students' lab assignments. Note that even the bridge-building exercise for potential engineering students mentioned earlier in this chapter serves that enculturation function.

Self-consciously building a research culture, beginning with a shared sense of purpose, presents a daunting challenge. The graduate education of most university social studies faculty has not, as both I (Shaver, 1982b) and Fraenkel (1998) have pointed out, prepared them well for the philosophical examination that is necessary. Nor has that education been for the most part imbued with much cognizance of research as a significant part of faculty role, except to meet university standards for promotion and tenure. The potential for research productivity if purpose and epistemology were shared rather universally in the field has received little, if any, attention.

The diffused perspective on research is not surprising, nor can it be condemned, in a field that is fundamentally service-oriented. The education of K–12 teachers is the major responsibility of social studies faculty, and the attendant interest in the efficacy of social studies education often leads to involvement in curriculum development and staff development in school districts. Research is not a high professional priority and, in fact, other professional commitments leave little time and energy for traditional "scientific" research activities. Priorities might shift and more time become available for research involvement if the generally accepted purpose for the research was consistent with social studies educators' professional interests and responsibilities.

Rather than "hankering after academic responsibility" (Simon, 1981, p. 130) by trying to meet university promotion and tenure criteria with pseudoscientific research, and spending time and energy contemplating whether the realist epistemology of science is valid and/or counterproductive for educational/social studies research, social studies educators might better take to heart the lesson from engineering: Science provides neither the only viable purpose or productive epistemology for research. With a purpose for research other than the understanding-of-nature, knowledge-building goals typically espoused for science, epistemology takes on a new character. No longer is wrangling about the validity and applicability of the assumptions of scientists pertinent; how to secure the knowledge necessary to accomplish appropriate professional goals becomes the challenge.

Despite the quarrels about the nature and purpose of social studies, there is, I believe, agreement among social studies educators about their central professional goal: It is to help social studies teachers, regardless of their teaching area or their position or lack of position on the nature of social studies, meet their instructional challenges.

What if, collectively, social studies educators self-consciously focused their research efforts on that goal, taking the design and implementation of artifacts and nonmaterial products to improve social studies education in the schools as our purpose? That practical, social service goal invokes technology, not science, and embodies a major shift in perspective—from "understanding about" to "designing for"—that would transform the

nature of research activities and the attendant epistemological considerations. Over time, with design and related research activities carried out
within a context of common purpose and eventual epistemological con-
cord, a social studies research community, akin to that of engineers but certainly different in significant ways, would emerge. Of special importance
would be the evolution of a research culture that would provide the framework for coordinated, long-term, programmatic design-related research
that could yield products with proven impacts on social studies outcomes.
In this scenario, the purpose-epistemology consensus that would eventually
develop might one day be explicated by an educationist Vincenti as different from those of science and engineering, but appropriate and productive
for social studies research.

What is the likelihood that such a research culture will develop, encompassing a professionally relevant purpose for social studies research and an
epistemology that is driven by that purpose? As Heilbroner's (1960) book
title, *The Future as History*, suggests so poignantly, our past experiences may
not determine, but they certainly condition, our future behavior. The lack
of progress in social studies education and research since James
Michener's (1939) optimistic appraisal, over 60 years ago, of the prospects
for the profession does not bode well for the future (Shaver, 1995). Unless
dramatic steps are taken to counteract the effects of a fragmented profession, essays like this one will be fitting commentary far into the future of
social studies education.

NOTES

1.   Within the variations of constructivism, it is important to distinguish disciplinary constructivism (also alluded to as social or metaphysical constructivism)
from personal constructivism (also referred to as psychological or cognitive constructivism) (Grandy, 1998, pp. 113–114; Phillips, 1998, p. 139, 2000, pp. 6–7;
Shaver 1992, pp. 1–2). The concern here is with disciplinary constructivism—i.e.,
commentary on the development of bodies of public knowledge—not with personal constructivism—i.e., a conception of an active learning process in which individuals construct their own portrayals of reality. The two conceptions are
independent in the sense that acceptance of one does not imply or necessitate
acceptance of the other.

2.   Similarly dysfunctional, Kuhn (1992) has argued, is the "strong program" of
constructivism, a companion of radical constructivism, in which reality is not
denied, but discussions by scientists of evidence, rational bases for interpretation,
and proximity to truth are taken to be "simply the rhetoric behind which the victo-
rious [scientific] party cloaks its power. What passes for scientific knowledge
becomes, then, simply the belief of the winners." That claim is "absurd: an example
of deconstruction gone mad." Less extreme constructivist positions are adequate
only if they address specifically how "observations of nature ... play a role in scientific development" (p. 9).

REFERENCES

Begley, S. (1997, Apr. 21). The science wars. *Newsweek*, pp. 54–57.

Begley, S. (1999, June 14). From both sides now. *Newsweek*, pp. 52–53.

Berger, B.M. (1994). Taking arms [Review of the book *Higher superstition: The academic left and its quarrels with science*]. *Science, 264*, 985–989.

Berson, M.J. (2000). Rethinking research and pedagogy in the social studies: The creation of caring connections through technology and advocacy. *Theory and Research in Social Education, 28*, 121–131.

Byrnes, J.P., & Torney-Purta, J.V. (1995). Naïve theories and decision making as part of higher order thinking in social studies. *Theory and Research in Social Education, 23*, 260–277.

Brophy, J. (1997). An "outsider's perspective" on social education. *Theory and Research in Social Education, 25*, 80–84

Cherryholmes, C.H. (1991). Critical research and social studies education. In J.P. Shaver (Ed.), *Handbook of research on social studies teaching and learning* (pp. 41–55). New York: Macmillan.

Cohen, J. (1988). *Statistical power analysis for the behavioral sciences* (2nd ed.). Hillsdale, NJ: Lawrence Erlbaum Associates.

Coulson, A.F.W. (1994). "Culture wars" [Letter to the editor]. *Science, 265*, 854–855.

Denzin, N.K., & Lincoln, Y.S. (Eds.). (In press). *Handbook of qualitative research* (2nd ed.). Thousand Oaks, CA: Sage.

Ehman, L.H. (1998). Trends in *Theory and Research in Social Education* from 1973 to 1997: Implications for goals and process. *Theory and Research in Social Education, 26*, 238–257.

Fraenkel, J.R. (1987). Toward improving research in social studies education. *Theory and Research in Social Education, 15*, 203–222.

Fraenkel, J.R. (1998). Some thoughts about social studies research. *Theory and Research in Social Education, 26*, 272–275.

Fraenkel, J.R., & Wallen, N.E. (1991). Quantitative research in social studies education. In J.P. Shaver (Ed.), *Handbook of research on social studies teaching and learning* (pp. 67–82). New York: Macmillan.

Gage, N.L. (1996). Confronting counsels of despair for the behavioral sciences. *Educational Researcher, 25*(3), 5–15, 22.

Gibbons, A.S. (n.d.). *The practice of instructional technology.* Unpublished manuscript. Department of Instructional Technology, Utah State University, Logan.

Glass, G.V (1976). Primary, secondary, and meta-analysis of research. *Educational Researcher, 5* (10), 3–8.

Grandy, R.E. (1998). Constructivisms and objectivity: Disentangling metaphysics from pedagogy. In M.R. Matthews (Ed.), *Constructivism in science education: A philosophical examination* (pp. 113–124). Dordrecht, The Netherlands: Kluwer Academic Publishers.

Griffith, A.D. (1999). Teaching social studies in Caribbean schools: Perceived problems of elementary school teachers. *Theory and Research in Social Studies Education, 27*, 375–395.

Guba, E.G. (1990). The alternative paradigm dialog. In E. G. Guba (Ed.), *The paradigm dialog* (pp. 17–27). Newbury Park, CA: Sage.

Hagan, W.J., Jr. (1994). "Culture wars" [Letter to the editor]. *Science, 265*, 853–854.

Hahn, C.L. (1996). Gender and political learning. *Theory and Research in Social Education, 24,* 8–35.

Heilbroner, R.L. (1960). *The future as history.* New York: Grove Press.

Houser, N.O. (1995). Social studies on the backburner: Views from the field. *Theory and Research in Social Education, 23,* 147–168.

Hughes, A.S. (1997). Toward a more thoughtful professional education for social studies teachers: Can problem-based learning contribute? *Theory and Research in Social Education, 25,* 431–445.

Jackson, P.W. (1993). Qualitative research and its public. *Qualitative Studies in Education, 6,* 227–231.

Kornfeld, J., & Marker, P.M. (1997). Classroom by classroom, school by school: A lens on the past, a vision of the future. *Theory and Research in Social Education, 25,* 492–499.

Kuhn, T.S. (1970). *The structure of scientific revolutions* (2nd ed.). Chicago: University of Chicago Press.

Kuhn, T.S. (1992). *The trouble with the historical philosophy of science.* The Robert and Maurine Rothschild Distinguished Lecture. Cambridge, MA: Department of the History of Science, Harvard University.

Leming, J.S. (1997). Social studies research and the interests of children. *Theory and Research in Social Education, 25,* 500–505.

Masterson, M. (1970). The nature of a paradigm. In I. Lakatos & A. Musgrave (Eds.), *Criticism and the growth of knowledge* (pp. 59–89). London: Cambridge University Press.

Melange: The irrelevance of philosophers of science. (1997, Feb.28). *The Chronicle of Higher Education, 43,* B6.

Metcalf, L.E. (1963). Research on teaching the social studies. In N.L. Gage (Ed.), *Handbook of research on teaching* (pp. 929–965). Chicago: Rand McNally.

Michener, J.A. (1939). The problem of the social studies. In J.A. Michener (Ed.), *The future of the social studies* (pp. 1–15). Washington, DC: National Council for the Social Studies. (Reprinted in *James Michener on the social studies: His writings in publications of the National Council for the Social Studies from 1938 to 1987* [pp. 29–35]. Washington, DC: National Council for the Social Studies.)

Miller, S.M., Nelson, M.W., & Moore, M.T. (1998). Caught in the paradigm gap: Qualitative researchers' lived experience and the politics of epistemology. *American Educational Research Journal, 35,* pp.377–416.

Mitchell, G., Evans, S., Daly, J., & Roach, P. (1997). Academic freedom and the preparation of social studies teachers. *Theory and Research in Social Studies Education, 25,* 54–66.

Nelson, J. & Shaver, J. P. (1985). On research in social education. In W. B. Stanley (Ed.), *Review of research in social studies education* (pp. 401–433). Washington, D.C.: National Council for the Social Studies.

Newmann, F.M. (1990). Qualities of thoughtful social studies classes: An empirical profile. *Journal of Curriculum Studies, 22,* 253–257.

Newmann, F.M. (1991). Promoting higher order thinking in social studies: Overview of a study of sixteen high school departments. *Theory and Research in Social Studies Education, 19,* 324–340.

Nola, R. (1998). Constructivism in science and in science education: A philosophical critique. In M.R. Matthews (Ed.), *Constructivism in science education: A philo-*

sophical examination (pp. 31–59). Dordrecht, The Netherlands: Kluwer Academic Publishers.

Oliver, D.W., & Shaver, J.P. (1974). *Teaching public issues in the high school.* Logan: Utah State University Press (originally published by Houghton Mifflin, 1966).

Phillips, D.C. (1998). Coming to terms with radical social constructivism. In M.R. Matthews (Ed.), *Constructivism in science education: A philosophical examination* (pp. 139–158). Dordrecht, The Netherlands: Kluwer Academic Publishers.

Phillips, D.C. (2000). An opinionated account of the constructivist landscape. In D.C. Phillips (Ed.), *Constructivism in education: Opinions and second opinions on controversial issues* (pp. 1–16). Ninety-ninth Yearbook of the National Society for the Study of Education, Part I. Chicago: University of Chicago Press.

Popkewitz, T.S. (1990). Whose future? Whose past? Notes on critical theory and methodology. In E.G. Guba (Ed.), *The paradigm dialogue* (pp. 46–66). Newbury Park, CA: Sage.

Popkewitz, T.S., & St. Maurice, H. (1991). Social studies education and theory: Science, knowledge, and history. In J.P. Shaver (Ed.), *Handbook of research on social studies teaching and learning* (pp. 27–40). New York: Macmillan.

Preissle-Goetz, J., & LeCompte, M.D. (1991). Qualitative research in social studies education. In J.P. Shaver (Ed.), *Handbook of research on social studies teaching and learning* (pp. 56–66). New York: Macmillan.

Prior, W. (1999). What it means to be a "good citizen" in Australia: Perceptions of teachers, students, and parents. *Theory and Research in Social Education, 27,* 215–248.

Ross, E. W. (1997). From the editor: *Theory and Research in Social Education* at a quarter century. *Theory and Research in Social Education, 25,* 6–8.

Saye, J.W., & Brush, T. (1999). Student engagement with social issues in a multimedia-supported learning environment. *Theory and Research in Social Education, 27,* 472–504.

Sechrest, L., McKnight, P., & McKnight, K. (1996). Calibration of measures for psychotherapy outcome studies. *American Psychologist, 51,* 1065–1071.

Shapiro, A.E. (1998, Feb. 20). Historians of science must again master scientific substance. *The Chronicle of Higher Education, 44,* B4–B5.

Shaver, J.P. (1979). The usefulness of educational research in curricular/instructional decision-making in social studies. *Theory and Research in Social Education, 7*(3), 21–46.

Shaver, J.P. (1982a, November). *Making research useful to teachers.* Invited paper presented at a general session, "Taking the Ivory Out of the Tower," annual meeting of the National Council for the Social Studies, Boston. (ED 224 754)

Shaver, J.P. (1982b). Reappraising the theoretical goals of research in social studies education. *Theory and Research in Social Studies Education, 9*(4), 1–16.

Shaver, J.P. (1985). Chance and nonsense: A conversation about interpreting tests of statistical significance, Part 2. *Phi Delta Kappan, 67,* 138–141. Erratum, 1986, *67,* 624.

Shaver, J.P. (1991). Quantitative reviewing of research. In J.P. Shaver (Ed.), *Handbook of research on social studies teaching and learning* (pp. 83–97). New York: Macmillan.

Shaver, J.P. (1992, July). *Epistemology and the education of social science teachers.* Paper presented at the International Conference on Subject-specific Teaching Methods and Teacher Education, Santiago de Compostela, Spain.

Shaver, J.P. (1993). What statistical significance testing is, and what it is not. *Journal of Experimental Education, 61*, 293–316.

Shaver, J.P. (1995). James Michener and the historical future of social studies. *Social Education, 59*, 446–450.

Shaver, J.P. (1997). The past and future of social studies as citizenship education and of research on social studies. *Theory and Research in Social Education, 25*, 210–215.

Shaver, J.P., & Larkins, A.G. (1973). Research on teaching social studies. In R.M.W. Travers (Ed.), *Second handbook of research on teaching* (pp. 1243–1262). Chicago: Rand McNally.

Silberman, C.E. (1970). *Crisis in the classroom: The remaking of American education.* New York: Random House.

Simon, H.A. (1981). *The sciences of the artificial* (2nd ed.). Cambridge, MA: MIT Press.

Singer, A. (1995). Challenging gender bias through a transformative high school social studies curriculum. *Theory and Research in Social Education, 23*, 234–259.

Stanley, W.B. (1992). *Curriculum for utopia: Social reconstructionism and critical pedagogy in the postmodern era.* Albany: State University of New York Press.

Tanner, D. (1998). The social consequences of bad research. *Phi Delta Kappan, 79*, 345–349.

tenDam, G., & Rijkschroeff, R. (1996). Teaching women's history in secondary education: Constructing gender identity. *Theory and Research in Social Education, 24*, 77–89.

Thomas, G. (1997). What's the use of theory? *Harvard Educational Review, 67*, 75–104.

Thomas, G. (1999). Hollow theory: A reply to Rajagopalan. *Harvard Educational Review, 9*, 51–66.

Thompson, B. (1998, April). *Five methodological errors in educational research: The pantheon of statistical significance and other faux pas.* Paper presented at the annual meeting of the American Educational Research Association, San Diego, April 15, 1998. Available: http://ACS.TAMU.EDU/-bbt6147/aeraaddr.htm.

Vincenti, W.G. (1990). *What engineers know and how they know it.* Baltimore: Johns Hopkins University Press.

Vinson, K.D. (1998). The "traditions" revisited: Instructional approach and high school social studies teachers. *Theory and Research in Social Education, 26*, 50–82.

Wade, R.C., & Saxe, D.W. (1996). Community service-learning in the social studies: Historical roots, empirical evidence, critical issues. *Theory and Research in Social Studies Education, 24*, 331–359.

CHAPTER 11

EPILOGUE

William B. Stanley

The experience of reviewing research in social studies education could lead one to conclude "the more things change, the more they stay the same." This sense of déjà vu is most apparent in the Cornbleth and Shaver chapters, but it is echoed in various ways in the other chapters as well. It is hard to deny the general lack of progress, if we measure progress in terms of the standards set by the authors in this book. However, we should note that the chapter authors have (rightfully so) set very high standards for the field. The available evidence indicates that programs reflecting such standards are the exception, not the norm. On the other hand, the authors also describe the social, political, and cultural contexts that constrain progress in the field.

It is not clear that any other curriculum area (e.g., English, math, science) has progressed significantly more than social studies over the past century when measured against the ideals posed by its intellectual leadership. In short, we can conclude that research on education, in general, has made less progress than we would like (Lagermann, 2000). But when we speak of "progress," we have introduced a political agenda. Clearly, there are very different and competing visions of progress that shape educational practice. Vinson and Ross discuss the impact of the standards and accountability movement on social studies. Proponents of standards regard as progress what Vinson and Ross describe as a problem. In her chapter, Cornbleth cites Jules Henry's contention that social studies are designed to make students stupid. In Henry's view, teaching for stupidity and docility was not an unanticipated consequence but a goal designed to help control the masses. Nelson, Santora, Merryfield, Parker, Levistik and Barton, and Berson, Lee, and Stuckdert all provide examples of how present forms of social studies education function to maintain the status quo, including forms of discrimination and the oppression of various groups. Yet the views represented by these authors do not reflect the dominant mainstream discourse on schooling. Rather, the authors in this volume have all problematized the current state of social studies education. While there are some significant differences among the various authors, all are critical of the status quo.

To the extent the critique of mainstream schooling (and social studies in particular) as antithetical to a democratic way of life is accurate, it begs the question of what should be done." There is no escape from the fundamental curriculum question, "what knowledge is of most worth?" or its corollary, "whose knowledge is of most worth?" Given this context, one might conclude that there is no way to avoid counter socialization in the process of educational reform. After all, does reform not entail trying to do something against the grain, an attempt to create social change? Of course this is a truism, but admitting as much does not resolve the issue. In practice, social studies reforms often degenerate into a value's contest, that is, the "good" reformer's values versus the "bad" values of those in power. In response to this issue, I believe the authors in this volume have all begun to move beyond the limited rhetoric of "counter-socialization."

Democracy as a way of life is a theme that runs through most of the chapters. As Parker explains, democracy is a work in progress, something each generation must claim anew. Democracy is not something already given, fully constructed, and ready to be transmitted to a passive citizenry. Nor is it something "natural" that humans do intrinsically. Indeed, democracy must be cultivated. Such cultivation requires a supportive environment possessing some minimum level of economic production and distribution, democratically motivated political institutions, and a supportive cultural climate. Put another way, we must learn a democratic way of life and have genuine opportunities to practice what we have learned. Some of the possible implications for social studies education are well described by the chapter authors. The suggestions raised in the chapters are by no means exhaustive, but the authors do point out many changes, which, if not sufficient for maintaining a democratic way of life, are certainly necessary. I do not suggest that there is a general agreement here as to what must be done. But let me summarize what I believe are some key points arising from the various positions taken in this book.

If we accept that democracy is a way of life, we must find an approach to education that supports this life form. Herein lies the negative dimension of so many counter socialization approaches to education, i.e., the claim to know the "right values" that will serve as a basis for a new social education program. Values such as "social justice," "freedom of speech and belief," "equality," and so on are typically offered as core values to provide a basis for educational reform. Aside from the inherent problems related to conflicts among core values and actually defining and operationalizing core values, it is not clear on what basis we can argue that such taken-for-granted values exist a priori. In human praxis, values emerge in the course of human history as we confront problems and must make decisions regarding how to live. In a democratic form of life, the determination of the social good and the structure necessary to achieve it is in the hands of citizens. Thus, while it is proper for social studies educators to ask students to confront social problems and devise approaches to social change, it is not our task to indoctrinate them to accept solutions we propose to create a new social order. To do so would undermine the very competence students need to become effective citizens in a democracy.

Of course, social studies education does not exist in a social vacuum. We all live in a world where core values defined by previous generations already exist. But no matter how strongly we, as social educators, feel about such values, it is our task to help the next generation to claim its own set of values–even if our hope is that their values will reflect our own. If we do not enable our students to critically examine and choose values for themselves, education degenerates into a form of dogmatic cultural transmission.

One might note the paradoxical nature of the position argued here. Is not the view that social studies education should seek to educate for a democratic form of life itself an imposed framework? The answer is yes. But I would add that such paradoxical forms of argument are intrinsic to curriculum theorizing (what knowledge is of most worth?) and philosophy itself. The key point is that there is an important difference between seeking to impose a particular social order based on taken-for-granted values and education designed to provide the conditions that will enable humans to develop the critical competence necessary to determine and act to realize their interests. While both educational approaches entail a framework, the first is designed to maintain the status quo, while the second seeks to create the possibility for social transformation.

What is needed is a new approach to the problem. As Dewey said as part of his critique of certain social reconstructionist positions:

> The upholders of indoctrination rest their adherence to the theory, in part, upon the fact that there is a great deal of indoctrination now going on in the schools, especially with reference to the dominant economic regime. These facts unfortunately *are* facts. But they do not prove that the right course is to seize upon the method of indoctrination and reverse its object. (Dewey, 1937 p. 37)

Dewey used the term "method of intelligence" or what others have called practical reasoning to describe the form of human competence necessary for democratic citizenship. Practical reasoning requires that we abandon what Dewey called the "quest for certainty." The highest form of human intelligence is

> associated with *judgment*; that is, with selection and arrangement of means to effect consequences and with choice of what we take as our ends. A man is intelligent not in virtue of having reason which grasps first and in demonstrable truth about fixed principles, in order to reason deductively from them to

the particulars which they govern, but in virtue of his capacity to estimate the possibilities of a situation and to act in accordance with his estimate. (Dewey, 1929, p. 70)

Practical reasoning refers to the inherently social and interpretive mode of behavior characteristic of human beings and required for praxis, defined as action for human betterment. The Greek word for this form of competence was *phronesis*. Unlike technical reasoning, which aims at achieving prespecified objectives, praxis aims at human well being, which by its nature must be open to reinterpretation. Consequently, practical reasoning can never be reduced to judgments about what we should do in accordance with a priori core values. Rather, practical reasoning is as much a matter of the competence to reformulate conceptions of our fundamental goals (or values) as it is an ability to carry out appropriate action in pursuit of those goals.

Practical reasoning is not merely another kind of critical thinking but the form of thought that is primary to the exercise of other kinds. It makes little sense to think through how to best resolve technical problems without first determining such problems are worth our attention. Thus, practical reasoning is not only something humans can do more or less well to make sense of their lives, it is part of what constitutes us as human beings. To the extent practical reasoning is not developed, one does not fully come to form as human. As such, it is simultaneously a basic human interest as well as competence. Here one can see the direct relationship between the cultivation of practical reasoning and the cultivation of a democratic form of life. Defined this way, practical reasoning is also the primary aim of social studies education (Stanley 1992, 2000). Without it, we can't have democratic citizenship or democracy.

The authors in this book have called our attention to a large number of conditions that disable the development of practical reasoning. Racism, sexism, homophobia, ethnocentrism, dogmatism, cultural narrowness, and the unequal distribution of wealth all function to undermine schooling for a democratic form of life. The approach to social studies entailed by a commitment to practical reasoning is not ambivalent. While it does not prescribe a priori values, it does argue for a democratic form of life that would enable all human beings to realize their full potential. This is an approach to education that would never be comfortable with the status quo, but would resist imposing some fixed or final conception of society. It rests on a deep democratic faith in the capacity of citizens to seek the social good. Social studies education can play an important part in this process by providing students with the experiences and opportunities necessary to develop their practical competence to function as democratic citizens.

REFERENCES

Dewey, J. (1929). *The quest for certainty.* New York: Capricorn Books.

Dewey, J. (1937). Education and social change. *The Social Frontier,* (3).

Lagermann, E.C. (2000). *An elusive science: The troubling history of educational research.* Chicago: The University of Chicago Press.

Stanley, W. B. (1992). *Curriculum for utopia: Social reconstructionism and critical pedagogy in the postmodern era.* Albany: State University of New York Press.

Stanley, W. B. (2000). Curriculum and the social order. In D.W. Hursh & E.W. Ross (Eds.), *Democratic social education: Social studies for social change* (pp. 65-72). London: Falmer Press.